PENGUIN BOOKS

Interpreting the Economy

Simon Briscoe was educated at Highgate School and Exeter University. Between 1981 and 1987 he worked at the Central Statistical Office, HM Treasury and the European Commission in Brussels. From 1987 to 1993 he was UK Economist at Greenwell Montagu, part of Midland Bank and subsequently HSBC. He then became UK Economist and head of bond analysis with S. G. Warburg Securities. In 1995 he joined Nikko Europe, the Japanese securities house, as chief economist. In 1997 he became managing director of research and was the European representative on the global investment strategy committee of Nikko Securities. In 1999 he became Statistics Editor at the *Financial Times*.

During his City career Simon Briscoe was highly ranked in a number of investor surveys (including number one positions in Extel and Institutional Investor). He was joint author (with Christopher Johnson) of *Measuring the Economy*, published by Penguin in 1995. He served on the Advisory Committee of the Office for National Statistics between 1996 and 1999, was elected to the Council of the Royal Statistical Society (in 1998), sat on the Council of the Society of Business Economists (until 1999) and continues to be the (inaugural) chairman of the Financial Statistics Users' Group. He was an adviser to the Treasury Committee of the House of Commons in 1998 for their study of EMU.

Interpreting the Economy
An Essential Guide to Economic Statistics

Simon Briscoe

PENGUIN BOOKS

For M, M and M

PENGUIN BOOKS

Published by the Penguin Group
Penguin Books Ltd, 27 Wrights Lane, London W8 5TZ, England
Penguin Putnam Inc., 375 Hudson Street, New York, New York 10014, USA
Penguin Books Australia Ltd, Ringwood, Victoria, Australia
Penguin Books Canada Ltd, 10 Alcorn Avenue, Toronto, Ontario, Canada M4V 3B2
Penguin Books (NZ) Ltd, Private Bag 102902, NSMC, Auckland, New Zealand

Penguin Books Ltd, Registered Offices: Harmondsworth, Middlesex, England

First published in Pelican Books under the title *Measuring the Economy* 1988
Reprinted in Penguin Books 1990
New edition 1995
This edition published under the current title 2000
10 9 8 7 6 5 4 3 2 1

Set in Adobe Minion and ITC Officina Sans
Typeset by Rowland Phototypesetting Ltd, Bury St Edmunds, Suffolk
Printed in Great Britain by Clays Ltd, St Ives plc

Contents

'The intelligent use of data requires that the user understands the context, provenance and quality of such data. Simon Briscoe's thoughtful and carefully researched text fills a need in this regard and is an essential book for users of UK economic statistics. Simon explodes the myth that statistics are neutral. The book provides a rich vein of material to be tapped by students and policy analysts. If it leads to more informed and wider use of the complex sources of economic data – and I believe that it will – then Simon's painstaking work will have been worthwhile.'

Professor Denise Lievesley,
President of the Royal Statistical Society

Preface

This book is born out of *Measuring the Economy*, which was first published in 1988 and reprinted in 1990. A new edition was published by Penguin in 1995. Simon Briscoe, who was joint author of the 1995 new edition, has taken the original concept forward in this new book which reflects the many changes of the last decade.

He would like to thank his colleagues at the *Financial Times*, and all his previous colleagues, for all their help, direct and indirect, in contributing to this book. He would particularly like to thank Rob Clements, Diane Coyle, Dave Fenwick, Julian Jessop, John Kidgell, David Mackie, Andrew Milligan, Mike Pepper, John Pullinger, David Ruffles, John Thorpe, Philip Turnbull, Pamela Webber and many others in the Office for National Statistics and Bank of England who helped in some way. The greatest thanks go to Christopher Johnson, who kindly acted as consultant editor for this new book, and Iain Jones.

Abbreviations

AES	Annual Employment Survey
AME	annually managed expenditure
BBA	British Bankers' Association
BCC	British Chambers of Commerce
BoP	balance of payments
BRC	British Retail Consortium
BSA	Building Societies Association
CBI	Confederation of British Industry
CIPS	Chartered Institute of Purchasing and Supply
COICOP	Classification of Individual Consumption by Purpose
COLI	cost of living index
CPI	consumer price index
CRB	Commodity Research Bureau
CSO	Central Statistical Office
D&B	Dun and Bradstreet
DEL	departmental expenditure limits
DMO	Debt Management Office
DTI	Department of Trade and Industry
EER	effective exchange rate
EMS	European Monetary System
ERI	effective rate index
ERM	Exchange Rate Mechanism
ESA95	European System of Accounts
EU	European Union
FEPI	final expenditure prices index
FES	Family Expenditure Survey
GCF	gross capital formation
GDP	Gross Domestic Product

GFCF	gross fixed capital formation
GNI	Gross National Income
GNP	Gross National Product
GSS	Government Statistical Service
GVA	gross value added
HICP	Harmonized Index of Consumer Prices
IDBR	Inter-departmental Business Register
ILO	International Labour Organisation
IOP	index of output of the production industries
JSA	Job Seeker's Allowance
LFS	Labour Force Survey
MFIs	monetary financial institutions
MPC	Monetary Policy Committee
MTFS	medium-term financial strategy
MWSS	Monthly Wages and Salaries Survey
NAIRU	non-accelerating inflation rate of unemployment
NES	New Earnings Survey
NIESR	National Institute of Economic and Social Research
NPISH	non-profit institutions serving households
ONS	Office for National Statistics
OPCS	Office of Population Censuses and Surveys
OTS	overseas trade statistics
PMI	Purchasing Managers' Index
PPI	producer price index
PPP	Purchasing Power Parity
PSBR	public sector borrowing requirement
PSFD	public sector financial deficit
PSL	private sector liquidity
PSNCR	public sector net cash requirement
RAB	resource accounting and budgeting
RPI	Retail Prices Index
RPIX	RPI eXcluding mortgage interest
RPIY	RPI excluding indirect taxes
RSS	Royal Statistical Society
SARY	seasonally adjusted RPI
SIC	Standard Industrial Classification
SNA93	System of National Accounting 1993
STES	short-term turnover employer survey
TME	total managed expenditure
TPI	Tax and Price Index

Introduction

Almost every day a new economic statistic is announced. An important sector of the information industry has grown up around the statistics, predicting, disseminating, analysing and disputing them. Financial analysts and traders in the City can add on or wipe off billions of pounds from the holdings of bonds, shares and currencies by the reaction to these economic indicators. Politicians attempt to interpret them so as to favour or rubbish government. Journalists make front-page news out of them. Employers, employees and trade unions fasten upon key numbers as an essential part of their dialogue.

This book explains those economic indicators that are announced in press notices, most of them once a month, some once a quarter. It also explains key financial market variables such as interest rates and exchange rates, which both influence and are in turn influenced by economic indicators. It therefore tends to focus on short-term changes in the economy, while putting them in a long-term perspective. It covers in less depth the wealth of economic and financial statistics which appear in government publications that are not of sufficient significance to merit press releases.

As well as describing and defining each of the main indicators, the book outlines their significance and the main economic factors which determine them, as well as citing some of the more erratic short-term factors which can cause them to depart from trend.

The first three chapters are more general in nature. The first describes some of the history of official statistics and explains some of the broader political issues that have arisen in recent years. Chapters 2 and 3 describe the issues surrounding the data and some of the statistical 'tools of the trade' (or tricks) to be aware of.

Thereafter, while the plan of each subject specific chapter differs somewhat according to the nature of the material, the aim is the same in each case. There is some explanation of why an indicator is important, looking at its impact on the economy and financial markets, followed by discussion of the meaning of the statistical concept and an explanation about how the figures are compiled. There is discussion of the recent history of the indicator and an illustration of how the statistics have moved in recent years.

Chapter 4 looks at the big picture – economic growth and the national accounts. The following chapters concern inflation, the labour market, consumers, business, overseas trade and, finally, money, public finances and financial markets.

The scope of this book is deliberately limited to the United Kingdom. It is true that the important indicators of other countries, notably the US, can be as important to our economy and financial markets as the UK's own. While many basic statistical methods and practices are common across countries, the often subtle differences are so important that a detailed description of other countries' statistics requires and deserves a separate book. Examples from other countries are regularly used to set UK statistics in context.

The prime source of all the information is the press notices. Most press notice material is later issued in hard copy publications but the original press notices can be of value by showing what the figures were as originally announced prior to revisions. The data given in examples were mostly those available in spring 1999.

This book is meant for school and university students (primarily of economics), professional economists and statisticians, politicians, civil servants, financial market analysts, journalists, stockbrokers and bankers, among others. Economists should bear in mind that much has been simplified for the intelligent lay person with a head for figures. Others should be reassured that concepts are explained so that familiarity with the subject, while desirable, is not essential. It is important to make statistics come alive by showing their relevance to economic and financial policy issues. The contents of this book make it easier to measure the performance of the government and of the private sector, so the book will appeal to anyone who reads the newspapers and whose main concerns are wider than statistical sources and methods.

1 | History and Politics

Publication of statistics is one of the government's tasks. It might therefore seem as if the government could use its monopoly in this field as a political advantage. It could distort, postpone and suppress figures that put its own economic performance in an unfavourable light. It could exaggerate, leak in advance and publicize figures that seem to be to its credit. Such extreme behaviour happens only in totalitarian regimes, but the reliability of official statistics used in political debate, especially on indicators like unemployment and inflation, has become a political issue.

In a democratic society, the objectivity and openness of official statistics should be beyond reproach. Like all democratic ideals, this one is only imperfectly realized in the UK and many other Western democracies. The British government has only very rarely been accused of 'fiddling the figures'. Indeed, when pressed, most critics can only think of a handful of examples of mistakes or deliberate distortions.

The more general problem relates to less explicit 'manipulation' and underfunding of the statistical service. The fear of manipulation is simply a consequence of the fact that successive governments have felt it necessary to control the statistical service rather than allow it to be independent. In practice, the manipulation which is known about normally takes the form of a selective use of statistics – the government, like any other user of statistics, will try to camouflage reality if it is unfavourable – meddling with the timing and content of publications. The selective use of statistics and the almost daily television and radio arguments between politicians about the meaning of statistics add to the atmosphere of scepticism.

Despite the lack of outright 'fiddling', the history of official statistics has been far from golden. To put it simply, three phases can be identified in the post-war period. The first period, up to the end of the 1970s, was a time of optimism as more and more statistics were published with seemingly no shortage of new resources being devoted to the task. The second period, lasting much of the 1980s, was the equivalent of the Dark Ages. As the 1990s progressed, confidence grew steadily, not least because of the prospect of greater independence, and that bodes well for the future.

POST-WAR OPTIMISM

It was a great step forward when the then Prime Minister, Winston Churchill, established the Central Statistical Office (CSO) in 1941, under its first director, Harry Campion. He was succeeded by Professor Claus Moser, who presided over a major expansion of official statistics, particularly in other government departments. This reflected the passion for statistics of Harold Wilson, who became Prime Minister in 1964, and it followed the recommendations of the now-defunct Parliamentary Estimates Committee in 1966. Their main recommendations were: the creation of the Business Statistics Office to collect data from businesses; the establishment of the Office of Population Censuses and Surveys to collect information from individuals and households; an enhanced role for the CSO in managing statistics across government; and the development of the Government Statistical Service (GSS). With this backing, the government statistics machine grew dramatically in the 1960s and 1970s, producing more and better information.

THE 'CUTS' OF THE 1980s

A far less glorious era descended in 1980, when the Government's approach to official statistics underwent a substantial change. In that year, there was a review of government statistical services under the auspices of Sir Derek Rayner (his team also reviewed other areas of government). On statistics, his main task was to economize on their cost and reduce the burden on the private sector of supplying statistics, mainly through form-filling. It was a blow to the democratic concept of statistics as a public good rather than a political tool.

The Rayner Report said: 'The primary duty of the CSO is to serve central government requirements . . . we have found the Office too heavily committed to serving the public at large.' The review was part of a wider initiative of the Thatcher Government to cut back on bureaucracy across the public sector. It raised questions about the need for a number of the social surveys, the extent of quality checking (criticizing the 'fulsome and perfectionist attention to technical detail'!), the value of research and the rising demands of the European Community. It sought to find private-sector players to plug gaps, cut subsidies to publications (forcing up the prices) and introduced the 'value for money' remit for the director.

There was nothing wrong with the principle of such reviews but in the prevailing climate there were vigorous reductions in statistical resources and activity. The staffing and administrative costs of official statistics were cut by about a quarter over five years, with the CSO's funding falling by a third. Within the limits imposed by the Rayner cuts, and the primary responsibility to ministers, the Government Statistical Service did its best to serve the public interest, but the quality of service suffered.

For nearly all the first fifty years of its life, the CSO was a department in the Cabinet Office. It was technically responsible to the Prime Minister, although in practice it worked closely with the Treasury, sharing the same building until the mid-1990s. In the late 1980s the CSO had a modest remit. It was, for example, directly responsible for publishing less than half the key macroeconomic press releases. The other departments that published key indicators in press notice form (because they were responsible for collecting data) included the Treasury, the Bank of England, the Department of Trade and Industry and the Department of Employment – and the CSO had little influence over them through the GSS structure.

NEW DAWN FOR OFFICIAL STATISTICS

The new era for official statistics dates from 1988 when a number of pressures came to a head. The trigger for change was the influential Treasury and Civil Service Committee of the House of Commons which, in its report on the March Budget, recommended that an investigation into improving reliability of economic statistics be carried out.

As the Committee noted, a number of weaknesses, such as discrepancies between the measures of GDP and the large balancing items and revisions, had led to the problems encountered in interpreting the state of the economy in the mid- to late 1980s. In particular, economic policy was found to have been too expansionary, because the Government did not know how rapidly GDP was growing in the mid-1980s. The economic boom of the mid-1980s (and subsequently the 'bust' of the late 1980s and early 1990s) was largely blamed on the incorrect policy pursued as a result of poor statistics giving a wrong impression.

There was, however, a broader undercurrent of criticism of government statistics during the 1980s. The government had been repeatedly accused of suppressing, abolishing, delaying and manipulating data for its own political ends. In 1989 Channel 4 broadcast a *Dispatches* investigation into the integrity of official statistics, which reported ten examples of interference with official data from many sectors including unemployment, poverty, the census, privatizations and the health service.

The programme included an interview with Sir John Boreham, who had been the director of the CSO until 1985. He said: 'There is a frontier zone in which the Government's desire to show that it is doing well, and the statistical service's desire to be objective and neutral, leads to constant skirmishing. Usually, ministers had an interest in making sure that what was published did not do them a great deal of harm.' He had earlier said (in an article in *Statistical News* in 1985): 'Where necessary we should try, by logic and diplomacy, to persuade colleagues and ministers of the risks of losing public confidence they would run if they suppressed, delayed or misused our statistics, or selected figures to satisfy their social, economic or political viewpoint.'

In June 1988 the Government announced an efficiency scrutiny into the improvements that could be made to government economic statistics. In November 1988 a review team concluded its study and the Government published a report entitled *Government Economic Statistics*. It made a number of recommendations, many of which were implemented. The CSO was established as an enlarged department in July 1989, incorporating the Business Statistics Office (previously part of the Department of Trade and Industry), and assuming responsibility for the Retail Prices Index and the Family Expenditure Survey. It was also set up as a separate department under the Chancellor of the Exchequer rather than as part of the Cabinet Office.

A number of further initiatives were subsequently announced. In May 1990 the then Chancellor of the Exchequer, John Major, launched the first of the so-called Chancellor's initiatives. This concentrated on improving statistics on services, companies and the balance of payments. The second phase in November 1991 under the subsequent Chancellor, Norman Lamont, built on the earlier changes and had as its centrepiece the launch of the CSO as an executive agency. The Conservative Government set up many executive agencies but the CSO was different from most in that it remained a government department in its own right, headed at Permanent Secretary level.

The Chancellor explained that there were two main aims in launching the CSO as an executive agency. First, he said, 'it put the focus on the quality of service provided to customers, inside and outside government'. Indeed, the CSO was allowed to 'consider requests to collect a wider range of data than that needed for the conduct of government business'. Second, he took the opportunity to set out 'publicly the arrangements to ensure the integrity and validity of UK official statistics'. It was made clear that 'ministers will ensure the freedom of the director to maintain and to demonstrate the integrity of the output'. These comments were backed up by detailed aims, objectives and targets. The move was designed to increase public confidence in the statistical output.

The Treasury said it needed data on a regular basis that are comprehensive in coverage, accurate, timely, coherent, not subject to large revision or bias and consistent with other information. The framework document set out targets in respect of all these features and it required the CSO's director to report to ministers annually, summarizing the extent to which targets had been met and what action was being taken, where targets had *not* been met, to remedy the situation. There was some extra cash as part of the initiative and the document suggested that the Treasury would view any further requests for additional resources favourably. Although substantial additional resources were never forthcoming the rhetoric was very different from that associated with the 'Rayner doctrine' in the 1980s.

In May 1992 the Government further clarified its position in a speech given by the Chancellor to the Confederation of British Industry (CBI). He emphasized that the Government required better statistics for its own use and that they should be 'for the benefit of business and for the public at large'. In addition, he hoped that 'the CSO's new framework document will dispel any remaining confusion' about the 'much misunderstood' White Paper from 1981. The 1993 White Paper on open government, part of the Citizen's Charter initiative, further spelt out the need for readily available data and included social as well as economic statistics.

The CSO devised and launched a mission statement in 1993. The overall aim was to ensure that CSO statistics are used, 'because our efforts are not worthwhile, however laudable they may be, unless decision-making, research or debate is influenced'. The four key principles were: communication with others, respecting providers of data, professionalism and integrity and valuing staff.

The changes put in place in the five years from 1988 undoubtedly represented a marked improvement, but it was not the end of the debate. While the greater use of statutory rather than voluntary surveys and the expansion of such inquiries were developments to be welcomed, the new framework left many unanswered questions. (See the introduction to *Measuring the Economy*, by Christopher Johnson and Simon Briscoe, published by Penguin in 1995, for a fuller description.)

It is always dangerous to be complacent about government statistics. Box 1.1 sets out some 'anecdotes' from the Chancellorship of Nigel Lawson (1983–9) to show how politicians feel about statistics. It shows that improvements in statistics must be seen and must be institutionalized – and not just spoken about – as they can easily be lost. In full awareness of the issues, the Royal Statistical Society (RSS), for instance, called in 1991 for greater centralization and control of statistics, an enhancement of methodological work, a National Statistical Commission and a UK Statistics Act. The set-up achieved by the mid-1990s went much of the way towards the ideal envisaged by the RSS, but it clearly fell short.

Box 1.1. **Views on statistics from Nigel Lawson**

The Lawson memoirs offer us several examples of how statistics get caught up in the business of politics. Lawson was not short of strong views about statistics. 'The practical problem, however, which is unlikely to go away, is that financial markets are always liable to react sharply to the latest piece of statistical information, however dubious its quality.'

The first example concerns the RPI. In a section headed 'The

ludicrous RPI', Lawson says that he 'was not helped by the composition of the generally accepted measure of inflation in the UK, the
RPI. This had been very foolishly amended during the early period
of the previous Labour government, in 1975, to include as a proxy
for the cost of owner-occupied housing the level of mortgage interest
payments.' He goes on to say that 'the inclusion of mortgage repay-
ments was both ludicrous and perverse . . . their inclusion meant
that the principal means of fighting inflation – raising interest rates
– shows as an increase in the rate of inflation'.

He continues: 'In a sane world the obvious answer would have
been to undo the mistaken 1975 change in the composition of the
RPI. But in the real world this is a good deal easier said than
done. The constituent parts of the RPI were determined not by the
government acting alone but on the advice of the RPI Advisory
Committee, a body at that time appointed by the Secretary of State
for Employment. The Committee was ostensibly set up to ensure
the government did not tamper with the RPI. In practice it reflected
the interplay of the various pressure groups which served on it.'

He concludes: 'the composition of the RPI advisory committee
was loaded against the government . . .' and felt that the chance of
reforming the RPI was low. So he decided to pursue other routes
such as publishing alternative measures of inflation simultaneously.
He already had a record of introducing alternative measures of
inflation. As Financial Secretary to the Treasury, he had introduced
the Tax and Prices Index in 1979.

The second example concerns the financial sector. In a section
titled 'They don't give you the figures', Lawson describes how when
he was Chancellor the responsibility for the financial sector was
divided between the Treasury (with responsibility for banks and
building societies), the Department of Trade and Industry (securities
and insurance industry) and the Bank of England. The subdivision
made little sense from a regulatory point of view and it naturally
made it difficult to compile and present worthwhile statistics on an
increasingly important sector of the economy.

Third, Lawson had strong views on the management of the CSO.
During the bulk of his Chancellorship the CSO came under the
control of the Cabinet Office, and therefore under the nominal
command of the Prime Minister. Lawson clearly felt that he and it

would be better under his control! 'The CSO was effectively outwith ministerial control altogether,' he writes. 'I have little doubt that this contributed to the deterioration in the reliability of the key statistics it provided. It was a monopoly producer of most economic statistics which felt itself under no obligation to meet the legitimate needs of its principal customer.' Not surprisingly, perhaps, the Chancellor was delighted with the conclusions of the 1988 Review that said that the CSO should come under his responsibility. As he says, they could then 'insist that the CSO's finite resources were devoted to the statistical series they most needed to steer the economy'.

'It is sometimes alleged', he claims, 'that the deterioration in the quality of the official statistics was due very largely to the cutbacks in staff and statistical coverage that the government imposed on the CSO in the early 1980s. In fact, most of the statistical series which were discontinued in 1980 and 1981 were appropriate to an age of detailed economic intervention, but not to one in which the government recognised that its task was to influence the economic framework. There was little point in burdening businessmen with the responsibility to report statistics that the government no longer required. In any case, apart from the failure to make the CSO responsible to its principal customer, the main reason for the deteriorating quality of the statistics was not staff shortages or discontinued series, but the deregulation of the economy in general and the liberalisation of the financial markets in particular.'

Critics of the Government viewed Lawson's role in a rather different light during the 1980s. He was described as having a cavalier attitude towards statistics; deciding that monetary statistics were more important than the 'real economy' statistics; realizing that real economy statistics would produce a gloomy message in those early years; desiring to cut government spending and the numbers of civil servants; and wanting to lighten the form-filling burden on industry. To the extent that these factors were the driving force behind the deterioration in statistical output during the 1980s, the reforms of the 1990s can be seen as an attempt to ensure that the cuts were not repeated.

(Quotations from Nigel Lawson,
The View from No. 11: Memoirs of a Tory Radical, Bantam Press, 1992)

CONTINUED IMPROVEMENTS IN THE 1990s

The initiatives of the early 1990s provided a platform for the CSO to encourage developments across the GSS. There were four areas in which the then head of the GSS, Bill McLennan, sought to make progress. (Indeed, the appointment of McLennan, an Australian statistician and widely viewed as a radical, was in itself probably a sign of willingness to change.) The first was to focus and co-ordinate the statistical work with Europe. It was clear that, following the ratification of the Maastricht Treaty of 1992, European affairs would have a growing impact on the UK's statistical work. The second area was the provision of up-to-date information on statistical sources. (Following the publication of a highly acclaimed guide two decades before, many users felt that the Government had failed in this respect.) Third was the development of a code of practice.

The fourth element, to investigate the overall efficiency and effectiveness of the GSS, including where there might be gaps in the overall statistical picture, produced the most significant conclusions. It was felt that the coverage of economic statistics was quite good and was improving as new initiatives came on stream. It was also felt that the provision of social statistics was reasonably good despite a fragmentation and inconsistency in the content and approach. Regional statistics, by contrast, were found to be lacking. It was from these investigations into the gaps in the official statistics, and after wide-ranging discussions across government, that the case for the creation of a new Office for National Statistics, combining the Central Statistical Office and the Office of Population Censuses and Surveys (OPCS), was born.

Accordingly, 1995 saw the start of another significant round of change. In January 1995 Kenneth Clarke, Chancellor of the Exchequer, and Virginia Bottomley, Secretary of State for Health, announced that they were considering the benefits of merging the OPCS and CSO. Following preliminary work, they announced in April that they did see benefits in the merger and launched a public consultation. The driving force for the proposals was to meet a widely perceived need for greater coherence and compatibility in government statistics, to improve the setting of statistical priorities, to improve presentation and to achieve easier public access.

The results of the consultation exercise were published in September

1995. The proposal received broad support from all sectors, including the Royal Statistical Society. There was clear support for greater integration between social and economic statistics; improved access to official statistics; combining the advantages of a decentralized system with a strong and independent co-ordinating agency; and providing benefits for all users, both government and non-government.

The key proposals were:

- The Agency (a government 'Next Steps' Agency) would be independent of any other government department and be accountable to the Chancellor of the Exchequer. (This did not represent a change for the CSO but it did raise concerns about whether a lower priority would be given to the work of the OPCS. The publication of a framework document setting out clear roles and functions was designed to counter this.)
- The changes should improve the quality of statistical support to government and non-government users. They should support the open government policies (see Box 1.2, 'Open government') and enable better-informed decisions to be taken about statistical priorities.
- The Agency would establish and maintain a central database of key economic and social statistics, produced to common classifications, definitions and standards.
- As well as providing statistics now required by government, it would ensure that statistics from the central database were made widely and speedily available to the public.
- The Agency would meet the perceived need for greater coherence and compatibility of government statistics, for improved presentation and for easier public access. Included as part of this was the publication of analyses and commentary bringing together statistics from different sources to present both national and sub-national pictures of trends and developments.
- The changes should enable gaps in government statistics to be identified more easily.
- The Agency would be in a stronger position to exploit technological development, including electronic dissemination.
- The proposals would not remove from departments any of their existing statistical responsibilities, although some changes would not be ruled out where they would be sensible and cost effective.

Box 1.2. **Open government**

The White Paper on Open government included the following comments.

'Official statistics contain a vast range of information about the economy and society. They are collected by government to inform debate, decision-making and research both within the government and by the wider community. They provide an objective perspective of the changes taking place in national life and allow comparisons between periods of time and geographical areas.

'Vital as this is, open access to official statistics provides the citizen with more than a picture of society. It offers a window on the work and performance of government itself, showing the scale of government activity in every area of public policy and allowing the impact of government policies and actions to be assessed.

'Reliable social and economic statistics are fundamental to the Citizen's Charter and to open government. It is the responsibility of government to provide them and to maintain public confidence in them.

'Since the Central Statistical Office became an agency it has announced certain improvements which mean that:

● All CSO statistics are now published as early as possible, with many being released much more quickly than before.
● CSO data are made available to all users at the same time, although ministers, and where appropriate the governor of the Bank of England, and some officials receive copies of key statistical releases one-and-a-half days in advance.
● The integrity of the statistics has been demonstrated by making it clear that the CSO is entirely responsible for the contents of its press releases, subject only to advance consultation with the Chancellor of the Exchequer or the Economic Secretary on changes in format.

'Other departments, in consultation with the head of the Government Statistical Service, are also introducing measures to help ensure the consistency of release practice for key official statistics.'

(from the 1993 White Paper, *Open Government*)'

- The existing CSO and OPCS policies and practices in respect of the confidentiality and security of data would continue.
- An advisory committee would be established to advise the head of the Agency and the Government Statistical Service on statistical issues and priorities.
- The new Agency would have a staff of about 3,200 (1,900 from OPCS – mostly in registration – and 1,300 from the CSO) and an annual budget of £125 million.
- The component parts would move to new premises at Drummond Gate, Pimlico in London in early 1996 and the new structure would commence from April 1996.

The most frequently identified concerns or areas where respondents sought reassurance were set out in the merger document. The key concerns were: the accountability and independence of the proposed agency; maintaining current CSO and OPCS services and standards; maintaining the confidentiality and security of data; improving accessibility within an appropriate charging policy; and clarifying the respective roles of the new agency and the private sector. These were addressed in the Government response and the Office for National Statistics (ONS) was subsequently born.

Coincidentally, the Employment Department was abolished during the consultation period, and responsibility for labour market statistics was transferred to the CSO. This transfer was widely welcomed as it fitted neatly with the proposed agency's agenda better to integrate social and economic statistics. Labour market statistics are, of course, important to both economic and social conditions. In addition, there had always been suspicions about the political motives of the Employment Department's statisticians, not least on account of the damage to the reputation of official statistics caused by the many changes to the definition of unemployment.

Dr Tim Holt, who had been appointed head of the CSO and head of the Government Statistical Service in July 1995, became the first Director of and launched the Office for National Statistics at the end of March 1996. He was also appointed as Registrar General. The framework document for the launch was issued with a foreword by Kenneth Clarke, the then Chancellor of the Exchequer, to whom the Director would ultimately report. The first business plan for the ONS, covering the period 1996/7 to 1998/9, set out the structure of the department in more detail along with the principal aims, objectives and issues it faced.

It is clear that compared to the dark days at the end of the 1980s, much had changed for the better and more improvements were promised. The 1990s were, however, a time of rapid change in information provision and dissemination, and government statisticians were finding the pace hard to keep up with. During this period, private-sector companies became increasingly involved in the collection and dissemination of official data. Most notably, the collection of the data for the RPI was put out to tender. Demands and expectations from users were none the less growing exponentially and many economic activities were becoming harder to measure. Against a background of constant reorganization and staffing difficulties – and, despite the rhetoric, continuing budget restraint – it was impossible for the ONS to fulfil its potential.

NEW LABOUR, NEW STATISTICS?

At the time of writing (mid-1999) the ONS was in the midst of the latest change. In May 1997 a Labour Government was elected. Its manifesto committed it to a comprehensive programme of constitutional reform as part of developing a new relationship between government and citizens based on openness and trust. One element was the commitment to an independent national statistical service.

Accordingly, in February 1998 the then Economic Secretary to the Treasury launched a Green Paper (*Statistics: A Matter of Trust*). Its key aims were widely welcomed even if there was some criticism of the content of the Green Paper itself. The debate in the Green Paper was seen as shallow. There were warnings that parliamentary time for legislation would be hard to find and that the government would have to look closely at the likely costs of any change. All of this hinted at modest change. In opposition, Labour had been a vocal supporter for improvements in official statistics. It began to appear that, once in government, enthusiasm was waning, perhaps offering further evidence of ministers' desire to exert control over statistics.

The Green Paper set out four possible models: strengthening existing arrangements; establishing a governing body for national statistics (a new concept which required definition as part of the process); establishing an independent Statistical Commission; and establishing a centralized

Statistical Office reporting directly to Parliament. The four models were not seen as being mutually exclusive. The consultation period closed at the end of May 1998 and it had been expected that the results of the consultation would be announced before the summer parliamentary recess.

The submission from the RSS (May 1998) concluded that there were merits in each of the models set out in the consultation paper. Rather than selecting one model, it set out a number of principles which it felt ought to guide the deliberations:

● The establishment and maintenance of the set of National Statistics, the scope and content of which would reflect public interest and continue to respond to needs over time. Independence and integrity would be assured by adopting the highest professional standards.
● There should be a cultural shift among those producing and using statistics, to include among other things an increased focus on the usefulness of outputs.
● The scope of National Statistics should include all statistics of public interest at the national, regional and local levels, regardless of the agency that produces them.
● A UK statistician should be appointed to have the ultimate professional authority for defining and auditing the accuracy, relevance and integrity of the statistics.
● A National Statistical Commission should be established to protect and promote the quality of National Statistics. It should be independent of any single producer and of political interference.
● An Act of Parliament should establish the powers, duties and rights of the UK statistician and of the Commission.
● A system of self-certification of quality and fitness for purpose, subject to audit by the UK statistician, would mean that only limited changes to statistical structures within government and agencies should be necessary.

The Government's proposals, in the form of a White Paper, were not published in 1998 as expected. Instead, two other initiatives dominated government time. First, the Treasury carried out a comprehensive spending review across government (in 1997 and into 1998) to evaluate public spending priorities for the remainder of the Parliament. The ONS was included and duly carried out its departmental spending review. This seemed to be largely a public relations exercise on the part of the Treasury and resulted in some apparently minor revised aims and objectives, but little else. Importantly, its budget allocations were largely unchanged.

Second, and more importantly, the Economic Secretary announced (in July 1998) an efficiency scrutiny by external management consultants to cover the whole of the ONS's operations. Its report was published in February 1999. The study envisaged a streamlining of activities and more private sector partnerships to allow the ONS to direct its professional resources to those areas – statistics and customer relations – where it has the largest contribution to make. It envisaged a drop of about 1,000 in ONS staffing from the prevailing level of 3,300. While many of these posts could be transferred to the private sector a number would be lost. It was estimated by the consultants that efficiency savings of £20 million a year, roughly 16 per cent of budget, could be achieved within several years. There was some scepticism as to whether the savings were achievable but the general principles and direction of the report were widely accepted and set a course for the ONS for the coming years.

Independently, the House of Commons Treasury Committee announced in May 1998 that it had established a subcommittee to scrutinize the departments and agencies for which the Chancellor of the Exchequer is responsible. In view of the government proposals to change the framework governing official statistics, set out in the Green Paper, the subcommittee decided that the ONS would be the subject of its first inquiry. The subcommittee published a critical report in December 1998, including twenty-two recommendations. The report did not want to pre-empt the consultation on the new framework but it did identify criteria which it said the new arrangements would need to satisfy. (The report was debated in the House of Commons in October 1999.)

These exercises on their own were probably sufficient to delay the publication of the White Paper, but an additional factor – the suspension of the average earnings index in November 1998 – implied further delay. The Treasury launched a review of the earnings series which subsequently reported in March 1999. (See Chapter 6, Box 6.4, for the details of this episode.)

The Government's White Paper 'Building Trust in Statistics', was eventually published in October 1999. The Economic Secretary, Melanie Johnson, launching the White Paper, said: 'Enhancing the quality and integrity of official statistics is at the heart of our new proposals.' The proposal to create a Statistics Commission which 'will be independent of both ministers and the producers of statistics' was widely welcomed – it was the option that emerged as the consensus from the consultation exercise.

There was, however, some concern expressed by the statistics community, including the Royal Statistical Society. First, the proposed scope of National Statistics was very narrow, with only the output of the Office for National Statistics being automatically included. In future, ministers would be able to include the output of their departments if they wished to do so. Second, the Treasury did not intend to enshrine the changes in legislation. Accordingly, it would be open to future governments to alter the arrangements. The Treasury promised a more detailed document, the Framework for National Statistics, by the end of 1999. That deadline was missed too, even though the plan remained to start the new structure in April 2000.

CONCLUSION

Government statistics have had a chequered history in the last two decades but it is probably right to be optimistic about the future. It must be noted that even the most well-intentioned government can be very slow to change bad habits. But the White Paper showed that departmental ministers working with their own statisticians still have considerable power and like to maintain the influence over the statistics that they produce. Government statisticians are now more prepared at least to talk about meeting the needs of non-government users. Public needs and demands are growing in such a way that further improvements in government statistics will prove irresistible in the years ahead.

2 | Data Issues

BACKGROUND TO THE INTEREST IN STATISTICAL DATA

Information has value. Governments and opposition parties want to know whether the Government's policies are succeeding. Companies want to know about their markets and their competitors. People who work in the financial markets want to know what is happening in the economy to judge whether asset prices will rise or fall. Researchers want to research and the media want firm foundations for their stories. Perhaps most importantly, citizens need to know about the world in which they live in order to make informed decisions.

It is important to remember that statistical data provide weekly, monthly, quarterly or annual snapshots of a constantly changing world. It would be too hard or tedious to follow this constant process every hour or every day. It is possible to imagine, however, some 'real-time' statistics for some economic data series in the way that we have real-time data for foreign exchange movements. There could be feeds from shop tills to give us data on retail sales or from tax offices to tell us about government receipts. But it is hardly practical in the near-term. In any case, the potential and actual distortions to very short-term movements could give incorrect steers from such data. By contrast, under the current system the release of data, when it happens, can provide undue focus for all concerned, leading to feverish attention by the markets and the media.

It is a fact of life, however, that the perfect data set for any given situation does not exist. It is always necessary to make do with what is available. This inevitably means we are forever engaged in a process of compromise, as a result of which the unwary can draw misleading conclusions. For example, we might look at credit card usage to learn more about the strength of consumer demand. If we do we must be aware that the fashion for reduced usage of cheques and increased usage of plastic means of payment will lead to a stronger trend in credit card usage than in retail sales. This chapter explains some of the issues that have to be addressed by users of macro-economic data.

FINANCIAL MARKETS, HUMANS AND HUMAN BEHAVIOUR

The way in which the markets focus on particular pieces of data can often be explained by human nature; specifically, the reaction to uncertainty. There is so much information available and so much confusion about what it means. It is therefore understandable that people prefer to give most weight to the tangible and the immediate, even though, in reality, one new piece of data is unlikely to add much to the world view.

Often one statistic becomes a totem, supposedly the key to understanding the economy. One example has been the near-obsessive focus in the 1990s on the publication of the US labour market report, often referred to as the non-farm payrolls data. Financial markets rarely move during the European morning, prior to 13.30 launch time (08.30 Eastern Standard Time in the US). Markets then trade frantically for ten or fifteen minutes before activity again fades away. None the less it is rare for payrolls numbers to have a lasting impact. This is partly because very strong or very weak data are usually dismissed as a statistical freak and partly because the labour market report has so many elements that there is bound to be some strength and some weakness visible to those looking for strength or weakness. The search for greater certainty is also seen in market and media reaction to comments from senior government officials. The markets are always trying to second-guess which particular piece of data is most important, with the effect that whenever a senior official refers to one piece of data, it becomes disproportionately important.

The focus on the short term seems to conflict with the avowed aim of most governments which is to set policy in a long-term context. The explanation for this lies in the realization that no one ever knows what the next crisis or ill wind will be. The hope of the analyst who crawls over every piece of data is that he will spot a new trend, the new big theme, before his peer group. Similarly, the analyst will hope to spot which data are currently being blown out of proportion.

DIFFERENT DATA ARE IMPORTANT AT DIFFERENT TIMES

In economics, as in any other business, fashions are constantly changing. Policy-makers, the financial markets and the media all find their focus shifting over often short periods of time. Concern about a particular issue seems very real at the time but can seem much less important just a few months later. For example, the principal concern for financial markets in 1997 was the extent of overheating in the US. That concern dissipated rapidly towards the end of the year and into 1998 as the extent of the financial crisis in emerging markets became clear.

There are three main reasons why attention might shift from one topic to another:

● Changes in the policy structure. The last two decades in the UK saw three very distinct policy targets. Money supply was in vogue in the early 1980s, followed by the exchange rate in the late 1980s and early 1990s, only to be superseded by retail price inflation from 1992 onwards. It is obvious that as the policy focus shifts so does the importance attached to different data. The authorities are not always explicit about what is of greatest interest to them, leaving the markets with an element of guesswork.
● The state of the economic cycle. When the cycle is more mature, observers tend to seek signs of inflation. As an economy drifts towards recession the attention will be on different variables, typically unemployment.
● Secular change. There was increased discussion during the 1990s about the so-called 'new paradigm' which suggested that the inflationary pressures globally were very weak. Accordingly, there was less interest shown in some of the leading indicators of inflation.

It would also be fair to say that in the short term, the attention span of many observers is such that a particular statistic rarely stays in the limelight for more than a few months.

EACH FINANCIAL MARKET HAS ITS OWN FAVOURITE DATA

Many different products are traded in the world's financial markets and each market follows certain data more closely than others.

● Commodity markets. The factors affecting supply – for example, labour availability, weather, war, political unrest – or demand – for example, economic growth, trade barriers – of commodities are most important.
● Bond and money markets. The most important variable is inflation as it affects both the outlook for short-term interest rates and the value of long-term fixed interest rate bonds. The key lead indicators of inflation are also important. The supply of government bonds is largely influenced by the need to raise money. Accordingly, the state of public sector deficits is watched closely.
● Equity markets. Economic growth is important, as during periods of strong economic growth most companies will perform well, increasing their profits, and merger activity will be increased. Domestically oriented companies will pay particular attention to consumer demand and the outlook for investment, while exporting companies will pay more attention to changes in the exchange rate.
● Currency markets. Any variables that throw light on possible changes in capital flows will be of interest. The trade deficit and differential trends in expected interest rates are perhaps the most important.

HOW ARE THE DATA RELEASED?

In the UK most of the important indicators are released by means of press notices. The Government Statistical Service (comprising the ONS and the statisticians in other government departments) refers to these as First Releases. The releases can be collected from the appropriate government department but are generally distributed by messenger in central London to a few agencies, newspapers, broadcasting stations and City firms. It is also possible to subscribe to these press releases and to receive them in the post a day or two after their release.

There is no reason why this information should not be made instantly available to anyone in the home or office who has the appropriate screen and telecommunications equipment. Indeed, in the early 1990s the CSO introduced a service called Statfax that enables anyone with a fax machine to dial in for copies of press releases. By 1999 the ONS was – belatedly – beginning to place their data releases on the Internet.

Most members of the public never see these press notices, but have to rely on the incomplete and selective versions of them which are released on wire services, radio and television, and in the next day's newspapers. Many members of the public buy the information in a variety of government statistical publications. By the time these publications appear, however, the following month's indicators in press release form may already make the publications out of date.

The last decade has seen a considerable tightening of the security surrounding the release of official data. The release time of the vast majority of press releases is now co-ordinated at 9.30 a.m. The strict embargo ensures that no one gets an unfair advantage, in the financial markets in particular, by seeing the information early. A small number of people (mainly government ministers and senior officials – the list is available from the ONS) see the data a day or two prior to its release. Accordingly, although information from official economic releases seldom leaks out of Whitehall in advance, there remain a small number of instances each year when ministers are suspected of leaking, usually with the desire to soften the blow of bad news.

HOW QUICK IS THE RESPONSE TO DATA?

The most rapid and dramatic responses to data are found in financial markets. Within the financial markets there are many different players who respond to the data over different time horizons. A trader on a futures exchange in the financial markets will respond immediately on seeing the headline figure of the data release. It is quite likely that within a minute or two the traders' (profitable or unprofitable) response to the data will be over.

Other employees of financial markets, sitting on banks' dealing floors, will respond to data over a period of several hours. These salesmen and traders will be interested in the immediate headline but will also be interested in analysis of the numbers. It is quite likely that the trader on the dealing floor will continue to respond to a data release for some hours after the impact moment. He will be interested in the analysis from his own company's economists and any response from investors in the market.

It is an important task of the City economist to make the post-release assessment of data. This will involve use of the screen-based news services available on dealing floors and the Internet, as well as, perhaps, telephoning and faxing the providers of the statistics to access any information that they are prepared to release.

The end investors, the clients of the dealing floor brokers, will receive the information flow but in many cases will not make investment decisions in the short term. Many pension funds only make major investment decisions every few weeks or months. These players in the market will often want to see a change in the trend in the data, which often means two or three observations. Their need for analysis in common with most private investors is much less urgent and they will normally be happy to soak up information from newspapers and the weekly and monthly circulars from economists.

Financial markets are now global and operate over three separate time zones: the Far East, Europe and the United States. The response to a piece of data is often different in different time zones. It is quite possible for investors in the US to have different expectations from their counterparts in Europe. Accordingly, it is not unknown for European data released in Europe in the early morning to have the first impact at the time of release and the second impact in the early afternoon, European time, when the US markets open.

Data releases are, of course, of interest to those working outside financial markets. The normal short-term transmission mechanism is through the media. The various electronic wire services will announce the data shortly after release, but it is television programmes and daily newspapers that have the greatest impact and reach the largest audiences. Beyond the media and the financial markets there are many users of economic data, but for those working for corporates or in research, time sensitivity is far less of an issue. The most common sources are hard copy versions of monthly or quarterly compendia of data and a variety of electronic data feeds.

Statements from the Government often accompany the release of important data. These 'political' press releases are distinct from the neutral statistical releases, but are often confused in the eyes and minds of readers. The financial markets always want to know how government policy will be affected by any data. As the Government very rarely reveals such information explicitly (especially not in the political press releases, which tend to be self-congratulatory in tone), markets have to rely on their own analysts, independent research groups and other commentators, for interpretation.

PERVERSE REACTIONS

Markets can react to the same piece of data in different ways in different circumstances. For example, the conventional wisdom is that higher interest rates will lead to a stronger currency. But the opposite may well also be the case, if the higher interest rates are seen as inappropriate, in some way damaging or indicative of a weak government. In such cases, overseas investors might sell bonds and equities, putting downward pressure on the currency. In the late 1990s the Japanese yen was strong despite a weak economy because Japanese institutions were having to repatriate capital.

DATA QUALITY

It is vital to appreciate that not all data are of the same quality. Accordingly, when forming an assessment of the state of the economy it is appropriate to give greater weight to trends that are appearing in data of higher quality. This book describes the relative merits of the data covered in each chapter. The key points to look for, however, are the following:

● The size and quality of the survey
● Revisions policy
● Timeliness
● Seasonal adjustment.

It stands to reason that if data are born of a small out of date sample survey, are subject to large revision, are published some months after the relevant time period and fail to adjust for seasonal factors, there will be less interest in the trends. There are many examples of how improvements in data quality have led to increased attention being paid to the numbers. The UK Labour Force Survey is one such example. At the start of the 1990s the survey was annual and was published nearly two years in arrears. It is now published monthly, on a rolling quarterly basis, soon after the end of the reference period and accordingly receives much more attention.

The attitude of the data producers also has a significant influence on the use that is made of the resulting product. Different cultures attach different priorities to making decent data publicly available. As a general rule, Anglo-Saxon countries score more highly in assessments of macro data. Even within countries there can be considerable differences between data sets. The differences normally reflect the varying traditions of the ministries and industries or the structure of regional government within the country. For example, some countries will make explicit allowance for black, informal or underground economy activity in the Gross Domestic Product (GDP) figures. There are rarely logical explanations for some raw data being subjected to more complex adjustments than others.

Unfortunately, it is becoming harder all the time to carry out statistical measurements, just as more importance is being attached to them. There are two principal reasons for this:

● First, deregulation of economic activity removes much of the direct access to private sector figures that the public sector used to have. The right not to fill in statistical returns is in itself a form of deregulation. There is a strong culture of lessening the burden of form-filling on smaller companies. Freedoms of this kind are usually obtained at the cost of statistical accuracy.
● Second, economic and financial innovation makes it harder to measure activity. There are many examples, but consider how the rapid pace of innovation in banking, the changing structure of the industrial and commercial companies sector (increased rates of mergers and acquisi-

tions activity and high levels of new starts), the arrival of e-commerce, increased international trade and outsourcing, and the blurring of the boundary between public and private sectors, have had an effect. All these developments cast doubts over the meaning, accuracy and worth of some of the related indicators.

There are, none the less, some benefits from technical change and modernization for statisticians. For example, statisticians are likely to have increased access to an ever-expanding number of databases, containing all sorts of information.

DATA SOURCES AND DEFINITIONS

It is important to be aware that some data are derived from administrative sources and others are collected through purpose-made surveys. The former may well have major limitations on their usefulness for analysis. It is quite unlikely, for example, that a definition that falls out of an administrative system will be precisely the same definition that a researcher or analyst would choose. Available data sets are nearly always proxies for the data that the analyst would ideally want. Where the official data on a subject are poor, there tends to be increased reliance on survey data. In the UK, a question from the CBI survey, for example, tends to be more closely followed if there is no official data equivalent.

It is not uncommon for statistics to change. When this happens, the series usually experiences a step change that is disruptive for analysis. There are three main reasons why change can occur:

- The rules and regulations of an administrative system can be changed.
- Statisticians can make changes to purpose-made surveys in order to improve data quality. Such changes are usually made with good intent but can none the less be disruptive.
- The government itself can also redefine indicators to suit its cause. Un-employment, monetary aggregates and public sector borrowing are examples of statistics that have been changed for political or policy reasons.

The best-known example of a high profile administrative data source with regular definition changes is the monthly measure of unemployment based on the benefit claimant count. Chapter 6 lists the major changes and discusses this problem in depth (see pp. 119–34). There are many other diverse examples, however. The conversion of a number of building societies to banks, mostly during 1997, has rendered building society data very hard to interpret.

Best practice is clearly to provide revised back data on the new definition, but this is not always done. The step changes in series can be frustrating for those analysing data over the medium-term. Indeed, many econometricians who are interested in the dynamic behaviour of the economy would rather have a poorly defined series that is time consistent than a better defined series which is inconsistent over time. But the time horizon for many in financial markets is sufficiently short for changes in definition to be readily forgotten.

Step changes can be frustrating for the analyst but arguably more dangerous are small, evolutionary changes to statistical series. These occur most frequently when sampling frame product boundaries change. For example, if the focus of a given company changes, returns from that company could change from being classified under one sector to being classified under another. Such modest changes are unlikely to be announced or even known about outside the office of the compilers, and will simply appear to the user of the statistic as a change in trend.

REVISIONS POLICY

There is a tendency to attach enormous importance to the latest data point when it is released. Many people ask simply whether the headline number in the latest month is higher or lower than the previous month. There is often considerable pressure to do this even though many data are subject to large revisions. For some data, the revision to the penultimate data point can be greater than the difference between the two last successive data points. For example, if the latest data showed a rise on the month of 0.3 per cent when −0.3 per cent was expected, the conclusion will be that the series is stronger than thought. But if, in the same release, the previous month's output is revised down by 0.6 per cent, the latest month is not strong. Indeed, the level of output in the latest month is exactly what the market had anticipated.

It would clearly be ideal if the initial estimates were never revised, but to wait for all possible information would mean a delay in publication that is unacceptable to users. Revisions are, therefore, a necessary burden.

There is a deliberate policy with some data never to revise the first estimate unless an obvious error has been made. One example is the UK RPI. In most cases, however, data are revised. In general, statistical authorities aim to keep revisions to a minimum and have usually been successful. By contrast, in some exceptional cases, it could almost be said that data are released deliberately 'wrong'. It is not unprecedented for statistical authorities (though it is very rare in the UK) to say, on the release of a piece of data, that when the revisions are published the estimate will be revised. One important example of such a practice is the data for manufacturing orders and production in Germany. The statistics office often says on data release that it expects a large future revision in a certain direction. It is difficult for interested parties to know what, for example, to make of a larger than expected fall in the latest month, but with the effective promise of an upward revision!

There is no short cut on the issue of revisions, except to learn what is likely with each data set. This is important as the trend in some series can change with the release of subsequent data. Some analysts still even try to forecast revisions to data that are already released. This is a difficult and imprecise science and it is often related to the casting of doubt on data accuracy if the original release is not close to expectations. Where there is known bias in the early data returns, the UK's ONS often allows for it in deriving the initial releases. Revisions can also occur when seasonal adjustments are changed – depending on series this will happen every month or quarter on a rolling basis or at one set time in the year.

PERIODICITY

Data are available for different time periods. While most of the economic data is available monthly or quarterly, some are available weekly or just annually. Some, of course, are not available at all!

Even when data appear to be for the same period, they are often not. Consider the following list that shows the periods covered by, for example, the January 1999 data:

- Trade figures and public sector borrowing – calendar month
- Retail sales – four week period from 28 December
- RPI – middle Tuesday
- CBI industrial trends survey – 17 December to 13 January
- CBI distributive trades survey – 7 January to 27 January
- Unemployment claimant count – 14 January
- Broad money supply – last day of the month
- Narrow money supply – average of the Wednesdays in the month.

Although this feature is statistically untidy, it probably causes only a little distortion to the data. Attention tends to be focused on data as they are released regardless of the time period to which they relate.

RELEASE MECHANISMS

The best practice for a national statistical office is to publish a timetable of data releases some months in advance and then to release the data at set times in line with that timetable, having not given the data to anyone beforehand. While some countries get close to this ideal state, the vast majority fall well short. In the case of most countries, the failure to achieve best practice has more to do with sloppiness and a lack of interest rather than anything more sinister and suspicious. The decentralized or federal structure of many countries can make it difficult for a central or national authority to co-ordinate data releases. For example, in Germany the consumer price index (CPI) is released first by each *Land* and only then can the national figure be calculated. In general, markets where interest in data is higher are usually found in countries where there are also pre-published calendars for release dates.

The release mechanisms for non-official data are even more varied. Some organizations do match best practice but the majority do not. Data are sometimes released overnight to the press and can find their way into the market ahead of official release. Some data do not have official release times, while others do but are deliberately leaked in advance of official publication. There have even been some examples when data could be bought early! In general, important data are released in sensible ways. There are some notable exceptions outside the UK, such as the unemployment figures for Germany and France, which are regularly leaked early.

TRUSTWORTHINESS

In most countries, the bulk of the most important economic data is trustworthy. In general, data can be relied upon if they are produced by the country's national statistical office. We should note, however, that the data produced by any organization will be spread over a wide quality range. There can also be significant quality variations within one data set, for example the various components of national accounts.

In some countries, however, there may be political interference. In developed democracies, the interference is much more likely to be very discreet and subtle, for example by failing to fund the collection of potentially sensitive statistics or to present them in a clear way, and, rarely, by the manipulation of figures that are published.

Data that are not published by the national statistical office can be much less reliable. It is always important to check the trustworthiness of data, as, if the quality of the data is very poor, the conclusions that can sensibly be drawn are limited. Sample sizes of some of the commercial surveys are just a fraction of the size of the official equivalent and they may not have complete coverage. Clearly, in some cases, trade associations for example can be very well placed to collect data. Form-filling is not a popular activity, however, so a survey that has little respect and no statutory backing might not have a good response rate.

The producers of statistics in a democracy rarely intend to deceive. The greater problem is a lack of professionalism coupled with a desire to get large headlines for the data. The latest data point in a monthly survey could easily be given some false significance by the sponsors. For example, they could describe it as the highest or lowest since the survey began even though the survey is only one or two years old! It is also quite possible that the organization producing the statistics, be it a government department, a trade association or any other producer, will have a vested interest and will focus on a positive feature of the data rather than the main message if that happens to be downbeat.

INTERNATIONAL COMPARISONS

The problems encountered when making comparisons between statistics within one country are magnified when comparing statistics from different countries. Statistics which on the face of it seem to be identical often turn out to be quite different. For example, consumer price indices (even in Europe where comparisons are made using a so-called harmonized index of consumer prices) will have different weights, relate to different time periods, have different sample sizes and structures, etc. A major step forward was made in late 1998 and early 1999, when European Union countries started to publish their national accounts on a common basis for the first time.

As administrative systems are invariably different in different countries, data derived from them will be on a different basis. Even data from specifically constructed questionnaires can elicit different responses in different countries. Employment surveys, for example, have to struggle with a different view of what constitutes work in different countries where family and business structures can be very different.

WHAT PRICE FORECASTS?

The bulk of economic forecasting activity concerns predicting the outcome over the next one to two years. But the importance of economic indicators is such that financial analysts carry out considerable research to try to forecast what the next press notice will show. Financial markets form expectations in advance of each announcement, based on some kind of average of the analysts' forecasts. If the figures are close to expectations, markets generally remain unaffected by the announcement. If they are very different, markets can be expected to react. Following analysts who diverge from the consensus can make money – if they are usually right.

There is no hard and fast way of making short-term forecasts. Normally, analysts will use a combination of methods to come up with a forecast that is plausible. The following components may each play a part:

- Erratics. Studying the previous data release for erratics, which might rebound in the following month, is often worthwhile. For example, if exports were particularly high in one month for no particular reason they might be compensatingly low in the following month. Indeed, the UK trade figures are presented in aggregate and 'excluding erratics', such as ships, aircraft and precious stones.
- Charts. Viewing the recent run of data in graphical form can often throw some light on the trend.
- Oddities. It is important to keep abreast of changes in the definition of statistical series. Changes to survey techniques or administrative rules that could affect the data are usually pre-announced and can be allowed for.
- Components. Some light can often be thrown on trends by looking at the published components of the aggregates.
- Econometric analysis. This involves allowing for the causal impact of other variables.
- Factual research. Patient research for apparently random factors may occasionally reap rewards. For example, the inflation analyst who buys his own vegetables and spots a glut of seasonal foods may steal a march on the competition as seasonal food prices have a large short-term impact on the RPI.

3 | Statistical Warnings and Tricks

Everybody collects, interprets or uses numerical information every day. The main function of statistical manipulation and its subsequent dissemination is to make some sense of information and thereby help in making decisions. The statistician needs to be able to put himself in the position of the user so that he can sift through the facts and pick out what is interesting and useful, and present it in a way which makes it easy to understand.

Statistics can, of course, be presented in such a way as to give a misleading or wrong impression. Sometimes the suppliers of information do have an 'agenda' and use the data to mislead, to give only one side of the story. Ultimately, a statistician is like any other employee working for an organization, and is unlikely to present data which are unfavourable for the organization. He can be expected, to borrow a phrase, to be economical with the truth. Normally, however, the intention is to be objective: statistics are generally presented in good faith. They do, none the less, present an opportunity to inflate, confuse and sensationalize. Ignorance and error can be as much of a problem as deliberate deception.

This chapter does not aim to be a textbook on statistical theory. It merely highlights some of the common themes or pitfalls that arise when dealing with economic statistics. Data, charts and trends are not always what they seem at first glance. Statements incorporating numbers often collapse under a second look. It should also prompt the reader to get in the habit of asking more frequently why the provider has chosen to present the data and in that particular way. Encouraging such self-discipline will lead to fewer instances of misinterpretation.

PRIMARY AND SECONDARY DATA

Primary data are collected by or on behalf of the person who is going to make use of the data. This normally involves conducting a survey using various sampling methods. Once data have been collected, processed and published they become secondary data. It is a simple fact of life that the vast bulk of data that will be used is secondary data. The use of secondary data does, however, have a number of advantages. Many of the data series have been collected for many years and can therefore show trends; there is a great variety of data; they are generally cheap to obtain; and large quantities are available on most topics.

As with any other second-hand product, it is none the less vital to know something about its history. It is only if you know about the nature of the collection, processing methods, accuracy levels, comparability and presentation that you can fully appreciate the reliability and meaning of the statistics.

DATA ACCURACY AND SPURIOUS ACCURACY

Perfect accuracy in statistical information is possible only very rarely. The type of data being measured and the uses to which it will be put will determine the accuracy that is required. There will be a point – a tolerance level – for every statistic where the degree of inaccuracy becomes unacceptable. (In statistical terms, the word 'error' is the difference between the approximation and the true figure, and does not mean a mistake.) The producers of statistics always need to make decisions about the scale of error that is acceptable. In most cases it is possible to reduce the size of the error, but often only at a high price in terms of collection costs.

An absolute error is the actual difference between the estimate or approximation and the true figure, and is measured in the units of the statistic. A relative error, by contrast, is an absolute error divided by the estimate, and is measured in percentage terms. When comparing errors from different series it is normally preferable to compare the relative errors.

Secondary data, usually presented in summary tables, will always contain approximations. Rounding is almost certain to have taken place in order to avoid the impression of spurious accuracy and the source ought to indicate what rounding has taken place. It might be that you need more detailed data, or that you could round the data further and still satisfy your needs. It is normal to round to the nearest whole number, so that 8.37 rounded to one decimal place would become 8.4. But occasionally a process called truncation, where unwanted final digits are omitted, is used. In this case, 8.37 would become 8.3.

Figures are often rounded to a given number of significant figures. Once the number of digits that are significant is stated, zeros will follow. For example, 10,533 rounded to three significant figures would be 10,500. It is important to remember that, when doing arithmetic with numbers which have been rounded to different degrees, the result can only be accurate to the least number of significant figures of any of the components.

The growth rates of most main economic indicators are presented to one decimal point. For example, UK retail sales are described as having risen by 2.1 per cent over the year, consistent with what seems to be the policy of the ONS in the UK. There are very few series which can justify a greater degree of accuracy than this, and there are perhaps some series, which at least on occasions, would justify further rounding, perhaps to the nearest quarter or half per cent.

Some series in other countries are occasionally published in greater detail, suggesting spurious accuracy. For example, it was reported that the National Statistics Institute of Spain announced in February 1999 that large store sales rose 58.11 per cent in December 1998 compared to November, and were up 8.10 per cent from a year earlier. There are many other examples of spurious accuracy, including the Brazilian jobless numbers and Peruvian inflation. Data are rarely the most useful for analysts if they are not seasonally adjusted and are presented with spurious accuracy.

In some countries data which normally would be available monthly might be available more frequently. If a country has been suffering from very high rates of inflation, for example, data on a monthly frequency might well be insufficient. In Russia, a report in May 1999 explained that the daily price rise had slowed to 0.078 per cent!

Interpretation of any data series requires a sense of likely accuracy to be kept in mind. A final and dramatic example of the dangers of data comes from China. It became clear in February 1999 that there had been some exaggeration of economic output in the regions. A spokesman for China's State Statistical Bureau said: 'Some local governments and officials overstate economic figures for their own political advantage, resulting in exaggerated statistics.' To offset these overstatements, the bureau used its own sampling in the regions and, as they put it, 'squeezed out the water' from the reported figures in order to get more reliable aggregates.

THE PERILS OF SAMPLING

It is desirable to base decisions on complete counts of companies, people and commodities. Anything less than a full count may be felt to include only part of the information and be open to a degree of approximation. In practice, 100 per cent surveys can be completed only in limited circumstances and normally a sample is required. Sampling does offer some advantages such as cost and time saving, and resource allocation. In practice, a high degree of reliability can be achieved if the sampling process is carried out professionally. Needless to say, it is important that users know the sample sizes and have some information about the sample design, so that appropriate weight can be given to the resulting statistics. In the extreme, if a survey announces that eight out of ten companies are expecting profits to rise, it might mean exactly that!

A basic test of whether a sample is random is, 'Does every member of the group being tested have an equal chance to be in it?' As a true random sample can be costly and time-consuming to carry out, and might not deliver sufficient numbers of small groups, a so-called stratified sample is usually used. Here the population is divided into groups and the sample taken within each group. It is always worth asking whether a survey was carried out in the street, door-to-door or over the telephone, as certain groups of people could be excluded by any one of these options. All surveys are battles of cost against bias.

It can also be informative to see a copy of the questionnaire. Are questions in such an order as to prompt a certain answer? Are people more likely to give you pleasing answers rather than seek confrontation? Also, put yourself in the position of the interviewer. If, as part of your stratified sample, you have to interview a middle-aged man in the street about drinking habits, are you more likely to choose a tramp or a clean-cut man in a suit? Certain sorts of people are much more likely not to be counted in a population census. There are formal statistical techniques for giving degrees of significance or sampling errors in a survey. Unfortunately these are very much the exception rather than the rule.

PRESENTATION OF STATISTICS

The type of presentation chosen should depend on the requirements and interest of the people receiving the information. Good presentation should be straightforward, bring out the important points, make the purpose clear and give an appropriate amount of detail and accuracy.

The first stage in presenting figures is normally the production of a table. Tables should always: have a clear concise title; offer brief but self-explanatory column- and row-headings; show the units of measurement; indicate the source of the data; and may have footnotes explaining any oddities. If tables omit any of these key features then there could well be a problem with the data.

Statistics can also be presented in any number of graphical and diagrammatic formats. Possibilities include histograms, line charts, frequency polygons, frequency curves, bar charts (of various sorts), pie charts, pictograms, cartograms, strata charts and various graphs including those with one or two logarithmic scales. The intention behind using graphs and charts is nearly always to inform but there can frequently be problems of distortion and deception. As with tables, we should ignore charts that are not fully labelled and sourced.

It is important to look at the scales and to think what the same information would look like if it were to be presented in a different format. Fig. 3.1 plots identical data in three different ways. This hypothetical series starts at 100, rises to 104 in time period two and 110 in time period three. Version (a) of the figure is clearly a far less dramatic representation than that shown in version (c). Also, beware of figures presented in two or three dimensions, most commonly bars of varying widths, as they can give misleading impressions.

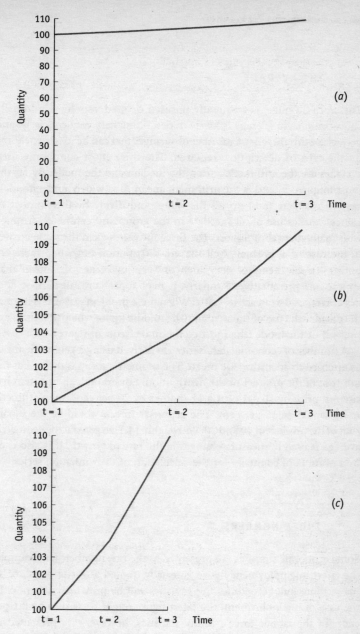

Fig. 3.1. Three graphical representations of the same hypothetical data

THE AVERAGE

The word 'average' is frequently misused or used very loosely in daily conversation. An average is a way of describing data very concisely, and because of this there are a number of averages that can be used depending on the type of description required. The three most commonly used averages are the arithmetic mean, the median and the mode. By far the most frequently used is the arithmetic mean. It is widely understood, is easy to calculate (add up all the values and divide by the number of values), makes use of all the data in the group and can be determined with mathematical precision. The three measures yield the same answer in the case of a 'normal', bell-shaped, distribution but when there are outliers, a few items of very high or very low value, the mean may appear unrepresentative. Similarly, it may appear unrealistic if it does not correspond to an actual value. When these problems arise, it is normal to consider the use of the median (the middle figure when all figures are ranked) or the mode (the most common or frequent figure).

A number of economic data series are derived using a geometric mean as opposed to an arithmetic mean. The geometric mean is defined as the nth root of the product of the distribution. For example, if one item has risen in price by 10 per cent and another by 20 per cent, the arithmetic mean would be 15 per cent. The geometric mean would be the square root of the product of 10 and 20, i.e. roughly 14.1. In general the geometric average is used to measure changes in the rate of growth. It is also used by a number of countries for the calculation of their inflation series.

INDEX NUMBERS

Some economic statistics are presented as the raw number. For example, the latest unemployment figure is usually quoted as a rise or fall of so many thousand. Sometimes the statistics will be presented as a rate. In the case of unemployment, the latest figure might be said to be 8.1 per cent (of the labour force). Many statistics, however, are presented as index numbers.

Box 3.1. **Example calculations of price indices**

Some hypothetical data relating to the purchase of cinema tickets and popcorn are shown in the table. Over the period shown, individuals increased their average monthly attendance at the cinema from two to three, during which time the price rose from three to five. The consumption of popcorn rose from one to three while the price remained stable at one.

Monthly sales of cinema tickets and popcorn

	Tickets	Popcorn
Number purchased:		
1990	2	1
1998	3	3
Price:		
1990	3	1
1998	5	1

In our example, the base weighted index is derived by multiplying the quantity of tickets in 1990 by the price in 1990 ($2 \times 3 = 6$) and adding the popcorn consumption in 1990 times the price of popcorn in 1990 ($1 \times 1 = 1$). The resulting 7 is converted into an index by dividing it by 7, to give the index 1.00. The index for 1998 is calculated by multiplying the number of tickets bought in 1990 by the price in 1998 ($2 \times 5 = 10$) and adding the quantity of popcorn bought in 1990 times the price in 1998 ($1 \times 1 = 1$). The resulting 11 is divided by 7 to give an index of 1.57.

The current weighted index is derived by multiplying the quantity of tickets in 1998 by the price in 1990 ($3 \times 3 = 9$) and adding the consumption of popcorn in 1998 times the price in 1990 ($3 \times 1 = 3$). The resulting 12 is converted into the base index of 1.00 by dividing by 12. The index for 1998 is calculated by multiplying the number of tickets bought in 1998 by the price in 1998 ($3 \times 5 = 15$) and adding the quantity of popcorn in 1998 times the price in 1998 ($3 \times 1 = 3$). The resulting 18 is divided by 12 to give an index of 1.50. Index numbers are frequently multiplied by 100 to give percentage points.

An index number is a measure designed to show changes over time more simply. It is a value expressed as a percentage of a given base figure. For example, 21.5 million television licences were sold in 1997 compared to 19.6 million in 1990. In index terms, licence sales would be 100 in 1990 and 109.7 in 1997, showing clearly an increase of 9.7 per cent. Index numbers have no units, which can be a distraction, and changes are easier to assess quickly as the base year usually starts at 100.

It is often necessary to combine two or more indices to form one composite index. A hypothetical example calculating an index relating to the monthly purchase of cinema tickets and popcorn is shown in Box 3.1.

There are essentially two ways of combining indices: a base weighted index, known as a Laspeyres index, or a current weighted index, known as a Paasche index. A base weighted index uses the same (the original) weights over the whole period while a current weighted series uses updated weights for each period. Neither form of calculation is right or wrong but for large series, base weighted indices are simpler to calculate. In practice, most indices are hybrids somewhere between pure base and current weighting. The UK RPI, for example, is a good compromise – it is an annually updated base weighted index. It is base weighted from month to month during the year and is current weighted from year to year as a new set of weights is introduced annually.

Whether an index is base weighted or current weighted is of little practical importance if the weights are updated regularly. Index numbers can become distorted if the weights are not frequently updated. The UK RPI weights are updated annually, but if they were not, as is the case in many other countries, sharp changes in one component could distort the index and lead to incorrect conclusions being drawn. Misinterpretation is rarely a major problem in the UK but can be a problem in other countries. The statistics office of Finland announced in early 1999 that they were reviewing the weightings of industrial production data. Since the weights were set in 1995, two of Finland's largest industries – forestry and electrotechnical (largely Telecom equipment) – had shown diverse growth trends, with the former falling fractionally and the latter increasing by over 100 per cent. The choice of statistical methodology can have a large impact on the resulting figures when there have been diverse movements such as these.

The base year, often called year one, will normally be at the start of the period under consideration. Occasionally, however, the base will have been chosen at some point in the middle or, exceptionally, at the end of the period under consideration. The choice of the mid-point can give the impression that the two series have converged and then diverged while the end-point can give an impression of convergence, both of which could be misleading. Fig. 3.2 (a) and (b) shows the indices of producer price input and output inflation in two different ways. Version (a), with the index based on 1995 = 100, allows a more intuitive assessment of inflation over the four-year period. It shows that from the starting point, input prices fell 20 per cent. The choice of base year can also introduce a bias. If a low year is chosen, the years that follow may appear particularly high; if a high year is chosen, the years that follow may appear low. It is always important to check where the base year is located.

If there is a need to compare two series, they will normally be converted to the same base year to facilitate comparison. The simple process of introducing a new reference date for a series has no effect, other than rounding, on the percentage movement between any pair of months. It is merely the re-scaling of the whole series up or down by a constant factor. The reference date need not have any connection with the weighting base dates.

MEASURING CHANGE

A single number or statistic is rarely of any interest on its own. Normally we will want to see a string of numbers or be given some indication of rates of change. For example, to be told that the US stock market rose by 127 points on a given day compared to a rise in the European market of 17 points would give a very clear impression of relative strength. However, if those rises were compared against the starting points or against a string of changes in recent days it would be clear that the initial conclusion was wrong. Table 3.1 sets out some examples of such changes. As the numbers in the table show, the percentage change is an easy way to interpret statistics. A percentage indicates the size of a change when the starting point is 100. As percentages are such a fundamental means of interpreting changes, it is essential to be comfortable with the basic calculations. These include presenting the change between two numbers as a percentage of either number, finding a given percentage of a number,

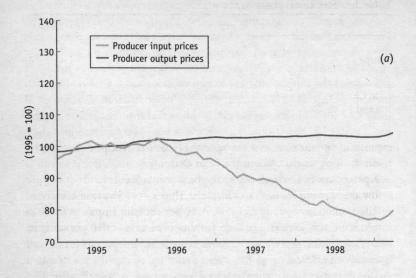

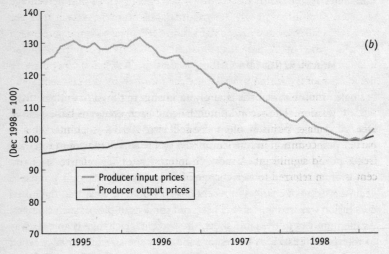

Fig. 3.2. Producer input and output price inflation plotted on two different bases

Table 3.1. Stockmarket changes

	Actual change	Level	Per cent change
US	+127	9311	1.4
Europe	+17	1231	1.4
UK	+79	5958	1.3

Note: Changes on 5 January 1999 of Dow Jones Industrial Average, FTSE Eurotop 300 and FTSE 100.

expressing one number as a percentage of another and working out the result of a given percentage increase or decrease.

A percentage rise followed by the same percentage fall results in a figure below the starting level. For example, a 10 per cent increase on pay of £10,000 would give pay of £11,000. A 10 per cent cut in pay of £11,000 would leave only £9,900. The same applies in reverse – a 10 per cent cut in pay of £10,000 would leave £9,000 from which a rise of 10 per cent would give £9,900.

Two examples of initially confusing terminology frequently arise. The first concerns the distinction between percentage points and percentage changes. If an inflation rate, for example, falls from 5 per cent to 4 per cent, it has fallen by one percentage point. The corresponding percentage fall is 20 per cent. A variant of this often crops up in reporting of the inflation numbers. It will often be said that the 'RPI fell 0.1 per cent' in the latest month, failing to make it clear *what* fell by 0.1 per cent – the index, the month on month change, the change in the m/m or the annual rate of inflation. The second potential confusion concerns basis points. One percentage point is often divided into 100 basis points. This is particularly common in financial circles where small changes in rates are frequent and significant. A move in interest rates of a quarter of 1 per cent is often referred to as a change of 25 basis points.

TIME SERIES

A time series consists of numerical data recorded at intervals of time, for example, weekly, monthly or annually. Most time series can be separated into fairly clear types of trend: the long-term or secular trend; cyclical fluctuations; seasonal variations; short-term movements; and irregular (random, non-recurring or residual) fluctuations. Time series analysis deploys a number of statistical techniques designed to separate out the various elements of the trend. Analysis of the trend can throw considerable light on the behaviour of the series.

SEASONAL ADJUSTMENT

The majority of economic figures show a seasonal pattern that repeats itself each year. For example, retail sales rise around the turn of the year as people prepare for Christmas and spend in the sales. The data show that retail sales are typically 50 per cent higher in December than in the average month. Similarly, factory output falls in the summer when many factories are closed for annual holidays.

A process called seasonal adjustment is used to adjust the raw or unadjusted data for the seasonal pattern. The seasonal adjustment process would analyse the monthly or quarterly patterns over a number of years so as to isolate the seasonal factor. That would then be used to increase or decrease observations in each period. Generally, no seasonal adjustment is needed when a monthly figure is compared with its equivalent in the previous year.

In the vast majority of cases, the process of seasonal adjustment vastly improves the ability to interpret the series. The statistical procedure of seasonal adjustment is complex, however, and has a large subjective element. It is therefore important to be aware of the manner in which the adjustment has been made. Needless to say some less scrupulous commentators will chose to focus on either the adjusted or unadjusted figure, which might be moving in different directions, subject to what suits them best in that month.

Fig. 3.3 shows the index of UK retail sales in adjusted and unadjusted form. There will be times when it is desirable to look at the unadjusted version of the data. It helps to explain, for example, why our high streets are so much busier and why retailers employ temporary staff in December. But it is clear that economic trends will be easier to see in the adjusted version.

It should be noted, however, that some series are not suited to seasonal

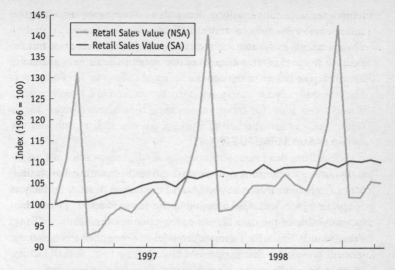

Fig. 3.3. A comparison of retail sales figures seasonally adjusted and unadjusted

adjustment (the UK RPI and the government borrowing numbers are two examples) and that the process does not necessarily produce a smooth series without distortions. Also, we should be aware that seasonal adjustment means different things to different producers of statistics. A seasonally adjusted series will sometimes include other adjustments designed to smooth the series, for example allowing for the number of working days and the timing of bank holidays. Some continental series are presented in 'calendar adjusted' form.

Table 3.2 sets out some adjusted and unadjusted figures for retail sales over a Christmas period to show some of the differences between the series. Several points are apparent:

- The unadjusted index (column one) shows the clear seasonal peak in November and December.
- The seasonally adjusted counterpart (column four) shows a much smoother trend.
- The month on month (% m/m) changes (columns three and six) give very different impressions, reflecting the nature of the series from which they are calculated. The former would be more useful for a

retailer trying to judge staffing demands or likely turnover, while the latter is preferable for economic analysis.

• The annual (% ann) rates (columns two and five) show similar trends. Because the annual rate compares one month's sales with the same month a year before, much of the seasonal difference is allowed for. The seasonally adjusted version is normally preferable for analysis since it might also allow for other known variations between years due to factors such as the number of working days in each month and the timing of bank holidays.

• It is clear from this example that seasonal adjustment does not necessarily deliver a smooth series. Normal month to month volatility, due for example to unseasonal weather and the timing of sales, and a host of special factors will still be visible in the adjusted series. Two special factors visible in the data shown in the table are the death of Diana, Princess of Wales, which suppressed sales in September 1997, and the football World Cup that suppressed sales in June 1998. Special factors, which reduce sales in one month, often give rise to a rebound in the following month.

Table 3.2. Comparison of adjusted and unadjusted retail sales

	Non-seasonally adjusted			Seasonally adjusted		
	Index	% ann	% m/m	Index	% ann	% m/m
1997:						
June	108.5	+5.7	+3.1	112.4	+6.4	+1.1
July	111.1	+7.3	+2.4	113.1	+7.8	+0.6
August	107.2	+6.0	−3.5	113.3	+6.4	+0.2
September	107.1	+4.2	−0.1	112.1	+4.9	−1.1
October	113.8	+6.3	+6.3	114.5	+6.6	+2.1
November	124.1	+4.9	+9.0	114.2	+5.2	−0.3
December	150.6	+7.0	+21.3	114.7	+6.2	+0.4
1998:						
January	105.7	+6.6	−29.8	116.1	+7.3	+1.2
February	106.1	+5.7	+0.4	114.9	+5.2	−1.0
March	108.5	+4.0	+2.3	115.6	+4.9	+0.6
April	112.2	+5.2	+3.4	115.3	+4.3	−0.3
May	112.3	+6.7	+0.9	117.7	+5.8	+2.1
June	112.0	+3.2	−0.3	115.9	+3.1	−1.5

Source: ONS (subject to revision, as at Q4 1998).

TURNING POINTS AND TRENDS

Economic trends go up and down, making it easy to present the latest figure in a series as good or bad according to which earlier figure it is compared with. Take as an example the hypothetical quarterly series over two years set out in Table 3.3. How should the second year's figures be presented? The first quarter of year 2 shows no change from the previous quarter, but a 6 per cent drop compared with the same quarter of the previous year. The second quarter shows a 2 per cent increase compared to the previous quarter, but a 2 per cent fall on the same quarter of the previous year. The third quarter also shows a 2 per cent increase on the previous quarter and on the same quarter of the previous year. The fourth quarter again shows a 2 per cent increase over the quarter, but a 6½ per cent increase compared with the same quarter of the previous year.

Growth through the year to the fourth quarter looks strong, yet if the quarterly index figures for each of the two years are averaged, they come to exactly the same figure of 97. This example illustrates that a figure is really only of interest if it is compared with another figure and that the choice of the other figure can heavily influence the impression gleaned. It also shows the desirability of looking simultaneously at several comparisons.

Table 3.3. Interpreting turning points

Time	Index	% change	
		Quarterly	Annual
Year 1: Q1	100	—	—
Q2	98	−2.0	—
Q3	96	−2.1	—
Q4	94	−2.1	—
Year 2: Q1	94	0.0	−6.0
Q2	96	2.1	−2.0
Q3	98	2.1	2.1
Q4	100	2.0	6.4
Year 1 average	97	—	—
Year 2 average	97	1.6	0.0

HOW TO SPOT A TREND

Different users of data have different needs, but a common theme for many is the desire to spot a turning point. Table 3.4 sets out some growth rates derived from the retail sales figures. This time the figures are of seasonally adjusted retail sales volumes, the series that was perhaps used above all others in the UK in the 1990s to judge the strength of consumer demand from month to month.

The table shows the most commonly referred to growth rates: the month on month (m/m) change, m/m annualized change, the annual growth rate, the month on month change of the three-month index, the three-month on three-month growth rate and the three-month annual rate. Note that the annual growth rate is different from the year on year growth rate. The former is one month compared to the same month a year before, while the latter is the last twelve months compared to the previous twelve months. This distinction is often ignored and 'year on year' is incorrectly used to describe 'annual'. In a data series with only annual observations, there is no difference between the two.

Occasionally it might be of interest to know what the change during the year to date has been. This is calculated by comparing the latest data point with the final data point of the previous year. This is not a common practice in the UK, but is in some other countries. One of the most prominent series for financial markets in the 1990s, German broad money supply (M3) growth, was presented in this way. The Bundesbank published the growth in the latest month compared to that at the end of the previous calendar year, in annualized percentage change form. Inevitably, this meant that the growth rate was very volatile – almost meaningless – in the early months of the year.

There are pros and cons to using each of the different measures. Often a particular sort of presentation is traditionally associated with a particular series. The US GDP figures, for example, are presented on a quarter on quarter annualized percentage change basis. Yet despite the shortcomings of this methodology and the difficulties that can arise when comparing those numbers with the equivalent number from other countries, presented in the more normal way (quarter compared to the same quarter

Table 3.4. Different growth rates for retail sales

	Index	m/m	Annualized	Annual	3m, m/m	3m/3m	3m annual
				%			
1997							
1	105.2	0.1	1.1	5.4	0.2	1.0	4.9
2	106.6	1.3	17.2	4.9	0.3	0.8	4.9
3	107.6	0.9	11.9	5.8	0.8	1.3	5.4
4	107.4	−0.2	−2.2	5.1	0.7	1.8	5.3
5	108.4	0.9	11.8	4.9	0.6	2.1	5.3
6	109.0	0.6	6.8	5.6	0.4	1.7	5.2
7	109.3	0.3	3.4	6.6	0.6	1.6	5.7
8	109.8	0.5	5.6	5.6	0.4	1.5	5.9
9	108.2	−1.5	−16.2	3.8	−0.2	0.8	5.3
10	110.6	2.2	30.1	5.7	0.4	0.6	5.1
11	110.1	−0.5	−5.3	4.3	0.1	0.2	4.6
12	111.0	0.8	10.3	5.6	0.9	1.3	5.2
1998							
1	112.0	0.9	11.4	6.5	0.4	1.4	5.4
2	111.3	−0.6	−7.2	4.4	0.4	1.6	5.5
3	111.4	0.1	1.1	3.5	0.1	0.9	4.8
4	111.3	−0.1	−1.1	3.6	−0.2	0.3	3.9
5	113.2	1.7	22.5	4.4	0.6	0.5	3.9
6	111.0	−1.9	−21.0	1.8	−0.1	0.2	3.3
7	112.2	1.1	13.8	2.7	0.3	0.7	3.0
8	112.5	0.3	3.3	2.5	−0.2	−0.1	2.3
9	112.2	−0.3	−3.2	3.7	0.4	0.4	2.9
10	111.8	−0.4	−4.2	1.1	−0.1	0.0	2.4
11	112.9	1.0	12.5	2.5	0.1	0.4	2.4
12	111.8	−1.0	−11.1	0.7	−0.1	−0.1	1.4

Notes: Col. 1: index, seasonally adjusted, volumes. Col. 2: m/m change. Col. 3: change on col. 2 annualized. Col. 4: month x compared to month x in the year before. Col. 5: 3m average of m/m in col. 2. Col. 6: last three months compared to previous three months. Col. 7: last three months compared to same three months a year before.
Source: ONS (data as at May 1999).

a year before), commentators continue to view those statistics on that basis. The best policy for thorough analysis is to look at several different growth rates before making firm conclusions about the trend.

A few general conclusions can be drawn from Table 3.4:

- The index itself is of little use (see column 1).
- Series such as retail sales are quite erratic from month to month (see column 2). They require some further analysis. This might be done in a 'formal' way, such as is seen in the table, or it could be more descriptive, saying, for example, that the annual rate in the latest month compares with such and such rates in the previous three months and the previous six months.
- The annualized month on month change exaggerates the erratic part of a series. Annualized rates are less frequently used in the UK than in the US, for example. While annualized rates make it easier to compare monthly changes with more familiar sounding annual rates, they can be highly misleading as many economic figures are highly erratic from month to month.
- The annual rate is useful but has some limitations (see section below).
- The moving average (calculated here in various forms over three months) is appealing for analysing those series which are erratic from month to month. The process of smoothing, however, does mean that turning points are likely to be spotted more slowly. This is especially so with a six month moving average.
- The purpose of most analysis is to understand what is going on in the economy. Accordingly, there is a desire to get behind the headline figures. Many series, including retail sales, have a number of break-downs of the total. It is possible, therefore, to see what is happening to food sales or non-food sales and to take out any component that might be erratic.
- It is invaluable to understand the construction of any statistical series that you want to analyse. For example, the series of retail sales volumes is derived from a survey of actual retail sales which is then deflated by the RPI. This means that an erratic month's RPI number can give rise to an erratic figure for retail sales volume even if the value figure looked 'normal'.
- There can be considerable value in looking at graphical presentations of data (see Fig. 3.4).

It is only with reference to several of the calculated series and probably several charts that anything meaningful can be said about the trend in sales. It is worth remembering the old adage that a difference is only a difference if it makes a difference. The claim of a change in trend will

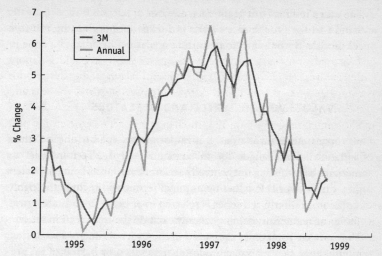

Fig. 3.4. The growth of retail sales – annual rate and three-month annual rate compared

be stronger if it is possible to answer the question 'Why now?' Be aware of making false correlations – many series are rising, or falling, at any one time, but it does not mean that the movements are in any way linked.

THE DANGER OF ANNUAL RATES

The trend in many economic statistics is assessed with reference to the annual growth rate. If it is the trend over a number of months which is of interest, the simple annual rate in each month will often be viewed. But there is a danger in paying too much attention to the change in the annual rate between one month and the month that follows. This is because a yearly comparison gives the same weight to what happened twelve months ago as to what happened in the latest month. A good example is provided by the press release for the RPI of September 1998. The two largest influences on the change in the annual rate between August and September were events from the September a year before (see

p. 116). As a result of this problem, a number of releases now give greater attention to the growth rate of the last three months on the previous three months or the same three months a year before.

VALUE, VOLUME, PRICE AND DEFLATORS

For proper time series analysis, it is important to separate out the effects of inflation from changes due to economic activity. Terminology can sometimes be confusing but generally series referred to as being in current prices, nominal prices, values or nominal terms, will include the effects of inflation. Similarly, if a series is referred to as being in constant prices, volumes or real terms, it will generally exclude the impact of inflation.

Volumes are sometimes measured in the units of the product such as the number of cars manufactured, journeys taken or barrels of oil produced. More often than not, however, volumes will be measured in the prices prevailing in a given year. At the end of the 1990s many of the UK's indicators were presented in terms of '1995 prices'. Such series are volume indicators, despite being in money units, because they have excluded the impact of price changes.

The difference between a volume and value series is a price series. The volume series can be derived by dividing the value series by the price index and the value series can be derived by multiplying the volume series by the price index.

COVERAGE AND COMPARABILITY

If statistics are being compared, it is important to be sure that they are comparable! If the statistics come from different sources, they may not be strictly comparable. The problem arises most frequently with the coverage of private sector surveys. Surveys from trade associations typically only refer to their members who may not be typical of the whole sector. For example, the CBI, the Institute of Directors and the Chambers of Commerce all deal with businesses, but they are different sorts of business.

There can also be differences in geographic coverage. Some statistics in the UK cover the whole of the UK, while others refer only to Great Britain or just England and Wales. The arrival of devolved assemblies in the UK will increase disparities in national statistics. Examples in other countries include the reunification of Germany when some statistics referred only to the west, which led to many statistical problems during the 1990s.

THE POWER OF COMPOUND INTEREST

It is impossible to end a section on basic statistics without a warning about the power of compound interest. If an initial amount of 100 is increased by 2 per cent in each time period, it might be thought, at first glance, that it would take fifty time periods to double to 200. In fact, the act of compounding, where each percentage increase is calculated from a higher base, means that it takes only thirty-five time periods for the original amount to double. Table 3.5 shows some doubling times and corresponding rates for monthly data.

Table 3.5. Doubling times and annualized rates

| Monthly % change | Doubling time | | Annualized rate (rise in a year) |
	Months	Years	
0.5	139	11.6	6.2
1.0	70	5.8	12.7
2.0	35	2.9	26.8
5.0	14	1.2	79.6
10.0	7	0.6	213.8

4 | Economic Growth

The rate of growth of the economy is the most important single indicator of a country's economic performance. Successive governments, especially since the inflationary problems of the 1970s, have convincingly argued that the control of inflation is the primary concern of government policy. None the less, governments clearly delight in economic growth and come under enormous pressure from all quarters when growth is absent.

It is important for the analyst to understand the GDP data set, as the so-called national accounts, from which the GDP numbers come, form the foundation for all economic analysis. A good understanding of the GDP framework will improve the understanding of links between saving and investment, the domestic economy and the external account, economic growth and inflation, the real economy and the financial economy, and so forth – in essence how all the bits of the economy fit together.

THE IMPORTANCE OF GROWTH

In fact, for all its talk of caution and stability, the Labour Government that was elected in 1997 seems to be more openly pro-growth than any for two decades. The opening sentence of the November 1998 Pre-Budget Report was: 'The Government's central economic objective is higher and stable levels of growth and employment.' The government is able to say this – and get away with it in the eyes of financial markets – because of the changes it has made to the long-term macro-economic framework. This includes giving the Bank of England operational independence to set interest rates to meet the government's inflation target (see Chapter 5) and the introduction of a new fiscal framework designed to control public finances (see Chapter 10).

By hiving off responsibility for inflation, and thereby essentially guaranteeing low inflation, the government is free to pursue its other policies, aimed at improving productivity, reducing unemployment and creating a 'fairer' society. It hopes to raise the sustainable growth rate in the economy and avoid the boom and bust cycles of the past.

GROWTH TRENDS

GDP has increased by an average of 2½ per cent a year at constant prices from 1955 to 1998. The average growth rate in each decade has been remarkably constant. In the 1950s, 1970s and 1980s, the annual growth rate averaged between 2¼ and 2½ per cent. In the 1960s the average growth rate was higher at 3¼ per cent. In the 1990s, up to 1998, the growth rate averaged just 2 per cent, but if 1990, the recession year, is excluded the growth rate from 1991 to 1998 averaged (again) 2½ per cent.

GDP growth has followed a smooth path since recovering from the early 1990s' recession (see Fig. 4.1). In the six years from 1993 to 1998, growth was between 2 and 3½ per cent every year except 1994, when it was over 4 per cent. This was an unusually stable time. The 1980s were more volatile – in the nine year period of growth, two years saw growth below 2 per cent and five saw growth over 3½ per cent. Growth was much more erratic and the spell ended, of course, with a deep and long recession. The last period of growth as stable as that of the last few years was in the 1960s and into the 1970s.

Strictly speaking, it is the per head growth of the economy which should be used as an indicator of the rise in human welfare. (Indeed, consumption or income per head would more accurately reflect living standards.) In many countries, population growth absorbs much of the economic growth, and welfare may rise little, or even fall, on a per head basis. In the UK, population grew by 25 per cent to 56 million in the forty years to 1971. Accordingly, 25 per cent growth in the economy would be required for the per capita economy to remain constant. In the last twenty years, the UK's population has been much more stable,

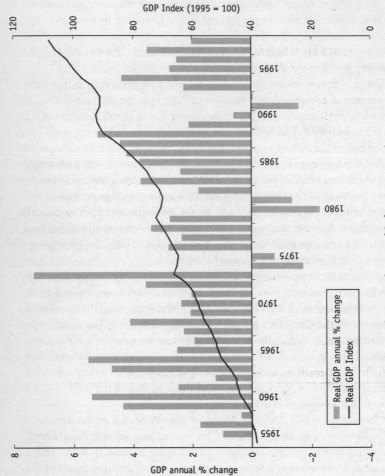

Fig. 4.1. Economic growth – annual rate and index

growing only modestly. Over that time therefore, average annual economic growth on a per head basis is little different (2 per cent) from aggregate growth (2¼ per cent).

INTERNATIONAL COMPARISONS

The growth rate is used to compare the UK's progress with that of other economies. Differences of a fraction of 1 per cent may affect positions in the league tables, even though they may be less than the average error in each country's statistics. The UK's growth rate was below average in the first half of the 1990s but above average in the second half. Japan's growth has been very erratic since the 'bubble economy' burst in the early 1990s. In the second half of the 1990s, the US was the global engine of growth and Euro-area countries were generally weaker (see Table 4.1).

The GDP figures, as opposed to the growth rates, can be used to ascertain which are the largest economies. Table 4.2 shows three rankings. The first ranking shows the world's largest, as judged by output at market prices. It shows that the US is by far the largest and Japan is clearly second, with the four main European economies following some way behind. The three largest economies, the US, Japan and Germany, are often referred to as the G3 group of countries. Adding France and the UK, gives the G5. And adding Italy and Canada produces the G7, even though Canada is actually ranked lower than seventh.

Table 4.1. Growth rates in different economies

	1990–94	1995	1996	1997	1998
US	1.7	2.3	3.4	3.9	3.9
Japan	2.1	1.5	5.1	1.4	−2.8
Germany	2.9	1.2	1.3	2.2	2.8
France	1.2	2.1	1.6	2.3	3.2
Italy	1.0	2.9	0.9	1.5	1.4
UK	1.2	2.8	2.6	3.5	2.1
Canada	1.1	2.2	1.2	3.8	3.0
TOTAL: G7	1.8	2.1	3.0	3.0	2.2

Source: OECD Economic Outlook, spring 1999.

Table 4.2. Countries ranked according to measures of GNP

| 1997 data | GNP, market prices | | GNP, PPP | GNP, PPP, per capita |
	$bn	Rank	Rank*	Rank**
US	7783	1	1	4
Japan	4812	2	3	8
Germany	2321	3	4	19
France	1542	4	6	15
UK	1231	5	7	20
Italy	1160	6	8	22
China	1055	7	2	135
Brazil	784	8	9	90
Canada	595	9	12	17
Spain	570	10	15	39
Korean Rep.	485	11	14	52
Netherlands	403	12	21	18
Russia	395	13	13	104
Australia	383	14	18	24
India	357	15	5	163

Notes: *Other countries appearing in the top twenty but not shown are: Mexico 10, Indonesia 11, Turkey 16, Thailand 17, Argentina 19 and Iran 20. **Several of the top countries are city-states or tax havens.
Source: World Bank, World Development Indices.

The second ranking, according to Purchasing Power Parity (PPP), gives a different picture. A number of countries, most notably China and India, move many places (respectively from 7th to 2nd and from 15th to 5th) up the rankings. PPP calculations essentially create a set of artificial prices, which are weighted averages of the relative prices that actually exist in the world. These prices are then normalized to ensure that US GDP is the same in market prices as in PPP prices. The new prices are then applied to given quantities of spending everywhere in the world.

In PPP calculations, therefore, a haircut of a given quality, for example, is the same price everywhere. As a haircut in China or India costs a fraction of the same haircut in the US, the result of this process is to boost the size of the economies where the price level is lower. PPP measures attempt to tell you about the real difference between standards of living across the world. PPP measures are useful in that they indicate that the standard of living in many of the world's less developed countries is not as low as conventional GDP figures would suggest. But if you want to measure a country's significance in the international economy, PPP calculations are largely irrelevant, and GDP at market prices is more appropriate. It is also fair to point out that the calculation of PPP rates is extremely difficult and impossible to do with any precision.

The third ranking shows the PPP calculations in per capita terms. This is a better measure of the comparative economic well being of the population in the country. On this basis the rankings are dramatically changed. Only the US and Japan remain in the top ten. The only other medium sized economies in the top ten are Singapore (3rd), Switzerland (7th), Hong Kong (9th) and Norway (10th). The remainder of the top ten is comprised of small city-states or tax havens.

GDP DATA – HISTORY AND COLLECTION PRINCIPLES

It was not until the 1930s that economists began to give satisfactory definitions of the economy whose growth was to be measured. Naturally that foreshadowed data collection and compilation. Official GDP figures for the UK first took on a recognizable form during the 1939–45 war. Annual figures for GDP are published back to 1946 and quarterly figures back to 1955. There are non-official estimates for GDP going further back. The Royal Economic Society has made estimates back to 1855 and *British Historical Statistics*, by B. R. Mitchell, has estimates back to 1830.

While the processes and practices of data collection have changed beyond recognition over the last fifty years, the basic ways of looking at economic activity have changed little. The three ways correspond to the alternative methods of estimating its size: by measuring total output, total incomes or total expenditure. The ONS still produces GDP figures with its income, expenditure and output components each quarter.

The income and expenditure components are most easily measured in money of the day, i.e. in current prices. The expenditure measure is also expressed in volume terms by deflating each year's figures by the increase in prices. The output components are most easily measured in terms of the volume of goods and services produced and are only available at constant prices in the short term.

At one level the use of three different methods (which, as far as possible, use independent sources of information) avoids reliance on one source and allows greater confidence in the overall estimation process. Inevitably, however, the estimates from each of the three calculations contain errors and omissions and do not produce an identical total. A reconciliation is, however, carried out through the construction of input–output balances, but these are not available immediately. In the 1998 *Blue Book*, for example, the accounts for 1997 were published but input–output balances were only available up to 1996. Accordingly there was an explicit discrepancy shown for 1997.

This is a far cry from the practice of the 1970s and 1980s. At that time the CSO published three different totals for GDP, one derived from each of the three separate measures. Accordingly, attention was focused as much on the differences between them as on trends in the economy, as measured by any one of the measures or by the average of the three. During the 1980s, the three measures were often quite different, fuelling the concern that the quality of the data was poor. Chapter 1 explained the evolving attitude towards official statistics and the extra resources now devoted to data collection. The compilation of input–output balances annually (albeit one year in arrears) rather than every five years, has sharply reduced the differences between the measures. It is now common practice to refer to GDP as a whole, as opposed to any of the three particular derivations of it.

THE INCOME APPROACH

The income approach provides estimates of GDP and its income component parts at current market prices. It adds up all the income of resident individuals and corporations. Some types of what might be thought of as income, like unemployment benefit and pensions, are not included. Although they provide individuals with money to spend, these payments are transfer payments, a redistribution of existing incomes, and do not themselves represent any addition to economic activity.

The main components of income are corporations' gross operating surplus, income from unincorporated enterprises, wages/salaries, employers' social insurance contributions, and taxes on production and imports. Subsidies on production are subtracted. Table 4.3 sets out the key numbers for 1998. Most incomes are subject to tax, so many of the figures are obtained from Inland Revenue sources. Due to delays in providing good quality estimates, other methods are used to complement and to provide initial figures. Within most of the components, an evasion adjustment is added to allow for income earned but not declared to the tax authorities. The income approach can only be used to calculate current price estimates because it is not possible to separate income components into prices and quantities in the same way as for goods and services.

Table 4.3. Components of GDP(I), 1998

	Current prices, £bn	Annual %
Compensation of employees	463.5	7.2
Gross operating surplus	186.8	−0.2
Public non-financial	4.3	2.8
Private non-financial	164.1	−1.0
Financial	18.4	6.7
Other income	72.9	−0.6
Gross value added	723.2	4.4
Taxes on production less subsidies	113.6	6.0
Statistical discrepancy	0.9	—
GDP at current market prices	837.6	4.6

Source: ONS, national accounts press release, March 1999.

THE EXPENDITURE APPROACH

The expenditure approach measures total expenditure on finished goods and services in the domestic economy. More formally, it is the sum of final uses of goods and services by resident institutional units, less the value of imports of goods and services. The total is obtained from the sum of final consumption expenditure by households, government and non-profit institutions on goods, services, gross capital formation (essentially investment but also including changes in inventories) and net exports of goods and services.

The data come from a wide variety of sources including expenditure surveys, the government's internal accounting system, surveys of traders and the administrative documents used for import and export. To avoid double counting in this approach it is important to classify consumption as either final or intermediate. Final consumption involves the consumption of goods purchased by the ultimate consumer or user and is called final (as opposed to intermediate) as the items cease to be part of the economic flow once purchased. Exports are regarded as final consumption since they are final as far as the UK economy is concerned. Imports of goods and services are deducted because they are not part of domestic production.

The expenditure approach provides estimates of GDP and its component parts in constant and current prices, as shown in Table 4.4. (The process of deflation used to derive constant price estimates is described below.) Note that GDP in current prices is the same whether measured by income or expenditure. The expenditure approach provides estimates of various measures of GDP. The largest, and most commonly used, measure, GDP at market prices, includes all taxes on production. GDP at basic prices includes only those taxes on production, such as business rates, which are not taxes on products. GDP at factor cost excludes all taxes on production.

Fig. 4.2 is an interesting graphical breakdown of the GDP numbers, showing the contribution that each part of the expenditure measure made

Table 4.4. Components of GDP(E), 1998

	Current prices		Constant 1995 prices	
	£bn	Ann. % change	£bn	Ann. % change
Final consumption:				
Households	523.5	5.0	486.2	2.8
Non-profit institutions	18.5	0.7	16.2	0.9
General government	152.4	3.6	145.1	1.5
Gross fixed capital				
formation	145.3	8.3	141.3	8.2
Change in inventories*	3.5	—	3.8	—
Total domestic expenditure	843.7	5.2	792.6	3.5
Exports	225.5	−1.6	243.6	3.1
Imports (less)	233.4	1.9	265.7	8.4
Statistical discrepancy	1.9	—	1.7	—
GDP at market prices	837.6	4.6	772.3	2.1

Note: *Includes change in valuables.
Source: ONS, national accounts press release, March 1999.

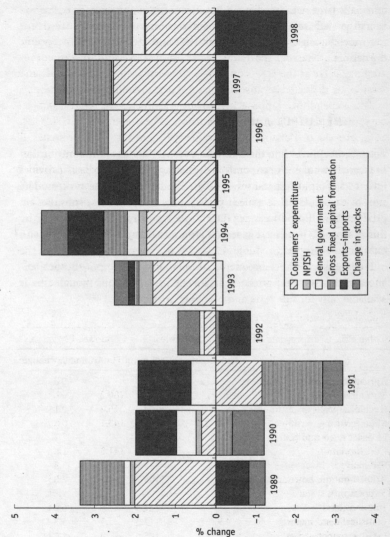

Fig. 4.2. Contributions to economic growth in each year

to GDP growth. In 1998, for example, the largest single contribution was consumers' expenditure (as in the two previous years). There was an unusually large negative contribution from net exports, which pulled the overall growth rate down. The positive contribution from investment was much stronger in the two years 1997 and 1998 than at any time in the decade.

THE OUTPUT APPROACH

The output approach to the estimation of GDP looks at the contribution to production of each economic unit; that is, the value at basic prices of their total output less the value of the inputs used in the process. The sum of this gross value added (GVA), plus taxes and less subsidies on products for all producers, is GDP at market prices. GDP measured by this approach is presented in seasonally adjusted index number form and only in constant prices. Table 4.5 shows the normal breakdown of the output measure. The subsequent compilation of the input–output balances allows the derivation of a current price version, though this is available only for full years and one year in arrears.

Table 4.5. Components of GDP(O), 1998

	Weight	1995 = 100	Annual % change
Agriculture, forestry and fishing	2	102.0	−0.4
Mining and quarrying (including oil)	3	104.3	2.1
Manufacturing	22	101.7	0.3
Electricity, gas and water	3	107.9	2.2
Construction	5	106.4	1.6
Services:	66	111.9	3.6
Distribution, hotels, catering	15	108.3	2.0
Transport, storage, communication	8	121.3	6.0
Business and finance	21	117.3	5.3
Government and other	22	105.6	1.9
GDP at market prices	100	108.5	2.4

Source: ONS, national accounts press release, March 1999, constant 1995 prices.

Estimates of output account for around 80 per cent of the total of the output measure, but a number of input indicators are used as a proxy where output (for example, of some public services) cannot easily be measured. Changes in the use of inputs, such as raw materials used or employment, generally provide acceptable estimates of output change over the short term. However, changes in the ratio of inputs to outputs can be caused by many factors, for example new production processes, over the longer term.

UK ACCOUNTS BY SECTOR

The UK sector accounts show the economic accounting framework in considerable detail in three different dimensions: the institutional sectors; the types of transaction; and the national and sector balance sheets. The six institutional sectors are non-financial corporations, financial corporations, general government (central and local government), households, non-profit institutions and the rest of the world. The first two of these sectors, together the corporate sector, have a number of subsectors reflecting the nature and ownership of the companies, i.e. public/private.

Sector classification differs from the industrial analysis (considered in Chapter 8). Sector classification divides the economy into institutional sectors according to their control, ownership and functions. Industrial analysis groups together economic units according to the main productive activity without reference to ownership. For example, doctors working in the private sector and the National Health Service would be categorized together in the industrial analysis but separately in the sector classification. The national accounts, which bring together all the sectors, show the relationships between different parts of the economy and between different types of activity.

The second dimension, the type of transaction, relates to the particular account within which the transaction appears, namely current, capital or financial. The third dimension, the balance sheet, or accumulation account, shows the changes that account for the difference between the beginning and end of the period. In theory, the net lending or borrowing from the capital account for each sector should equal the net borrowing or lending from the financial account. Consolidating the current and accumulation accounts would present a data set not dissimilar to many presentations of commercial accounts.

Table 4.6 is a summary of table A from the 1998 *Blue Book*. It shows the three GDP measures split by sector and the net financial transactions which are required for the sectors to balance. The first two columns show that non-financial corporations generate the bulk of the output and income in the economy. The two largest components of GDP(I) are the compensation of employees and the gross operating surplus. So it is no surprise that non-financial corporations, which contribute most of output, also have the highest wage bills and the greatest operating surplus. The third column, GDP(E), shows that it is households (the recipients of the wages) which make up the bulk of final consumption. Public sector spending and fixed capital consumption, essentially corporate investment, make up the rest of expenditure.

Our summary table does not show the many thousands of distributive transactions between sectors, the 'lubrication' in the economy, that bring about these totals. To illustrate these flows, we may focus on two of the largest. First, the lending and borrowing of money. In 1995 financial corporations had around £1,000 billion of loans outstanding and financial assets of about £3,500 billion. Together they received net interest payments from the other sectors totalling nearly £50 billion. Second, the net flows of taxation and public expenditure. The *Blue Book* shows that general government spent £264 billion on a variety of social transfers and benefits in 1995. The tax receipts for these payments came largely from the

Table 4.6. The components of GDP, 1995, £bn

	GDP(O)	GDP(I)	GDP(E)	Net financial transactions
Non-financial corporations	428.2	428.2	74.1	2.2
Financial corporations	41.0	41.0	5.0	8.6
General government	75.3	75.3	154.3	−41.2
Households	115.0	115.0	482.0	27.1
Not sectorized	53.0	53.0	0	0
Rest of the world	0	0	−2.8	3.2
UK economy	712.6	712.6	712.6	0

Source: ONS *Blue Book* (1998), table A.

household sector but also from corporates and, to a lesser extent, the rest of the world. (The contribution to GDP(E) in Table 4.6 is only £154 billion as transfer payments are not counted.)

The final column of the table shows net financial transactions, in other words the net transactions in financial assets and liabilities that were required during the course of the year. The table shows that government was a net borrower in 1995 and that the household sector was the largest creditor. These are the tax flows discussed above. As the detailed tables in the *Blue Book* show, households in fact built up deposits with financial institutions that then bought government bonds, allowing government to spend the proceeds.

GROSS NATIONAL DISPOSABLE INCOME

GDP is normally the aggregate of greatest interest, but on occasions it is appropriate to look at some of the others which are available. One alternative is Gross National Income (GNI), which represents the total disposable income of the country's residents. (It was called Gross National Product, GNP, until the change in the accounts in 1998. GNP, as such, does not exist in the new set of accounts but will still be referred to for a transitional phase while it remains the basis for the assessment of countries' contributions to the EU budget.)

GNI is derived from GDP by adjusting for net income from abroad, in effect by making three adjustments. First, it is necessary to add net employment income and net property income from the rest of the world. Second, flows into and out of the country which are not concerned with economic production need to be netted off. These current transfers include items such as transactions with the European Union, overseas aid and private gifts. Third, disposable income is affected by terms of trade. As some of the expenditure by UK residents is on imported goods and services and some of the income of residents derives from the export of goods and services, changes in the exchange rate which affect import and export prices affect the income of residents.

CONSTANT PRICE GDP

Although current price GDP is often the easiest to understand intuitively, it is usually constant price GDP which is of most interest. The constant price series shows the change in GDP after the effects of inflation have been removed. The conversion makes it easier to see whether more goods and services are being produced now than at some time in the past. In the constant price series, transactions are revalued for all years to a fixed price level, that is, to the average prices of a selected year (known as the base year). The base year was last set in 1998, at 1995. Ideally, the base year should be chosen because it closely reflects the price structure of the period under consideration. In practice it is normally reset every five years in line with international convention. Normally this is perfectly acceptable, but if there is something unusual about the base year it can severely affect all comparisons that are made.

Re-basing follows the need to update the pricing structure used in the constant price calculation. As time passes some goods escalate in price more rapidly than others. Accordingly, the relative prices of goods and services in the base year become less representative and the changes in measured volume will become less representative of recent growth. For most types of expenditure, re-basing has the effect of reducing the estimates of growth slightly in the later periods. Consumers tend, on average, to increase their consumption of the goods and services whose unit prices have fallen or grown the least, in substitution for goods and services whose unit prices have grown more. In re-basing, the weight given to the products whose consumption has been increased will be increased, and vice versa for those where consumption has been reduced.

Re-basing does not mean that the whole series of constant price estimates (some going back as far as 1948) are recalculated using the relative weights of the new base year. This would impose inappropriate weights on the estimates for earlier periods, just as failure to re-base would impose inappropriate weights on the latest years. So currently, although constant price or volume estimates are expressed as 'at 1995 prices', more appropriate pricing structures will have been used for series prior to 1994. For these, 1995 is only used as a reference year. It is convenient to reset constant price series to 100 every few years to facilitate the mental arithmetic of inter-year comparisons.

In order to link all of the constant price estimates a process called chain linking is used. Each series is divided into several blocks of years and within each block all constant price figures are calculated with reference to the same base year. A linking factor is obtained for each of the link years (the first and last in each block) so that the whole series may be shown with reference to the latest base year. The European Union has recommended that countries move to a chain linked set of estimates of volume growth, with the weights used being updated annually rather than every five years. The UK practice is widely accepted for many statistical series, but despite a legal requirement to change the move is not imminent.

ACCURACY

Estimates of GDP are built from numerous sources of information: business surveys, household and other social surveys, administrative information and survey data. Data are collected monthly, quarterly, annually and in some cases from *ad hoc* surveys. Some of the resulting estimates which feed into GDP will be firmly based while others will be on weaker foundations. Sampling errors can be calculated for estimates derived from random samples but errors due to limitations of coverage and measurement problems are impossible to know. Reliable estimates of error are, accordingly, very difficult to estimate for many of the components of GDP.

The extra resources now devoted to national accounting allow the many interrelationships within the system to be explored, and internal consistency checks and data validation to be carried out. Accordingly the ONS is more confident now than perhaps ever before about the quality of GDP data. While it is clearly very difficult to comment on the accuracy of GDP estimates, the ONS, sadly, makes no attempt. While the principal official measure of reliability is to use evidence from analyses of revisions, most users of other countries' data know from experience that the UK data are among the best.

TESTING FOR BIAS

The ONS regularly monitors revisions to growth rates of the components of GDP for bias. It has published several analyses of revisions (in *Economic Trends*), comparing the initial quarterly estimates and the corresponding estimates published three years later. The latest analysis, published in 1996, showed that only three or four (depending on the time horizon chosen) of the twenty-three components showed an indication of bias. The results are less worrying than they may appear at first because the analysis examined data only up to 1992 and accordingly failed to take any real account of improvements in data collection which took place in the 1990s. It would be expected that the next such analysis will provide more encouraging results. The ONS has found no reason thus far to put in bias correction factors.

Once input–output balances are published, the accounts will, by definition, balance. In the intervening period (the input–output balances are published for full years only, eighteen months in arrears) a statistical discrepancy item is shown in the accounts. This item provides a measure of reliability as it reflects errors and omissions in the account. In this context, the publication of numbers to the nearest £1 million seems to offer precision that is not warranted by the evidence. This practice is, however, justified on the grounds that some of the estimates in the tables are fairly precise and any significant rounding would compound errors for those who are preparing derived statistics. It is a shame that the ONS does not provide more robust quality warnings for its data.

ESA95 – THE NEW SYSTEM OF NATIONAL ACCOUNTS

The summer of 1998 saw not only the publication of the annual *Blue Book* (including the data up to 1997) but also the launch of UK national accounts consistent with the European System of Accounts (ESA95). The changes were considerable. They were described by the ONS as the most extensive changes to the accounts since the *Blue Book* was first published in 1952. The ONS took the opportunity of the introduction of ESA95 to make a number of other changes. Examples include:

- Re-basing to 1995.
- Inclusion of data from the new Inter-departmental Business Register (by replacing a number of separate registers, gaps and double-counting have been reduced).
- Other methodological changes (notably, improved measurement of government output and new assessments of tax evasion), including some new surveys.
- Data revisions, the need for which became clear during this major process of overhaul.

The introduction of these changes inevitably revised the level and recent growth path of GDP. Table 4.7 summarizes the main changes to growth rates and gives their source. The introduction of ESA95 did more to alter the structure of the accounts and the terminology than the numbers themselves. The bulk of the change in the growth rate in recent years was accounted for by the new business register, the new measurement of government output and the act of re-basing.

The new system of European accounts is based on, but a little more specific in parts than, the System of National Accounts 1993 (SNA93), sponsored by all the major international economic organizations, which is being adopted worldwide. There was, realistically, little option for the UK but to adopt the new system. The system used by the UK up to 1998 was in any case ready for an overhaul, but European legislation now requires member states to submit to the European Commission ESA95

Table 4.7. Revisions to GDP annual growth rates in 1998

	1991–3 average	1994	1995	1996	1997
Old measure	−0.4	4.3	2.7	2.2	3.4
New measure	0.9	4.4	2.8	2.6	3.5
Change	1.3	0.1	0.1	0.4	0.1
of which:					
ESA	−0.2	−0.1	0.1	−0.1	0.1
Rebasing	0.0	0.0	−0.1	−0.2	−0.4
Non-ESA	1.5	0.1	0.1	0.6	0.4

Source: ONS *Blue Book*, 1998, table C.

accounts from April 1999. Countries remain free, of course, to present accounts in whatever format chosen for domestic purposes but a good case would be needed to prepare two sets of accounts on different definitions.

Further details of the differences between the new and old accounting frameworks can be found in a range of documents published by the ONS in 1998, notably the 1998 *Blue Book* and the *UK National Accounts Concepts, Sources and Methods*. Changes include:

● New institutional sectors were created replacing the old. This has led to some reclassifications. For example, partnerships have been recognized as 'quasi corporations' and have moved from the personal sector to the corporate sector.

● Much of the language has changed. For example, Gross National Product became Gross National Income, stocks became inventories and the balance of payments became the current external balance.

● There were some subtle but important methodological changes. For example, in the new system, value added is measured at basic prices (including taxes and subsidies on production but not on products) rather than, as in the previous system, at factor cost (excluding all taxes and subsidies on production).

● One of the most important definitional changes concerned capital formation or investment. The scope of capital formation has been extended with the effect of increasing GDP by redefining spending from intermediate consumption (i.e. not counted as final expenditure) to capital expenditure. Spending on mineral exploration, cultivated assets, artistic originals, computer software, work in progress in the service industries and valuables, is now all included in capital expenditure.

While many of the underlying data series are unchanged, they are grouped differently and they look very different. The change came as something of a shock to seasoned analysts and also required a considerable effort over several years from the ONS. The new accounts meant that those maintaining econometric models had a massive data updating and recalibration exercise. There has been some criticism of the new accounts in that they provide too little useful information and plenty of largely irrelevant detail on the government sector. This has compounded the problems associated with classification changes between the public and private sectors, which has always bedevilled analysis of the public/private split.

The introduction of the new set of accounts has also led to a refocusing on new variables. The UK authorities henceforth will use GDP at constant market prices as the key indicator of the state of the economy, in common with other EU member states. The previous key indicator, GDP at factor cost, is not a concept used in the new system. All the components to calculate it, however, are still available and the ONS has said it will continue to provide 'gross value added' at current and constant factor cost while demand continues.

Box 4.1. **Bank of England assessment of national accounts changes**

The following comments come from the November 1998 Bank of England *Inflation Report*. They illustrate the sort of issues that concern market practitioners.

'The level of GDP at current market prices in 1997 is now £15.4 billion higher than under the previous set of accounts. The introduction of the ESA95, which resulted in revisions as far back as 1948, accounted for £2.4 billion, but had only a negligible impact on recent growth rates.

'In real terms, cumulative GDP growth between 1991 Q1 [first quarter] and 1998 Q2 is now estimated to be nearly two per cent higher than previously thought. Rebasing is estimated to have reduced real GDP growth by 0.7 percentage points since 1995, implying that other changes to the data would have left GDP growth 2.6 per cent higher since 1991 Q1. Average annual growth of real GDP in the last decade is now 2.2 per cent, compared with 2.0 per cent in the previous accounts. The revisions to GDP occur principally in two time periods. Around two-thirds of the upward revision occurs between 1991 and 1993, which reduces the measured depth of the recession. And growth is higher since 1994, and particularly since 1996.

'The upward revision to GDP, particularly since 1996, mainly reflects higher fixed investment, which affects both the demand and supply sides of the economy. The peak in GDP growth now occurs in 1997 Q4, one quarter later than previously thought. But the slowdown in domestic demand, and particularly in household expenditure, since 1997 Q4 is more marked. Growth in household expenditure in the year to 1998 Q2 is now estimated to have been 2.8 per cent, compared with 3.8 per cent in the previous accounts. By contrast, the contribution to growth from net trade is now less negative. This is primarily owing to higher exports of services. Investment income has also been revised up, significantly reducing the current account deficit in 1997 and 1998 Q1.

'On the output side, the relative sizes of broad industrial groups have changed. The weight of manufacturing in the economy has fallen, but the service sector's weight has risen to almost two-thirds of the economy. Over the recovery as a whole, cumulative service sector growth has been revised up by 1.5 percentage points. That largely reflects a methodological improvement to the measure of government output. Manufacturing output since 1992 Q2 is unchanged, but was 0.7 percentage points higher between 1997 Q3 and 1998 Q2. Nonetheless, the divergence between ONS and survey data since 1995, which has been highlighted in the past, still remains a puzzle.'

WHAT IS INCLUDED IN THE UK'S GDP?

The economy of the United Kingdom is made up of institutional units which have a centre of economic interest in the UK economic territory. In most cases the decision to include or exclude a unit is fairly obvious, but at the margin there will always be difficult decisions to make. The economic territory includes air space and territorial waters and any free zones coming under UK customs control, military bases, embassies and so forth. It excludes the offshore islands, such as the Channel Islands and the Isle of Man (which are not members of the European Union). The concept of economic interest largely rests on residency.

The issue of exactly what production to include in GDP is more contentious. In its widest sense, economic activity could cover all activities resulting in the production of goods or services and so encompass some activities which are very difficult to measure. The so-called 'production boundary' is defined to include all activities where an output is owned and produced by an institutional unit, for which payment or other compensation has to be made to enable a change of ownership to take place. This definition has the advantage of omitting purely natural processes. Perhaps less attractively, it also excludes the production of services for own final consumption, notably household domestic and personal services such as cleaning, cooking and the care of children and the infirm. The purchase of some of these services by some people is clearly included in the statistics while in most cases the activity is excluded.

Once the boundary is agreed, some items in it are not measured because they cannot be, giving rise to a number of inconsistencies with understandable pragmatic origins. For example, the produce of farms consumed by the farmer's own household is included in GDP, because estimates are available, but produce from gardens or allotments is excluded, as estimates have been impossible to derive. Such inconsistencies may be irritating but so long as the definition is consistent over time, growth rates will still be meaningful and reliable. There is greater uncertainty about the so-called 'black economy', such as criminal or unrecorded activity, that occurs within the boundary, for which no allowance is currently made in the accounts.

One final issue concerns the term 'gross', as used in Gross Domestic Product. In this context 'gross' means that the figures do not allow for capital consumption or depreciation. Capital goods do not get used up straightaway in the production process but wear out or become obsolete over time. Due to the difficulty in obtaining reliable estimates of capital depreciation, no allowance is made. Accordingly, GDP does not give a true picture of value added in the economy.

It is also worth noting that a country's measured GDP will be larger than its true income, as its wealth is running down. This can be a serious defect if irreplaceable natural resources are being used up rapidly. The best example would be that of an oil producing country which has high growth rates as a result of taking oil out of the ground. Clearly, oil will not be available indefinitely. The same problem, however, applies to most countries, say in the case of viable land or fishing stocks, on a smaller scale.

DATA SOURCES

As explained above, the data that make up the GDP numbers come from every imaginable source. The sources are constantly changing and have changed dramatically in the last decade, as indicated in Chapter 1. Box 4.2 sets out some of the typical sources of the information. An important source is the surveys carried out by the ONS. In 1997, for example, the ONS conducted seventy-nine surveys of businesses, issuing nearly 1.3 million inquiry forms. In addition to this, there were surveys of individuals and households and surveys conducted by other government departments.

Box 4.2. **Sources for GDP data**

GDP(O)

Production industries (27%)	Monthly ONS index of production series. Trade association surveys. Deflation using producer price indices.
Construction (5%)	Quarterly survey of work done.
Distribution, hotels, catering, repairs (15%)	Retail turnover as proxy supplemented by delivery and production indices where possible. Vehicle registrations and delivery of petrol. VAT system. Annual catering inquiry.
Transport and communication (8%)	Passenger journeys/miles, goods/miles and deflated turnover figures for rail, road and air. Interpolation of annual figures and turnover data for sea. Turnover for telecoms. Post Office activity.
Business services and finance (21%)	Cheques cleared, size of deposits, building society advances, housing market turnover, expenditure on insurance, turnover and employment.
Government and other services (22%)	Employment, wage bill, VAT turnover of venues, spending on sport, hairdressing and gambling.

GDP(E)

	% of GDP(E)
Family Expenditure Survey	20
National Food Survey	10
International passenger survey	2
Retail sales (durables, clothing, household goods etc.)	15
Various vehicle surveys	5
Trade associations, government departments (rail, bus, gas, petrol, ice cream etc.)	13
Receipts data (local authority housing, rents, rates etc.)	13
Interpolation from annual data	12

In addition: government spending figures, surveys for capital spending and stocks, overseas trade figures, CAA data, surveys of pay, surveys of 'City' activities and surveys of company profits.

Source: ONS methodological paper no. 3. GDP(O) % figures are the 1995 weights.

WHAT DATA ARE PUBLISHED?

Culminating with the publication of the new national accounting framework in 1998, the GDP data have probably undergone much greater changes in both style and substance of publication than has been the case for any of the other indicators.

There are three press releases for each quarter. The first, called 'GDP preliminary estimate', is published just three weeks after the end of the quarter. It gives an index number for GDP in constant prices only, and calculates the economy's quarterly and annual growth rates in the latest period. Very little detail is given in the release, reflecting the provisional and sketchy nature of the data. The growth of the service component, roughly two-thirds of total output compared to production industries' one-quarter, is shown. The estimates of the output of the production industries are derived from the monthly industrial output release (which is discussed in Chapter 8). Construction and agriculture, for which there is very little information at this stage, account for the remaining 7 per cent of the economy's output.

The release is eagerly awaited, as it is believed that the Monetary Policy Committee of the Bank of England, which sets interest rates, pays great attention to the growth of the economy. In response to the desire to know about the growth rate in the economy several organizations have at times published monthly estimates of GDP. The National Institute of Economic and Social Research (NIESR) estimate, published since 1998, receives considerable press attention. Using a selection of ONS data and projections for the latest month, NIESR publishes a quarterly estimate for GDP three weeks ahead of the ONS.

The second of the press releases, called 'UK output, income and expenditure', is available roughly a month later, some seven weeks after the end of the quarter. This release includes a revised estimate of GDP growth in the recent quarter, but also gives plenty of new information. The revisions to the initial estimates of growth in GDP have been modest in recent years (typically no more than 0.1 per cent) following the extra resources that have been allocated to the task during the 1990s. Accordingly, most attention is focused on the new information.

There are essentially five pieces of new information in this release. These are:

● The first current price estimates of GDP that allow the derivation of the implied GDP deflator, which, as an index of home costs, is the broadest measure of inflation in the economy.
● A break-down among the nine industrial categories of the constant price output measure given in the first of the releases.
● The first estimate of the income measure of GDP in current prices.
● A break-down of the expenditure measure of GDP in current and constant prices.
● A break-down of inventories by industrial sector.

There is enough information in this release to derive a reasonable picture of the state of the economy in the latest quarter.

The last in the series of three releases, 'Quarterly national accounts', is published a month later, just before the end of the following quarter. The release provides much more detail of the GDP break-down, including twenty tables (as opposed to one and six respectively in the previous two releases), as well as revisions to the earlier estimates. The highlights in this release are the break-downs of household final consumption (i.e. consumers' expenditure), service sector output, investment, the detail of the household accounts (which leads to the savings ratio) and information about the (private, non-financial) corporate sector's performance, including profits.

The third release also includes a table of alignment adjustments. As explained above, the three alternative ways of deriving GDP are most unlikely to yield exactly the same estimate. However, as the output approach is considered to provide the best estimate of quarter to quarter movements, the income and expenditure totals tend to be adjusted to reflect the movements in output. This process of alignment is complex but adjustments tend to be made to stockbuilding (in the expenditure analysis) and the gross operating surplus of companies (in the income analysis), as these components are believed to have the widest error margins. The release also includes some analysis of revisions.

Some weeks later, in the second half of the fourth month after the end of a quarter, the ONS publishes *UK Economic Accounts*. This booklet includes more than a hundred pages of tables detailing the national accounts data. The first section sets out the main aggregates in tables which are broadly familiar from the earlier releases. The next three sections set out the current, capital and financial accounts along with the financial balance sheets. The final section relates to the balance of payments. These tables present a picture of the economy, and in considerable detail. Only a couple of weeks later, the first estimates of the following quarter's GDP are published. (There are several other supporting releases which are dealt with in other chapters.)

FORECASTING GDP

There are a number of approaches to forecasting GDP. The traditional method is to construct an econometric model of the whole economy, in which numerous equations embody theories about the behaviour of each part. An alternative is to seek a very simple, perhaps even single equation, model of the economy. This could aim to explain changes in GDP using a small number of variables such as interest rates and the budget deficit.

A third approach is to extrapolate the recent trend of GDP, allowing for short-term disturbances, medium-term cyclical fluctuations and long-term changes in variables which affect the growth rate. A number of forecasting bodies, generally either academic or commercial forecasters, use a variant on the first method while the majority of City commentators use the third method.

The key feature of any model is that it provides an opportunity to bring together in a consistent and systematic way the large amount of information relevant to forecasting. Models are thus a framework, not a substitute, for judgement. Any forecasting exercise requires a full understanding of the data, both the latest trends and the intricacies of the series themselves.

It is important to appreciate that different forecasters are usually trying to focus on different parts of the economy and over different horizons. While economists mostly look at the same basic data and concepts, the focus will range from interest rate and currency developments over the coming days and weeks to trends in manufacturing or relative regional prosperity, for example, over a decade or more. Some companies, such as utilities, with large capital investment plans might forecast over the next quarter of a century. The Treasury itself, for example, puts more resources than usual into forecasts of the public finances, which is not surprising given the central role of tax and spend decisions in policy making. That said, most forecasting relates to the general health of the economy – growth, inflation, unemployment etc. – over the next two years.

Some forecasting, however, is very short term. This is not easy as GDP can be erratic from quarter to quarter, even after seasonal adjustment. For example, over the seven quarters from the third quarter of 1996, GDP grew by 0.6 per cent, 0.6 per cent, 1.1 per cent, 1.1 per cent, 1.0 per cent, 0.6 per cent and 0.7 per cent. It was difficult to forecast the rise in the first quarter of 1997 and the fall in the fourth quarter of 1997. A forecaster might reasonably be expecting a rise or a fall but getting the extent and the timing right is difficult. Such sharp fluctuations in the data from quarter to quarter can have an impact on policy and market sentiment. Accordingly, some forecasters try to assess the impact of exceptional events, such as strikes or sharp changes in weather, in an attempt to improve the forecast.

Forecasting the path of GDP beyond the next quarter, and over the next year or two, is a far more challenging exercise and one to which greater resources are devoted. When the growth rate is steady, the task of forecasting appears relatively easy. At the start of 1998, roughly half of the forty or so published forecasts were expecting growth during the year of between 2¼ and 2¾ per cent. A handful of forecasters expected growth below 2 per cent and a similar number expected growth over 3 per cent. In the event the early 1999 estimates of growth in 1998 were between 2 and 2½ per cent and there was little to choose between rival forecasters.

More often than not, however, the economy is not growing in line with trend and the forecasts are far more uncertain. The tendency to be backward looking and assume that growth will return to trend in the period ahead, means that many fail to predict either the severity of recessions or the extent of booms. For example, at the beginning of 1991, the range of +1 per cent to −1 per cent encompassed most forecasters. The average was looking for no change. While the data now show a fall in GDP of 1½ per cent, at one point the economy was recorded to have shrunk by over 2 per cent. The same tendency also accounted for the failure of many to spot the recovery phase. There was, for example, also a 2 percentage-point range of expectations for growth, from no change to +2 per cent, at the start of 1993. The statistics currently show growth of 2¼ per cent for 1993.

The ability to predict so-called 'turning points' in the economic cycle, when a period of growth gives way to slow down or vice versa, is elusive. Predicting turning points conflicts with the natural human tendency, and that of models, to base the future on the immediate past. The last decade has seen some extremes of growth, from a 5¼ per cent rise in 1988 to a 1½ per cent fall in 1991 and a 4½ per cent rise in 1994. This period proved a severe test for forecasters and it is fair to say that none was covered in glory over the whole period.

It is quite normal for forecasters to have 'axes to grind'. These axes can be to the benefit or the detriment of their forecasts. Some forecasters have a natural bias towards, or prior belief in, high growth rates or low inflation rates and will therefore appear to be more right at certain times in the economic cycle. Some users of forecasts, for example fund managers, are sometimes perfectly happy to have forecasts with known biases. Presented with a naturally bullish and naturally bearish forecast, readers can then judge the merits of the opposing arguments and come to their own conclusions about the likely outcome.

Other forecasters occasionally spot themes which can be influential on the economic outlook over a period of time. For example, the conversion (through the process of demutualization or purchase by other organizations) of many building societies into banks during 1997, with the attendant consumer windfalls, led to several quarters of strong consumer spending. It is probably fair to say that those forecasters who realized the potential impact of this change were those who had the superior forecasts. Certainly the 'story' attached to their forecasts would have been more plausible if it allowed for this factor.

It is important to be aware of political bias in government forecasts. Most famously, in the recession of 1990 to 1991, the then Chancellor of the Exchequer, Norman Lamont, never once published a forecast of continuing recession. The Treasury always thought that the latest quarterly fall in GDP would be the last. It is easy to understand why he became so well known for the failure of his 'green shoots of recovery' to sprout.

To be fair to the Treasury, the quality of their forecasts deteriorated at that time largely due to the poor quality of the data, as discussed in Chapter 1. It is hard to know what is coming next year if you do not know where you are starting from! It was also a time of unprecedented change in the behaviour of the personal sector in response to institutional and structural changes in the economy. Further, Treasury studies have shown that their forecasts did not compare unfavourably with forecasts from other institutions. Indeed, the differences between forecasters are often small compared to the differences between the average forecast and the eventual out-turn, reflecting the comfort that most forecasters feel in having a consensus forecast.

Forecasts for periods beyond the next year or two become progressively more hazardous. The Treasury itself only forecasts the coming eighteen months and usually refers to growth projections for future years as assumptions. Longer-term forecasts normally depend upon some estimate of the potential underlying growth rate of the economy. Such a growth rate must be sustainable in the sense that it could occur year in year out without inflation picking up, the balance of payments moving into large deficit or other problems arising. The sustainable growth rate is currently estimated at around 2 to 2½ per cent for the UK economy.

5 | Inflation

The language of inflation can be confusing due to the loose or ambiguous use of words. Generally, however, there is said to be inflation when there is a broad-based and sustained rise in prices in the economy. The rate of increase in prices may be gradual (creeping inflation) or large and accelerating (hyperinflation). If the rate of inflation is falling, there is said to be disinflation. Occasionally prices actually fall, which is called negative inflation or deflation. Deflation is also used to describe recession, i.e. a fall in the level of national income, which is often accompanied by falling prices.

Price indices are frequently referred to as deflators and are used to convert, i.e. deflate, figures in current prices into constant prices. This statistical process, which is also called deflation, is distinct from the process of deflation in the economy.

THE VARIOUS MEASURES OF INFLATION

There are many price indicators measuring different prices or groups of prices. An oil price index, for example, measures the change in the price of oil. If not otherwise specified, inflation normally refers to an index of consumer prices. Some of the more common indicators are shown in Box 5.1. They are arranged loosely in the order in which inflationary pressures are transmitted through the economy. A sharp rise in the price of basic materials will feed through to intermediate and then into retail prices and the GDP deflator.

Box 5.1. **The main measures of inflation**

The Retail Prices Index (RPI) is the most frequently used measure, but the following are also often used.

Basic indicators:

- The gold price (and other precious metals)
- The price of oil
- Commodity prices and composite commodity indices (which are compiled by many organizations)

Intermediate indicators:

- Producer (or wholesale) input and output prices
- Business surveys. Many trade associations publish measures of inflation relevant to their economic activity.
- Export and import prices
- Construction costs and prices
- Labour market indicators, such as average earnings and unit labour costs
- House prices
- Investment and industrial assets
- Share prices

Final or broad indicators (in addition to the RPI):

- Consumers' expenditure deflator
- GDP deflator
- Final expenditure prices index (FEPI)
- Tax and Price Index (TPI)
- Harmonized CPI (HICP)

The inflation rate varies dramatically according to the definition chosen (see Table 5.1). The basic and intermediate measures of inflation are far more volatile than the final measures. Each of the more important indicators is discussed towards the end of this chapter, but most attention will be focused on consumer inflation, as measured by the RPI.

Table 5.1. Comparison of various measures of inflation

	Average 1986–90	Average 1991–5	1996	1997	1998
Gold ($, troy oz.)	5.0	0.3	0.9	−14.7	−10.9
Oil price (Brent)	4.8	−3.6	20.0	−2.6	−30.7
Commodity index*	−0.4	7.2	−5.2	−2.9	−18.6
Producer input prices	−1.4	2.6	−1.2	−8.3	−9.0
Producer output prices	3.9	3.8	2.6	1.0	0.5
Export prices**	1.8	5.4	−0.3	−5.6	−4.0
Import prices**	1.6	5.4	0.2	−6.3	−5.9
Ave. earnings growth	8.6	4.7	3.5	4.2	5.1
Unit labour costs	7.3	2.5	2.0	2.8	3.9
House price index†	14.3	−2.2	4.3	6.4	5.5
Share price, FTSE 100	12.9	8.8	14.5	22.5	20.8
Consumers exp. def.	5.0	4.2	2.9	2.5	2.0
GDP deflator	6.0	3.5	3.3	2.5	2.5
Tax and Price Index	4.5	3.3	1.4	2.1	3.2

Notes: for a comparison of the various measures of RPI inflation see Table 5.2.
*Economist, all items, £ terms. **Excluding oil and erratics. †Halifax.
Sources: ONS and Datastream.

POLICY BACKGROUND

The control of inflation is a top policy priority in all developed countries. This is because a high rate of inflation is thought to:

- blur relative price movements, distorting economic behaviour and introducing inefficiencies;
- encourage speculation in property and commodities rather than long-term investment in companies;
- introduce an additional major uncertainty, discouraging long-term business planning;
- redistribute income, in particular, pensioners on fixed incomes suffer while wage earners benefit;
- create an imbalance between saving and borrowing – saving becomes unattractive and borrowing becomes lower-risk as the real value of a fixed nominal debt falls;

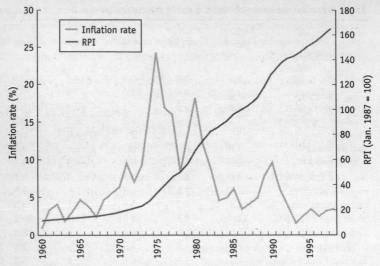

Fig. 5.1. Retail price inflation – annual rate and index

• damage international trade if exports become more expensive.

In general, if inflation is seen to be rising or turns out to be higher than expected, economic policy – fiscal or monetary – will be tightened in order to bring inflation down. If inflation is lower than expected or there is a threat of deflation, economic policy will generally be eased.

In the extreme, high rates of inflation can cause a loss of confidence in the currency. The threat to stability from the oil price shocks of the 1970s prompted governments in the developed world to give increased attention to the control of inflation. This manifested itself in many countries in the increased freedom given to the non-political, more independent, central banks to run monetary policy, i.e. the raising and lowering of interest rates, in such a way as to control inflation. There are many common themes between the structures that each country has established, but there are also important differences. Each country's system reflects its own social, political and economic circumstances and history.

The UK, perhaps more slowly than many countries, has followed this route. Nigel Lawson, the former Chancellor of the Exchequer, described inflation in 1986 as the judge and jury of economic policy. However, there were no serious anti-inflationary measures pursued in the UK in the 1980s and the economic boom at the end of the decade saw a sharp rise in inflation (see Fig 5.1). The 1990s saw more serious attempts to pursue low and stable rates of inflation. There are three notable landmarks:

● 1990 – Joining the exchange rate mechanism of the ERM, pegging the currency to the Deutschmark.
● 1992 – Setting an inflation target of 1–4 per cent for RPIX as the centrepiece of economic policy (following sterling's exit from the ERM). This was accompanied by an increasingly public role for the Bank of England, notably through the publication of its inflation report.
● 1997 – Handing over responsibility for achieving the inflation target (2½ per cent as measured by the RPIX) to the Bank of England (see Box 5.2).

Box 5.2. **The UK policy framework**

On the first working day of the new Labour Government (6 May 1997) the Chancellor held a press conference to announce changes in the institutional framework for monetary policy. The key components were:

● The Bank of England to be given 'operational responsibility for setting interest rates'.
● The Bank's policy objective 'to deliver price stability as defined by the government's inflation target and, without prejudice to this objective, to support the government's policy, including its objectives for growth and employment'.
● Interest rate decisions to be made by a new Monetary Policy Committee (MPC) comprising the governor, the two deputy governors and six members, of which four are not Bank staff. The committee is to meet monthly and the Bank will continue to publish its quarterly inflation report.

The framework and the remit have evolved since the initial announcement but the main aspects are still similar to the Chancellor's statement in 1997.

The policy framework in each country is unique in its detail, but they all have broadly the same aim and that is to control inflation. UK inflation was lower in the 1990s than it had been for several decades, partly reflecting policy changes and partly the global environment.

Governments have typically not set a target of, or sought, zero inflation. This is partly because there is a high economic cost, notably in the form of rising unemployment, to reduce inflation once a rate in low single figures has already been achieved. A little inflation, say 2–3 per cent, is accepted and can even be thought of as being helpful to the economy. It is also suspected that due to a bias in the statistics, mainly a failure to allow fully for quality improvements, a published rate of 1–2 per cent is consistent with price stability (see p. 104).

Some flexibility on the part of policy-makers is also required from time to time. There are occasions when it is appropriate to tolerate higher rates of inflation for a short period of time. If a country is undergoing structural economic change, a short period of higher inflation can be a small price to pay for significant long-term gains. Examples might include: the reunification of Germany; financial deregulation in the UK in the

---

Box 5.3. **A brief history of UK retail price inflation**

The records of price changes of staple commodities going back to the Middle Ages can be used to provide a rough and ready idea of inflation trends. But it was not until the national cost of living index was set up in 1914 that there was any formal collection of trends in retail prices.

High rates of inflation, year after year, are a relatively modern phenomenon. In the century 1850–1950, prices fell in thirty-five years and rose in sixty-five, of which ten were war years. The price level was about the same in 1900 as it had been in 1850, despite the fluctuations in between. It multiplied three-and-a-half times between 1900 and 1950, but the annual average inflation rate for that period was still only 2½ per cent.

It was only in the late 1960s that inflation rose above 5 per cent for a number of years. The inflation rate averaged 13½ per cent in the 1970s and 7 per cent in the 1980s. Inflation was much lower in the 1990s, indeed the headline rate was only above 4 per cent in a handful of months.

1980s; the introduction of market economies in eastern European countries in the 1990s; or the catching up of Ireland and Spain with other countries in the run-up to EMU.

It is also true that to cut inflation too quickly to return to a satisfactory rate can be damaging in terms of disruption to the economy. One example would be the attempt of a number of EU countries to satisfy the Maastricht criteria for EMU entry by 1998. As a result of the tough policy that had to be pursued, growth rates, especially in Germany and Italy, were restrained well below the trend level. Expectations of inflation in society can take many years to change.

THE RETAIL PRICES INDEX

Everything that consumers buy has a price and that price varies over time. The best-known measure of consumer price changes in the UK is the Retail Prices Index (RPI). It is one of the most widely publicized of all UK economic indicators. Most other countries refer to the main measure of consumer inflation as either the consumer price index (CPI) or the cost of living index. While there are technically differences between these measures, the terms are frequently used to mean the same thing.

The RPI measures the rate of change of prices for a typical basket of goods and services that are bought regularly by consumers. No single consumer conforms to that spending pattern and no two people or households spend their money in exactly the same way, but the RPI aims to be close to the experience of inflation for many people. It prices the same goods and services every month, indicating how much it costs to maintain the same purchases over time.

The RPI rate of inflation is referred to as the 'headline rate', though users will often refer to other inflation rates which are sub-components of the total. The most common forms are:

- RPIX. This is the RPI eXcluding mortgage interest. It is the measure that the government has set the Bank of England to target. It is frequently referred to as the underlying inflation rate.
- RPIY. This excludes mortgage interest and local authority and indirect taxes. It measures inflation excluding government driven price changes

and is probably the best measure of underlying inflation in the economy. This measure was 'created' by the Bank of England in the early 1990s and its calculation was subsequently taken over by the ONS.

● Rossi index. This is used for the uprating of state income related benefits and is currently defined as the RPI less mortgage interest payments, rent and council tax. These items are excluded, as benefit recipients are unlikely to be paying significant housing costs. It is named after a social security minister of the early 1980s.

The RPI monthly press release sets out an additional dozen sub-components, including all items excluding food, consumer durables and personal expenditure. (The Rossi index is not published in the press release.) The Bank of England, in its quarterly inflation report, refers to a number of other RPI variants. These include the HARP and THARP measures (RPIX and RPIY including an allowance for owner occupied housing costs) and the median and trimmed mean indices. The trimmed mean removes the largest and smallest 15 per cent of price changes and tends to produce a lower rate of inflation than the RPIX as there are typically more large increases than large decreases in prices. The Bank looks at these various rates (which are not published by the ONS) to improve its understanding of the inflationary dynamics within the economy.

THE HARMONIZED INDEX OF CONSUMER PRICES – HICP

As its name suggests, the Harmonized Index of Consumer Prices attempts to harmonize practices and definitions across the countries of the European Union and is best used for international comparisons. The origins of this measure lie in the steps in the 1990s towards economic and monetary union (EMU) in Europe. One of the economic convergence criteria for EMU set out in the 1992 Maastricht Treaty concerned price stability. To qualify for EMU a country had to have an average rate of inflation over a period of one year that did not exceed, by more than one-and-a-half percentage points, that of the three best performing member states. Price stability had to be measured by means of comparable consumer price indices.

The process of harmonization has been a long and difficult one for Eurostat, the European Commission's statistical arm, as many countries were unwilling to change their long-standing practices. They were able to publish interim indices from 1996 and the first set of harmonized indices from 1997. Even so, there are still a number of differences between the countries' harmonized indices which need to be resolved in the years ahead.

The UK HICP uses the same basic price collections as the RPI, but there are a number of areas where the methodologies differ. The main differences are:

● The HICP is based on the international classification system, COICOP, whereas the RPI uses its own distinct system. For instance, under Classification of Individual Consumption by Purpose (COICOP), 'alcoholic beverages' comprises off-sales only, while sales of alcohol in bars and restaurants are included under 'catering'. By contrast, in the RPI all expenditure on alcohol is included under the one heading of 'alcohol'.
● A number of RPI components are excluded, most notably owner-occupiers' housing costs, house depreciation and council tax (which together make up about 10 per cent of the RPI) and others such as private education and medical fees.
● The HICP series for personal computers and new cars are explicitly adjusted for quality changes.
● The HICP uses the geometric mean to aggregate prices at their lowest level while the RPI uses arithmetic means.
● The HICP uses weights for spending by the whole population, while the RPI excludes some pensioners and high earners.
● The HICP is a revisable index while the RPI is never revised.

The UK HICP has consistently reported a lower rate of inflation than the RPI and its various sub-indices. At the beginning of 1999, there was a difference of 1 per cent between the RPIX (2½ per cent) and the HICP (1½ per cent). Half of this was accounted for by the formula effect, 0.4 per cent by the owner-occupied housing component, with other coverage differences accounting for the remaining 0.1 per cent. Since the introduction of this measure, pressure has been growing on the government to use it for monetary policy targeting so as to put the UK on an equal footing with other EU countries.

At the start of 1999, a handful of the fifteen countries in the European

Union reported harmonized inflation rates between 1 and 2 per cent, broadly in line with the UK's 1½ per cent. While several countries reported a higher rate, the weighted average for the European Union was just 1 per cent, being pulled down by the low rates, around ¼ per cent, in France and Germany, the two largest countries.

Table 5.2. Comparisons of RPI, its sub-indices and the HICP

	Average 1987–91	Average 1992–6	1997	1998
RPI	6.4	2.7	3.1	3.4
RPIX	5.8	3.2	2.8	2.7
RPIY	6.2	2.7	2.2	2.1
HICP*	n.a.	n.a.	1.8	1.6
Rossi index**	6.2	3.1	2.5	2.2

Notes: *HICP did not exist before 1996. **Given on 1998 definition, excludes 1987.
Source: ONS.

THE TAX AND PRICE INDEX (TPI)

The TPI measures how much the average person's gross income needs to change to buy the basket of goods allowing for the average amount of income tax and National Insurance paid on the earnings. The TPI is barely affected by a shift between direct and indirect taxation, which would distort the RPI as consumer prices rose. It is for this reason that the TPI was developed in the early 1980s, so that the shift to indirect taxation would not make inflation look so bad. It is clearly different from the RPI and is appropriate for different uses. Most economists will compare the TPI with average earnings. If the latter is rising more rapidly, there is a rise in the real purchasing value of gross earnings.

THE USES OF INFLATION DATA

Measures of consumer price inflation are the most rapidly available guide to national inflation and are used, therefore, both for international comparisons and for interpreting other price changes. Prices are often said to be rising by more or less than the rate of consumer price inflation. The RPI is widely used in the social sciences and finance to deflate amounts in money terms so as to express them in real terms, taking out that part of a change which is due purely to rising prices rather than rising quantities. One fundamental advantage that the RPI has over other official measures of inflation is that the data are never revised.

Inflation is also a performance measure for the Bank of England. As explained above, the government sets the framework for macro-economic management in terms of the annual change in the RPIX. The government also uses the annual increase in the RPI to:

- Index many tax allowances each year in the Budget. Allowances are raised in line with inflation to keep their value to the taxpayer constant.
- Uprate certain social security benefits. The annual rate of the RPI in September is generally used to uprate benefits and pensions for the year starting in the following April. (The RPI is used for non-income-related benefits while income-related benefits are revised in line with the Rossi index.)
- Increase the principal value of index-linked gilt-edged securities and National Savings certificates. To say that something is index-linked means that its value changes in line with the RPI.

More generally, the RPI is used in a variety of areas:

- Pay claims. Employees generally bargain for an increase in line with inflation, plus some real increase to allow for other factors such as productivity.
- The regulation of utilities. The prices that many of the regulated privatized utilities can charge are constrained to rise by no more than a rate dependent on the RPI.
- Miscellaneous contracts and regulations. Many contracts and statutory instruments link payments to changes in the RPI. Examples can be found in areas as diverse as housing, broadcasting and the waterways.

THE HISTORY OF THE RPI INDEX

Although there were occasional official comparisons of food prices in the late nineteenth century, the history of the RPI can be traced back to 1914, when the government first began a systematic and continuous monitoring of the increase in the cost of living. The index was very crude; it used out-of-date weights relating to urban working-class households and was influenced by highly subjective assessments of what constituted legitimate expenditure for a working-class family.

Criticism of the index grew through the 1920s and 1930s, as a result of which a significant revamp was started in 1936. By the time the results became available, war had broken out and the upgrading had to wait until 1946. The resulting 1947 interim index was in turn replaced by a new index of retail prices in 1956. The RPI took its present form in 1962, when the components began to be given new weights each year in line with changes in family expenditure.

INDEX TECHNICALS

The RPI in any month is an index number, such as 164.4, which it was in December 1998. This has no meaning on its own but does allow comparison with the same index at a different point in time, most frequently the same month a year before. The index itself is restarted at 100 from time to time, most recently in January 1987, and before that in 1974 and 1962. It is as if the price of the basket of goods and services used for the RPI was set at 100 units in those base months, and then increased by the percentage increase shown by the whole basket.

At one level the construction of a price index might seem quite simple. The RPI is, after all, just a weighted average of several prices. In practice, however, there are many technical issues to resolve and the resulting inflation rates can vary enormously according to how the issues are resolved.

Due to the importance of the RPI, the government has always sought to follow best practice and be open about the construction of the index and any changes to it. Accordingly, the Cost of Living Advisory Committee was established in 1946 to advise the government on the construction of the index. This has been replaced by the Retail Prices Index Advisory Committee.

The committees have produced a number of reports over the last fifty years as the index has evolved. Recent reports have covered topics such as altering the sub-divisions of the RPI and ruling on whether and how to include the price of holidays, new cars, various fees and subscriptions, and financial services. Including new items and ensuring the best possible treatment is clearly desirable but often poses major measurement problems. The Committee last met in 1994. There is no clear-cut rule for the involvement of the Committee, however. Some potentially large changes have been made, such as the inclusion of computers in the index, without reference to the Committee. Curiously, the RPI is the only statistic that still remains under the direct control of the Chancellor.

Each item is given a weight in the basket, which is the percentage of household spending according to the Family Expenditure Survey (FES). The total is set at 1,000 units and each item is given a weight equal to parts out of 1,000. The weights are updated annually, which is more frequent than in most other countries. In this respect the index is reasonably up-to-date. In other respects, which are discussed below, the index is not as up-to-date as it could be.

The weights of the major groupings are given in Table 5.3. Some of the weights may seem surprisingly small or large compared to personal experience, but they are based on the FES. Sub-divisions are available from the ONS. For example, the food component (128 out of 1,000 in 1999) is broken down into thirty categories, such as bread (5 parts per 1,000), fresh milk (6 parts) and bacon (2 parts). It is interesting to see how the weight of some components has fallen quite sharply. Generally these are the 'basic' items, such as food, where the percentage of total expenditure falls as incomes rise, or products where the relative prices have fallen, such as fuel and light. The proportion of expenditure on services has risen as incomes have increased. Expenditure on housing has risen in good part because the relative price has risen (see Table 5.4 on p. 102 below).

Using the weights, it is possible to calculate the contribution of each component to total inflation. For example, food prices rose by 2.5 per cent in the year to December 1998 and its weight was 130 per 1,000 (13.0

Table 5.3. RPI weights by major component

	1987	1993	1999
Food	167	144	128
Catering	46	45	51
Alcohol	76	78	69
Tobacco	38	35	31
Housing	157	164	193
Fuel and light	61	46	34
Household goods	73	79	74
Household services	44	47	57
Clothing and footwear	74	58	55
Personal goods and services	38	39	40
Motoring expenditure	127	136	139
Fares and other travel costs	22	21	21
Leisure goods	47	46	47
Leisure services	30	62	61
TOTAL RPI	1000	1000	1000

Notes: The major components underwent significant redefinition in 1987 making comparisons with earlier periods difficult. The increase in the weight for leisure services in 1993 reflects the inclusion of holidays in the index.
Source: ONS.

per cent). Multiplying the two (2.5 × 0.130 = 0.325) shows that just over 0.3 per cent of the 2.8 per cent inflation rate in December was due to food.

The reference population for the RPI comprises all private households excluding those pensioner households that derive at least three-quarters of their total income from state pensions and benefits, and high income households. The latter are defined as those households whose total income lies within the top 4 per cent of all households. These groups are excluded as their expenditure patterns are deemed not typical, in the context of the aims of the RPI.

This means that about 15 per cent of households and about 14 per cent of household expenditure, as measured by the FES, are excluded from the RPI. A slightly larger proportion of total consumer expenditure is excluded from the RPI. Certain categories, such as expenditure by those living in institutions and expenditure of UK residents abroad, are excluded from the FES.

The RPI measures the price of goods and services paid for by consumers. Anything free at the point of consumption is, therefore, outside the scope of the RPI. Accordingly, items such as state education and visits to doctors under the NHS are excluded. A variety of other expenditures are also excluded, such as cash gifts, gambling, savings, life assurance, illegal transactions, repayment of loans, house purchase and major home improvements. (The RPI technical manual issued by the ONS gives full details of the scope of the RPI.)

The key features of the collection process are:

- About 120,000 price quotations are taken each month.
- There are around 650 representative items in the RPI.
- Specific representative items are chosen to represent price movements in the RPI basket. For example, prices of lamb are collected for 'loin chops with bone' and 'shoulder with bone'. Other joints, such as loins and shoulders without bone, are not priced and it is assumed that their price movements are close to those of the goods that are priced.
- The details of the items (for example, 'Dining room chair, without arms', 'Swimming pool admission, standard, for adult, off peak', or 'Butter, home produced, 250g') are reviewed each year in January.
- More price quotations are collected for items which exhibit large price variability than for those that are more stable.
- The sampling procedures used for price collection were overhauled in 1995. Prior to this date, the location of the sampling points reflected the location of the offices of the civil servants that carried out the price collection. Following the contracting out of the price collection in the mid-1990s, nearly 150 locations were selected as part of a stratified random sample with stratification by region and size. The original five year contract expired at the end of 1999 and was successfully re-tendered.
- Prices are collected on 'Index day', normally the second or third Tuesday in each month.
- Most prices are collected locally and usually by visiting the outlets (some are collected by phone). Some national prices are collected centrally.
- The price usually used is that for a cash transaction.
- Discounts are ignored unless they are universally available. Money-off coupons, free gifts, 'extras' and loyalty bonuses are also ignored.

● Sale prices are recorded if they are 'normal' sales, as opposed to reductions related to the closing down of an outlet, the sale of faulty goods or the sale of perishables approaching their sell-by date.

HOUSING COSTS

The longest running debate on weights has concerned the treatment of housing costs. Most people feel that housing costs should be included as they have a major impact on the budgets of most households. Accordingly, failure to include housing costs could give rise to a credibility gap for users. But the issues are not easy, and housing offers a good example of how pragmatic solutions are required for complex conceptual and measurement issues.

For rented accommodation, the conceptual difficulties are modest and the rental amount can be included. Similarly the costs of home maintenance and the normal household bills, including council tax (Band D figures are used and updated each April), present few problems. But for house purchase, the issues are much more complex. Typical problems encountered by including owner-occupied costs in the RPI include:

● Only a small part of the value of the average house is mortgaged so mortgage payments understate the full rental value of the service provided by the house.
● What importance should be given to the cost of the house?
● Interest rates are volatile, adding undesirable volatility to the RPI.
● Rising – or falling – house prices are not taken into account.
● It is impossible to allow for the investment component of a house purchase.
● If payments to lenders are included in the RPI, it could be argued that receipts should also be included. (They are not currently included.)
● Increasingly complex methods of mortgage finance make accurate measurement hard.
● Mortgage payments are a cost of credit and such payments are excluded from the RPI. It would be intuitively unsound to measure the price of a piece of furniture by the credit payment associated with its purchase.
● Inclusion of mortgage rates induces a perversity in that the rate of

inflation rises when the government raises interest rates with the specific intention of bringing inflation under control.

The UK solution is typically pragmatic. Mortgage interest payments have been included in the index in one form or another to represent the cost of owner-occupied housing since 1975. Mortgage interest payments are measured using a model of the payments being made for mortgages by an average index household. The key steps in the calculation are set out in Box 5.4. The net effect of this process is that the RPI does adjust slowly over time to changes in house prices, mortgage debt outstanding and interest rates.

Box 5.4. **Owner-occupier housing costs**

The key steps in the calculation are:

- estimate the average price of all houses bought on mortgages in each month since 1975
- exclude those bought by the top 4 per cent of earners
- make some estimation for the latest month due to the unavailability of data
- multiply house prices in each month by the assumed proportion of the mortgage that was borrowed for house purchase
- adjust for the proportion of the capital amount outstanding
- adjust the resulting average current debt outstanding on mortgages of different ages for tax relief
- sum the average debts for each month to give the average amount of mortgage outstanding for owner-occupying households
- multiply by the average mortgage interest rate (net or gross as appropriate) charged by the largest banks and building societies
- apply scaling factors for the number of index households that are owner-occupiers and have lived in their houses for less than twenty-five years

The January payment determines the weight for the year and the parameters are reviewed annually or after five years.

A depreciation component has been added since January 1995 to represent the expenditure that is required to maintain the property at constant quality, as the intention of the RPI is to measure prices at constant quality.

The vigorous debate during the 1980s about the merits of including owner-occupied housing has been defused by the increased attention for policy purposes now given to measures such as the RPIX and HICP, which exclude mortgage interest payments. Many countries have excluded housing costs from the measurement of consumer inflation altogether. They have taken the view that the measurement issues are insurmountable; there is no internationally accepted form of treatment; and that owner-occupation is not a significant feature of their economy (something that is not true in the UK).

Table 5.4 shows the movements in the various housing measures. Two points are noteworthy:

- Housing costs generally rise faster than non-housing costs (see first column of table).
- Prices associated with housing are far more volatile than non-housing costs.

The numbers seem to justify the decision of many countries to take the 'easy route' by excluding housing costs. It also explains why the inclusion of housing can be contentious.

There are many issues other than housing which require careful resolution. Examples include the inclusion of products available in only part of the year, mid-year changes in availability of a product, rebates and quality improvements in goods and services. These are discussed in the ONS *RPI Technical Manual*.

Table 5.4. The RPI and housing costs

	Average 1987–98	1995	1996	1997	1998
RPI	4.4	3.4	2.5	3.1	3.4
RPIX	4.2	2.8	2.9	2.8	2.7
RPI ex-housing	4.0	2.7	2.7	2.4	2.1
RPI components:					
Housing	6.5	6.7	1.4	6.5	8.9
Rent	7.2	5.6	4.6	3.4	3.0
Mortgage interest	9.4	15.9	−7.9	12.8	21.3
House prices	5.4	−1.5	4.3	6.4	5.5

Note: RPI weights in 1998 per 1,000: rents 47, mortgage interest 45, other housing 105, making a total of 197 for housing.
Source: ONS and Halifax.

SEASONAL ADJUSTMENT OF THE RPI

The RPI is not seasonally adjusted. The principal reasons for not adjusting the RPI are:

- The process of seasonal adjustment would lead to revisions even if the unadjusted series do not alter.
- The RPI is strongly affected by mortgage interest payments which are erratic and non-seasonal so the resulting series would not be smooth.
- Much of the seasonality is due to annual tax changes, which many do not regard as genuine seasonality.
- The annual change in the seasonally adjusted series could differ from that for the unadjusted series, causing confusion with regard to the statutory and contractual uses of the RPI.

The lack of seasonal adjustment can, however, lead to some difficulty in interpreting the inflation rate. The use of more contemporaneous measures of inflation, such as the three month moving average, has failed to become popular because of the month to month erratic components within the RPI. In particular, the weather can dramatically affect the prices of seasonal foods and the timing of sales and annual price changes can affect the prices of clothing and household goods. By way of example, seasonal food prices fell by 6 per cent in the first two months of 1997 and rose by 8 per cent in the following three months. The RPI measure excluding seasonal food is a rough and ready 'seasonally adjusted' version of the index.

The ONS announced in May 1999 that they would start publishing a seasonally adjusted series for RPIY, to be called SARY. This positive move was deemed possible because most of the effect of annual tax changes is removed from the RPIY, there are no statutory uses of the RPIY, and it was considered that minor revisions to the series would not cause any problems. To avoid any confusion with the unadjusted series, the ONS decided not to include the adjusted series in the consumer prices press release, but at the time of writing it is available from them on request.

RPI REVIEW

In February 1999, the ONS announced a three-year review of some of the technical aspects of the RPI. The announcement followed the publication of the Boskin Report in the US in 1996, which suggested consumer price inflation in the US was overstated by 1.1 per cent. Issues to be covered by the ONS review include the earlier inclusion of some new goods and services, the impact of discounts on shop and product selection, the choice of sampling locations and the measurement of quality changes.

The review will also assess whether the use of the geometric, as opposed to the arithmetic, mean method should be adopted. A decision to move to the geometric mean method could take as much as half of 1 per cent off the inflation rate. (See section on HICP, p. 92 above.) The ONS argues, probably quite rightly, that, with the exception of the choice of geometric or arithmetic calculation, the scale of bias from the sources identified in the US is likely to be much more modest in the UK.

The review highlights the fact that the appropriateness of a price index depends on the uses to which it is being put. There cannot be a single best measure for all purposes. It is important to note that the RPI is not a cost of living index (COLI). A COLI is the answer to the question: 'What is the minimum cost, at this month's prices, of achieving the level of utility actually attained in the base period?' It is extremely difficult to compute such an index and even those countries which claim to have a cost of living index do not fulfil all the true conditions. That said, the RPI was not designed to be a COLI, with its stress on a minimum price, and so bias in the RPI should not be assessed in the context of a COLI. Most people have a life experience or mental picture of inflation that falls between the theoretical RPI and COLI, as they will shop around to a limited extent if one shop raises its prices.

WHAT DATA ARE PUBLISHED?

There is a wealth of information available in the RPI data set. Inevitably, only a small portion of it is published as a matter of course by the ONS. The monthly press release (published mid-month, following the end of the reference month, i.e. about a month after the index day) is reasonably comprehensive. Up until the end of 1998, there was one release for the RPI and one for the HICP. From January 1999, these were merged into a single release called consumer price indices. This was a welcome development as the release now presents a fuller picture of the inflationary position in the country.

It is unfortunate that the release does not publish the weights of each component in the index. If it did, it would highlight that the release continues to give too much attention to relatively small components and insufficient attention to larger and more important components. There are, for example, thirty-six sub-components shown within the food and alcoholic drink sections, yet only eight components shown in the motoring and leisure services component, which together have roughly the same weight. It seems inevitable that attention will increasingly be focused on the components of the harmonized index, as opposed to the RPI, as analysts and commentators become more familiar with it.

Additional break-downs are published in other ONS publications, notably the *Business Monitor MM23* (published two months after the end of the reference month).

WHAT ARE THE RECENT TRENDS IN INFLATION?

Several points emerge from Table 5.5:

- There has been a gentle decline in the rate of inflation over the last decade. All the components, except tobacco (which has been hit hard by tax increases), have shown a decline over the period, even though some rose in 1998.
- The higher rates of inflation tend to be associated with services, while

Table 5.5. Average annual rates of inflation by component

	Average 1987–91	Average 1992–6	1997	1998
Food	5.1	2.4	0.1	1.3
Catering	7.9	4.8	3.7	3.9
Alcohol	7.4	4.0	2.8	3.4
Tobacco	6.1	8.1	2.8	8.6
Housing	11.5	1.1	6.5	8.9
Fuel and light	4.6	1.6	−3.1	−4.3
Household goods	4.7	2.3	1.2	1.3
Household services	6.2	1.9	1.8	2.7
Clothing and footwear	3.6	0.2	0.7	−0.6
Personal goods and services	7.0	4.2	3.6	4.7
Motoring expenditure	5.9	3.9	5.3	3.1
Fares and other travel costs	7.5	3.9	3.3	2.2
Leisure goods	3.7	1.0	0.2	−2.2
Leisure services	8.1	4.6	4.9	4.4
TOTAL RPI	6.4	2.7	3.1	3.4

Source: ONS.

lower rates tend to be associated with goods. This reflects the relative increase in the price of labour which forms a larger part of total cost in services, the choice between imports or home production which potentially drives down prices overall, and the increased demand for services as wealth increases. Leisure goods and clothing and footwear prices were notably weak in 1998.

● The inflation rates remained low in the mid- to late 1990s despite the strength of the economy. The only strength in the last few years has come from housing and tobacco, and motoring, which was pushed up by petrol tax increases. Fig. 5.2 shows the trend in inflation for the RPI and the two main underlying measures.

FORECASTING INFLATION

The Bank of England produces the most thorough assessment of the prospects for inflation in the UK in its quarterly inflation report. The report explains publicly the reasoning for interest rate decisions and the

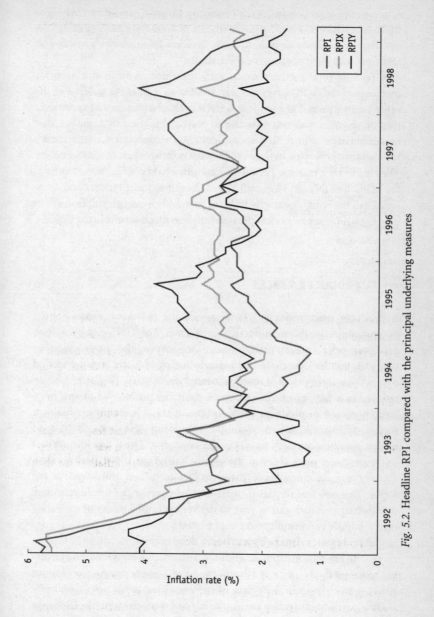

Fig. 5.2. Headline RPI compared with the principal underlying measures

Inflation rate (%)

RPI
RPIX
RPIY

1992   1993   1994   1995   1996   1997   1998

process of preparation helps the Monetary Policy Committee (MPC) to make its decisions. Very few governments or monetary policy authorities elsewhere can claim to present such detailed forecasts for growth and inflation with such thorough explanations.

A reading of the report along with the minutes from the monthly meetings of the MPC gives as clear an idea as is possible to have of the inflationary process. The emphasis given to the various factors varies over time as events move on. It is the unpredictability of that change that makes inflation forecasting so difficult. As a consequence, the bank's forecasts are presented in terms of fan charts rather than as spot forecasts. The House of Commons Treasury Committee held confirmation hearings for MPC members in 1998 and 1999. The subsequent reports and some articles in the Bank's quarterly bulletin gave additional information about how the MPC members view the transmission mechanisms in the process.

PRODUCER PRICES

A producer price index (PPI) measures the prices of goods bought by companies in the manufacturing process. The ONS publishes two producer price indices each month. One covers the input prices of materials and fuel purchased by manufacturing industry and the second covers the output prices of manufacturers' home sales. The latter is often referred to as factory gate prices. Some countries produce wholesale price indices instead of producer price indices. Although manufacturing is a modest and shrinking part of the UK's economy, the series give a good indication of inflationary trends in the economy. There was less interest in the producer price series in the second half of the 1990s, perhaps than at any time since wholesale price indices were first published in the 1950s. This was due in part to their limited coverage of whole economy inflationary pressure and in part to the very subdued prices of manufacturers' inputs and outputs over that period.

Materials and fuel make up less than a third of manufacturing industry's costs, with labour contributing about two-thirds. So, even for manufacturing, changes in the price of labour can have a greater impact on output prices than changes in the prices of commodities. Input prices are more volatile partly because they are imported, and thus vary with the exchange

Table 5.6. Weights for the producer price input series

	Weight	% change, year to February 1999	% change, January to February 1999
Fuel	11	−0.4	−1.4
Crude oil	10	−27.3	−7.5
Food manufacturing, home produced	18	1.0	2.4
Food manufacturing, imported	8	−7.1	−1.0
Other home produced	2	2.2	0.0
Imported metals	10	−13.4	1.4
Imported chemicals	16	−6.2	−1.2
Other imported materials	25	−4.2	−0.7
TOTAL	100	−6.4	−0.7

Source: ONS, producer prices first release, February 1999.

rate, and partly because commodity prices themselves are volatile. Table 5.6 shows the weights for the producer price series and some monthly and annual growth rates to illustrate the volatility of the series.

As with most other price indices, the series are regularly re-weighted to allow for the changing relative prices of different sectors of output and input. Generally, the PPI is re-weighted and re-based (to 100) every five years. The series was last re-based towards the end of 1998 when the index year was set at 1995. (Note that a re-weighting every five years is in contrast to the re-weighting of the RPI which is annual.) In the summer of 1999 the ONS embarked on a two year programme, fundamentally overhauling the way the producer price data are collected and series calculated.

The ONS surveys about 3,500 companies each month. It is extremely comprehensive, asking for the prices of about 10,000 items. The survey seeks the prices being quoted on new orders for home, as opposed to overseas, sales. The survey is meant to reflect the average prices over the month. Since 1992 the survey has been compulsory. It shows the net position for inputs, removing transactions between manufacturers. Purchases of capital goods are excluded since the manufacturer is considered to be the end user of the product. VAT is excluded since most companies can recover that cost, but excise duties are included. The index is a measure of home costs but does include the price of imported items, which make up around half the index.

The release is one of the first in the monthly cycle to be published, coming only a week or so after the end of the month to which it relates. In part due to this swift publication schedule, the producer price indices, unlike the RPI, are revised as more responses to each survey return and as seasonal adjustments are amended. In general, however, the revisions are modest – especially now that the inflation rate is so low.

Output price inflation had more or less disappeared by the end of 1998 having been historically very low in the preceding couple of years. Indeed, excluding excise duties, output inflation was between 0 and –1 per cent throughout 1998. This weakness reflected input prices falling for three years, and a lack of manufacturers' pricing power as consumers and retailers sought increasingly competitive prices (see Fig. 5.3).

Each producer prices press release contains several separate series. The input and output series are published in both a headline and a so-called underlying form, which excludes the food, beverages, tobacco and petroleum industries components. The main reason for excluding these items from the underlying index (about a third of the total) is that they are volatile and subject to changes in tax rates. In addition, most of the series are published both in seasonally adjusted and unadjusted form. Food has a high weight in the input index and seasonal food prices, in particular, are especially volatile. This range of indicators is useful for thorough analysis but does lead to some confusion and difficulty at the moment of release as they rarely all point in the same direction. The press release also offers an industry break-down into about thirty sub-sectors.

Financial markets tend to focus most on the underlying output price series, either in the form of the annual rate or the three-month on three-month rate. Markets tend to pay little attention to the input price data on a month to month basis, not least because it is one of the most difficult of all the statistics to predict in advance.

As the economy – and the RPI, in particular – has become more service oriented, the producer price indices, which focus exclusively on manufacturing, have become less important for commentators and financial markets. There has also been a suspicion that, as the economy has become more open and price setting more sensitive to market conditions, the PPI has failed to pick up some of the price discounting. Many respondents are thought to submit list, rather than actual, prices. Some

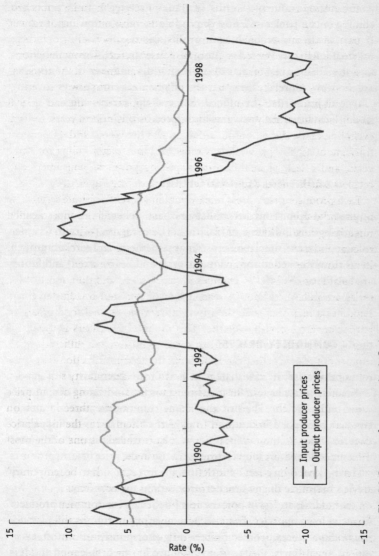

Fig. 5.3. Input and output price inflation

Input producer prices
Output producer prices

1990   1992   1994   1996   1998

Rate (%)

15
10
5
0
-5
-10
-15

commentators still focus on the difference in the movement of the input and output series. That difference is viewed as an indicator of manufacturing industry's 'terms of trade'. Clearly, if input prices are falling, yet companies still find it possible to raise output prices, their terms of trade, and probably their profits, will rise.

A decade ago there were few alternative data sources. The main options were the CBI survey of manufacturing and a number of commodity indices. Now, however, there are several private sector surveys covering a range of industries. The official data and the surveys together give a good indication of the price pressures faced by business.

LABOUR MARKET INDICATORS

A variety of labour market indicators have become the most keenly watched leading indicators of inflation. These are dealt with in Chapter 6. Unemployment, unit labour costs, pay settlements and earnings growth are all closely linked to the economic cycle and both current and future inflation rates.

COMMODITY PRICES

Commodities are the raw materials used in the manufacture of goods. Commodity prices have in the past been good lead indicators of manufacturing output prices. The prices of some commodities, mainly metals, have also been good indicators of the level of demand in industrialized countries. Many of the commodities which are traded actively, and whose prices are followed, are foods. Although a rise in the price of farm products will have a knock-on effect on inflation, the impact tends to be temporary and less indicative of any broader pressures in the economy.

Commodities are less important now for the same reasons that producer prices are less important. Even so, a number of institutions still produce commodity indices. These indices vary enormously in almost every respect. Accordingly, they tend not to move in synchronization and it is vital to understand the coverage of each. Some indices exclude precious metals, oil, or commodities not traded on open markets. The weight given to the commodities in each index depends upon the purpose of the index – to measure a country's cost pressures, to monitor the terms of trade, or (as in the case of the Commodity Research Bureau, CRB) a simple desire to give each commodity an equal weight. Commodity indices are available frequently and, in some cases, in real-time. They tend only to be of interest to financial markets when there has been a sharp movement.

Some economists argue that the gold price is a helpful indicator of inflationary pressures. It probably was so a decade or two ago, but most analysts now realize that a number of the major influences on the gold price have little to do with growth or inflation in the world economy. Two of the world's largest producers, South Africa and Russia, were both politically turbulent during the 1990s. Stocks of gold were also very high, several-fold higher than annual production. In addition, uncertainty about the future levels of the core holdings of central banks was distorting the price.

There has been a similar reduction in importance attached to the oil price. The oil shocks of the 1970s had a dramatic effect on global inflation and the course of economies but such dramatic volatility was not repeated in the 1980s and 1990s. The era of generally more stables prices along with a number of factors – the discovery of more reserves coupled with improved technology, a weakening of Opec, increased attention to conservation, the substitution of other fuels – have reduced the attention paid to the oil price.

NATIONAL ACCOUNTS PRICE INDICES

The so-called implied deflators relating to the national accounts receive surprisingly little attention in financial markets. Traditionally, the main two deflators are those for GDP and consumers' expenditure, but a deflator may be derived for any series where there is an estimate in current and constant prices. While most price indices are constructed directly by collecting prices and weighting these together, the deflators derived from national accounts data are simply price series implied by the difference between current and constant price estimates of aggregates.

The ONS publications offer, surprisingly, very few implied deflators. The *Blue Book* gives implied deflators for a dozen components of the expenditure measure of GDP, but these are only available annually and for complete years. The quarterly cycle of GDP releases gives implied deflators for only three of the aggregate measures of GDP.

It is a shame that more is not made of the consumers' expenditure deflator. It has some disadvantages. For example, it is published only quarterly, with a three month lag, and remains subject to revision. On the other hand, it has a number of attractions over other measures of consumer price inflation. First, it covers the whole of consumers' expenditure as defined in the national accounts. The RPI excludes top income households and pensioners largely dependent on social benefits and reflects the prices of only a basket of goods. Second, it uses expenditure weights of the current year, rather than those of the base year. It shows price increases of the actual goods and services purchased in that year, taking into account changes in weights due to switching from more expensive to cheaper goods and services.

It is rare for the RPI and consumers' expenditure deflator to diverge markedly, except in the very short term. But an understanding of the processes in the economy will always be improved by considering the additional information that is available from additional series. Analysts will generally use the RPI for comparisons going back to 1962, when it was first published in its current form (although its predecessor series provide data back to the First World War). Consumers' expenditure deflator data is available back to 1938.

FINAL EXPENDITURE PRICES INDEX

In the second half of the 1990s, the ONS started work on a new price index. The development work reflected user demand for an inflation measure which would:

● Cover the economy more widely than the RPI
● Be published monthly and be timely
● Be subject to minimal revisions only
● Reflect directly measured prices.

Such a measure would be used for developing a greater understanding of the inflation process as part of macro-economic analysis, and many other functions such as deflating nominal sums and indexing contract payments. The resulting final expenditure prices index, FEPI, was first published at the end of 1997. It is based on the national accounts concept of Total Domestic Expenditure, excluding changes in stocks. The transactions covered are final purchases by UK residents, including private consumption, investment and government expenditure.

The FEPI is calculated monthly, not seasonally adjusted, reflects market prices, is base weighted and chain linked. Many of the actual deflators used in the national accounts are being used directly in the FEPI, but some new indicators have been found, for items such as government expenditure. At the time of writing, the series was viewed as 'experimental' and was available on request but not published in an ONS First Release. It is the intention of the ONS that it will be more widely available in due course.

POINTERS FOR INFLATION

- A 'good' rate of inflation. The definition of what is a good or satisfactory rate of inflation depends upon the measure chosen and the precise circumstances. In general, however, a rate of between 1 and 3 per cent would be considered adequate in most developed countries. Materially higher or lower rates of inflation would point to an economy that is growing too strongly or growing insufficiently.
- Plenty of information. Inflation is one of the areas where there is a good selection of UK data (official and unofficial) available, compared to many other areas of the economy. The same cannot be said for all other countries.
- Raw materials are less important. The prices of raw materials generally fluctuate by much more than prices of finished goods. As raw materials on average account for only about 10 per cent of the cost of a product, and some fluctuation in the prices of raw materials is absorbed by the companies, this is not a real cause for concern. Accordingly, a 5 per cent change in the price of oil or gold is far less significant (or worrying) than a 5 per cent change in retail prices.

- Raw materials are more volatile. The prices of raw materials generally fluctuate by much more than prices of finished goods. Many companies will only revise their list prices once or twice a year or when the product range is changed. This factor goes a long way to explain the traditional jump in the month on month index in January.
- Levels and rates. We should distinguish clearly between a fall in the level of prices and a fall in the rate of inflation. If the inflation rate declines but remains positive, prices are still rising.
- Variable lags mean difficult relationships. While the sequence of cost pressures is reasonably clear, the long and variable lags in the economy mean that there are no simple fixed relationships between any of the price indicators. On occasions, for example during periods of strong economic growth, raw material price increases can feed through quickly to retail prices. At other times, significant raw material price changes seem to have no impact at all on retail prices.
- Which RPI component? We should ensure that we are looking at the right measure of the RPI. We can often learn something about the inflationary pressures in the economy by looking at the way the different measures are moving.
- Exclude mortgage costs for most analysis. The inclusion of the mortgage rate in the headline RPI can often give a misleading impression of the real inflation trend. Mortgage rates are closely related to official interest rates; accordingly, when official interest rates are raised to bear down on inflation the mortgage component of the RPI also rises, with the result that inflation is increased. This is why most analysts now look at the RPIX in preference to the RPI.
- Beware of base effects. The yearly comparison gives as much weight to what happened twelve months ago as to what happened in the latest month. For example, the RPI press release for September 1998 said: 'The largest downward effect on all the items 12 month rates came from housing costs . . . as a result of last year's increases in mortgage interest payments dropping out of the 12 month comparison. There was a strong, partially offsetting, upward effect from fuel and light charges as the effect of last year's reduction on household fuel bills dropped out of the 12 month comparison.' Clearly, the events of the latest month are far more important in assessing inflation than the events of a year ago.
- Volatile components. Some components of the RPI have particularly

volatile prices. Petrol, for example, which comprises nearly 4 per cent of the index, can have a marked impact on the inflation rate. A 10 per cent price rise adds around 0.4 per cent to the inflation rate. An increase in inflation for a specific reason like this need not necessarily have an impact on policy.

● Target obsession. Since the introduction of the 2½ per cent inflation target there has been an obsessive, sometimes ridiculous, attention paid to minute changes in the inflation rate. This has led to some bizarre newspaper headlines. In February 1999, when the January inflation number was released, one story had the headline 'Potato defended over chip blip in the economy'! The targeted measure of inflation had risen to 2.6 per cent from 2.5 per cent and one of the principal causes had been the price of potatoes, including frozen chips. Clearly, such temporary and seasonal factors should not have a lasting impact on market sentiment.

● Annual price changes. The prices of many goods change at regular times during the year. For example, public transport charges, local authority taxes, accommodation rentals and utility bills normally change only once a year. As the changes are often in April, that month usually sees the largest month on month jump in the RPI index. (As the jump is comparable in size each April, the annual rate rarely reflects this feature.)

● Tax changes. Changes of indirect taxes can also have a significant impact on the inflation rate. Alcoholic drink and tobacco make up about a tenth of the index. As such a large part of the total product price is accounted for by duties, tax changes are highly significant around Budget time. A 5 per cent duty rise can add ¼–½ per cent to the RPI.

● The month on month change is meaningless. Due to the various factors above, the month on month changes are of little analytical use. In the last five years, month on month changes have varied between a fall of 0.8 per cent and a rise of 1.7 per cent. Grossing up, or annualizing, this change, as occurs in some other countries, can be very misleading.

● RPIs for different income/social groups are not available. Pensioner indices (for one and two pensioner households) are available on a quarterly basis from the ONS. The weights are adjusted according to typical spending patterns. It is unfortunate that more sub-indices are not published for other 'typical' groups. It would be easy to imagine a

family index, a single person's index or an index for those living in
council property. There is a strong argument that such additional
indices would add credibility to the inflation numbers (by making it
easier for individuals to identify with a particular inflation rate) and
be useful for directing government policy. Some private research groups
have published income group RPIs from time to time.

● No regional RPI figures are published. This is in contrast to many
other countries. The inflation figures for other countries are often
derived on a city by city basis or for regions within a federal state. In
Germany, for example, inflation rates are published for the *Länder*
before the national rate is available. Similarly, in Italy and Switzerland,
city rates are available before the national rate. None the less, while
the method of data collection in the UK would at first sight seem to
lend itself to publication of RPI numbers on a regional basis, the ONS
claims that it would be difficult and expensive. The possibility of
publishing regional figures was considered by the RPI Advisory Committee in 1971, but was not taken any further by the Department of
Employment, which at that time controlled the RPI. It would be
possible to publish not only the regional differences in price changes
over time but also to measure the differences in price levels between
regions.

6 | The Labour Market

Labour market data are important for a variety of reasons. Over the long term, the size and structure of the working population is an important indicator of pressures on an economy. An increase in the number of people of working age points to either an enhanced productive potential for the economy or higher unemployment. Similarly, the economy must grow at least as fast as the population if output per head is not going to fall.

In the shorter term, employment and unemployment numbers are excellent indicators of the state of the economic cycle even if the labour market lags behind the cycle by some months. A low rate of unemployment relative to recent years points to inflationary pressures. In contrast, higher rates of unemployment suggest an output gap, with the scope for policy relaxation and a faster rate of growth. Movements in the growth of earnings are also the key to making economic policy judgements.

The most conspicuous labour market statistic in Britain is that for unemployment. For many decades unemployment was the focal point for many in politics and economics and it was often cited by voters as the most important policy issue facing the country. The combination of the policy focus shifting away from full employment to inflation and the improved availability of other labour market data during the 1990s, means that the unemployment figure itself is now of less importance than a decade or two ago. The release of the monthly unemployment figures still attracts considerable attention, however.

Despite the importance of labour market data, they are notoriously difficult to measure accurately. Unemployment and the other data on the labour market, such as employment, earnings and productivity, appear in one compendious monthly press release from the ONS, which forms the basis of this chapter. There are a number of other useful data sources, notably the *Labour Force Survey* (LFS) quarterly supplement and *Labour Market Trends*, a monthly 'magazine' produced by the ONS with help from the Department for Education and Employment, the Employment Service and the Department of Trade and Industry.

There are frequent calls for additional labour market data, despite improvements in the data set over the last decade. Problem areas include:

● Pay settlements. Very little is known about them, despite the government's frequent exhortations against excessive pay increases.
● Non-pay components of remuneration. Benefits in kind of various sorts are increasingly common but are not explicitly measured.
● General measures of labour market performance. The link between pay, productivity and employment is one example.
● Service sector data.
● Poor linkage between sources. It is a shame that the major sources – the benefit system and the LFS – are not linked (for example, by using the register of claimants as a sampling frame for part of the LFS).
● Labour market dynamics. For example, the transition from economic inactivity to activity or the dramatic rise in the receipt of sickness benefit by people of working age.

The strength of demand reflects the way that labour market information bridges social as well as economic policy. Much of the additional recent demand reflects the difficulties in assessing the extent of poverty, measuring social exclusion or the shortfall in work, which have been given a higher priority since the election of the Labour Government in 1997. It is not unreasonable to believe that the fundamental changes in the labour market in recent years – the rise of women in employment, the increase in flexible working hours, increased employment in services, an increase in temporary employment and career breaks, and so on – have prompted many users to question the usefulness of conventional measures.

Labour market data may sometimes show apparently conflicting pictures. Accordingly, sensible interpretation requires knowledge of the concepts behind the data. (The ONS has produced several useful guides to this effect – see Sources.) Labour market data are obtained from three main sources: the Labour Force Survey, employer surveys and administrative records. Each source has its strengths and limitations. In contrast to most of the other data releases discussed in this book, many of the labour market data are available on a regional and local basis. New data are published every month although some data are available only quarterly. It is important to note, however, that data in any given release can often correspond to different reference periods. Some data refer to the average over a period while other series refer to a particular day in the month.

Box 6.1. **The Labour Force Survey**

The LFS is the largest regular household survey in the United Kingdom. LFS interviews are conducted continuously throughout the year. In any three-month period, a nationally representative sample of approximately 120,000 people aged 16 or over in around 61,000 households is interviewed. Each household is interviewed five times at three-monthly intervals. In all but the most sparsely populated areas of the country, the initial interview is face-to-face by an interviewer visiting the address. The other interviews are conducted over the phone.

The LFS was carried out every two years from 1973 to 1983. The concepts and definitions of the International Labour Organisation (ILO), an agency of the United Nations, were first used in 1984 from which point the survey was conducted on an annual basis, with the results available for every spring quarter. The survey moved to a continuous basis in the spring of 1992 with average quarterly results being published four times a year. From April 1998 the results have been published twelve times a year for the average of the latest three consecutive months. Data are published around six weeks after the end of period to which they refer.

The LFS produces coherent labour market information on the basis of internationally standard concepts and definitions. It is a rich source of data on a wide variety of labour market and personal characteristics. It allows pictures of the labour market, such as that shown in Fig. 6.1, to be drawn up. However, it is a sample survey and is therefore subject to sampling variability. The LFS suffers not only from non-response but also from 'proxy' reporting where one member of a household answers questions on behalf of other members. Definitional problems also arise, for example, with the definition of part-time work, those temporarily ill or laid off, and home workers. The classification of an individual as in employment if they do just one hour of work in a week is often questioned. Different regions, cultures and religions will often give different answers to these questions. The monthly press release sets out the 95 per cent confidence intervals for estimates from the LFS.

UNEMPLOYMENT

Unemployment is not only an important statistic but also one of the most highly disputed. Unemployment might sound like a simple concept but it is not and there are many different ways of defining it. Unfortunately, the UK's traditional definition, the claimant count, has been changed so many times in the last twenty years that confidence in all statistics, not only those for unemployment, has been undermined.

It is clearly insufficient to say that anyone who is not working is unemployed. There are millions of pensioners who are retired and millions of housewives who prefer not to enter the labour market. We do not normally think of them as unemployed. Keynes was the first to develop the concept of involuntary unemployment to describe those who wanted to work at the prevailing rates of pay but were unable to find such work. This definition has broadly survived to the current time but more precise criteria are now used, including claiming unemployment benefit, seeking work, and wanting a job, while, of course, being available for work and not working. Different definitions of unemployment can usually be categorized with reference to these and similar criteria. Although the numbers in each of the categories are independent, there is often a high correlation between trends in employment as measured by any definition.

There are two official measures of unemployment that are regularly available in the UK – the claimant count and the Labour Force Survey. The measure most frequently referred to is the monthly claimant count, which is a by-product of the administrative system for paying out unemployment related benefits. The alternative measure, from the Labour

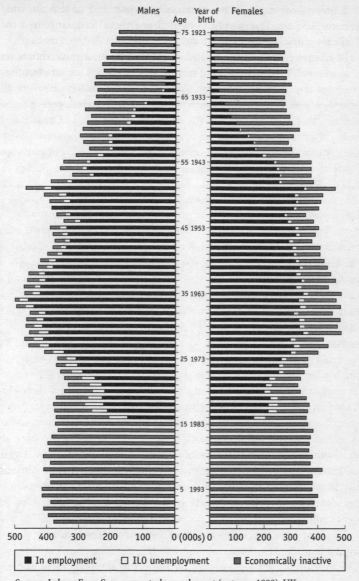

Males   Year of   Females
Age   birth

75 1923

65 1933

55 1943

45 1953

35 1963

25 1973

15 1983

5 1993

500   400   300   200   100   0 (000s) 0   100   200   300   400   500

■ In employment   □ ILO unemployment   ▨ Economically inactive

Source: Labour Force Survey quarterly supplement (autumn 1998), UK

Fig. 6.1. Population structure by age, sex and economic activity

Force Survey, was largely ignored a decade ago, but is attracting increasing attention now that the survey is carried out more frequently and the results are published in a more timely fashion.

The relative advantages and disadvantages of the two measures are set out in Box 6.2. It is interesting to note that, like the UK, most countries have both a registrant count of some sort and a survey measure of unemployment. In general, the survey method is preferred, and in those countries that have a monthly survey, such as the USA, Canada and Japan, little use is made of the register measure. In other countries, with an infrequent survey, the registrant count assumes increasing importance despite the deficiencies of the measure. As the Labour Force Survey in

---

Box 6.2. **Advantages and disadvantages of claimant count and LFS**

Claimant count

Advantages	Disadvantages
• Available quickly	• Frequent definitional changes reflecting changed eligibility rules for benefits
• Available monthly	
• Relatively inexpensive	
• Exact and accurate	• Not internationally standardized
• Modest revisions	
• Small area figures available	• Negligible information about or break-down of the unemployed
• Long data history available	

Labour Force Survey

Advantages	Disadvantages
• Common definition (ILO)	• Costly
• Internationally comparable	• Available only on a three-month rolling basis
• Allows detailed analysis of labour market trends	• Less timely publication
	• No small area analysis
	• Only annual data prior to 1992
	• Subject to sampling error and revisions

the UK has increased in frequency and grows in familiarity, it is expected that the measure of unemployment that comes from it will supplant that from the claimant count. But habits of a lifetime are not changed overnight and it will take some years for the LFS measure to become as popular. The use of the LFS measure of unemployment would be greatly increased if its timelessness was the same as the claimant count's.

The two measures have a quite different coverage of unemployment. The claimant count is based on the computer records of those claiming unemployment-related benefits, currently Job Seeker's Allowance (JSA) and National Insurance credits. To qualify, people must declare they are out of work, yet available for and actively seeking work in the week in which the claim is made. The claimant count relates to a specific day in the middle of the month, usually the second Thursday. It excludes a number of people who might be considered to be unemployed. For example, people who are looking for work but do not claim benefit (such as married women), school leavers with a guaranteed place in the future on a training scheme, those on government training schemes including the New Deal, and those receiving invalidity benefits who are still of working age. The claimant count has practical difficulties, too. It will, for example, include fraudulent claimers of benefit who do work, and exclude those entitled to benefit but who fail to claim.

In contrast, the LFS defines the unemployed as those without paid jobs, who say they want and are available for work and have sought work in the last four weeks. The LFS definition pays no regard to whether the individual is entitled to or actually receiving benefit. Indeed, the LFS excludes some of the benefit-claiming unemployed, most notably those receiving benefit who are not looking for, or are not available to start, work. It also excludes those in work but earning insufficient to disqualify them from benefits – an individual counts as employed in the LFS if they do just one hour of work in a week.

There is clearly no 'right' definition of unemployment, but the difference in the trend of unemployment on these two main measures has generally been small given the definitional differences. Certainly, the peaks and troughs in the two measures have usually occurred at the same time. The claimant count measure does, however, seem to be more sensitive to the economic cycle. At the last two cyclical peaks of unemployment, in 1986 and 1993, the two measures were close, within 100,000 of each other. At the subsequent troughs, in 1990 and 1998, the gap between the two was over 400,000 (see Fig. 6.2).

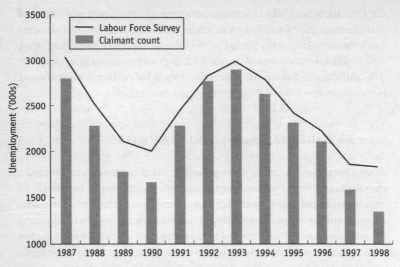

Fig. 6.2. Unemployment – Labour Force Survey and claimant count measures compared

This phenomenon could be explained by a number of factors. If the 'natural' difference between the two measures is around 400,000, the narrowing at times of higher unemployment could be explained by more of those without jobs choosing to claim benefit. It is also known that as the economy improves, more people are encouraged to look for work, and therefore leave inactivity for ILO-defined unemployment. These people might well not be eligible for social benefits or choose not to claim them. Alternatively, if the 'natural' gap is close to zero, the more dramatic fall in claimant unemployment at times of economic boom could be explained by claimants' greater enthusiasm to seek work. It has been argued that since the supply of labour into the labour market seems to depend on the state of the labour market itself (more people want well paid, attractive jobs than unpleasant, poorly paid jobs, and will come forward if they are available), the LFS is weakened, especially as a measure of unemployment.

Periodically, the ONS publishes (in *Labour Market Trends*) a reconciliation of the two measures of unemployment (covering GB, not the UK). The reconciliation published in March 1998 covered the data up to the summer of 1996. At that time, seasonally adjusted unemployment on the

LFS measure was 2.25 million (a rounded figure), compared with the claimant count's 2.04 million. The modest difference between the numbers is all the more surprising given that, of the 2.25 million LFS unemployed, 1.47 million were claimants and 0.79 million were non-claimants. Of the 2.04 million claimants, only 1.49 million were ILO-defined unemployed.

A RANGE OF UNEMPLOYMENT NUMBERS

There have been calls over the years for the government to publish a spectrum of unemployment measures. One model would be the U1 to U6 measures published by the US Bureau of Labor Statistics. U1 includes only people unemployed for longer than fifteen weeks while U6 includes marginally attached workers and part-timers wanting full-time work. The rates were 1¼ and 7½ per cent respectively in spring 1999. The official measure, U3, was 4½ per cent. Publishing a range of measures, each of which might be the best measure for a different purpose, could defuse the argument about definition. It would mean that users could apply a definition that they felt comfortable with or that suited their particular needs. It would be preferable to have clearly defined official alternative measures rather than encourage, by default, commentators to create their own, less well understood, measures.

Those with an interest in maximizing the unemployment problem often refer to the 'hidden million' of unemployed, in other words those people included in the LFS measure but not in the claimant count. (The figure stood at ¾ million in 1999.) Those respondents say that they are available for and seeking work and so seem to be unemployed, but are not on Job Seeker's Allowance.

The Labour Force Survey offers the possibility of more complex measures from its analysis of those people who are economically inactive. This shows that, at the end of 1998, in addition to the 1.8 million unemployed, there were 2.3 million people who said they wanted a job. The majority of these people are not available to start work or are not actively seeking work, perhaps because they are sick, students or looking after the family home. None the less, it shows that there is a pool of potential workers who would take a job if circumstances were different. The 1999 Budget referred to the 4 million people who want to work but do not. This group is probably better referred to as potential employees rather than unemployed, and it represents a measure of under-employment in the economy.

It is just as easy and plausible to come up with more restrictive definitions of unemployment. An argument could be put that people at the younger or older end of the working age range, those with their partner in work or those who have been unemployed for only three or six months, could be excluded. Indeed, the Labour Government elected in 1997 did exactly this. Their New Deal, welfare-to-work programme, makes it very difficult for youngsters under 25 years old to claim unemployment benefit other than in the very short term. This change in the administrative system has had a dramatic impact on the usefulness of the unemployment statistics.

Table 6.1 shows some possible measures of unemployment that the ONS could publish with relative ease if it so chose. It is based loosely on similar measures that have been published in the UK by the Unemploy-ment Unit and the Employment Policy Institute, and in the US by the Bureau of Labor Statistics. The measures currently published in the UK are shown here as U1 and U6 (though the ONS does publish most of the components that are required to derive the other measures).

Researchers from Sheffield Hallam University produced a measure of so-called 'real unemployment'. They added those unemployed (but not

Table 6.1. Possible measures of unemployment

		Millions	
		Number	Cumulative
U0	Unemployed over age 25	1.2	1.2
U1	+ unemployed under 25s	0.6	1.8
U2	+ available to start but not looking	0.7	2.5
U3	+ other inactive who want a job	1.4	3.9
U4	+ those on government schemes	0.2	4.1
U5	+ part-timers who want full-time work	0.7	4.8
U6	Claimant count	1.3	n.a.
U7	CC and LFS (U1 + U6 excluding overlap)	c.2.3	n.a.
U8	Working population claiming benefits	6.1	n.a.

Notes: U0–U5 and U7: LFS, ONS, spring 1999; U6: Benefits Agency; U8: DSS August 1998.

claiming benefit) and those on government schemes, to the registered unemployed. In addition, they estimated the excess numbers of early retirees and the excess number of permanently sick. According to this methodology, in January 1997 the real level of unemployment was 3.9 million compared to the claimant count figure of 1.8 million (equivalent to a rate of 14.2 per cent compared to 6.4 per cent).

The concept of matched and unmatched aspirations has received more attention in recent years. An individual who is economically inactive but does not want a job has a matched aspiration, while an inactive or unemployed person who wants a job has an unmatched aspiration. Information about genuine aspirations would give a much clearer assessment of possible labour market tightness and reduce the ambiguity about what constitutes employment, unemployment and inactivity.

It is also possible to play down the unemployment figures by suggesting that many of the unemployed are doing paid work in the black economy. It is, of course, impossible to know how many fraudulent claimants of unemployment benefit there are, but surveys and analyses over the last twenty years have put the figure at between 3 and 10 per cent of benefit recipients. Estimates made by the Unemployment Unit in 1999 suggest that nearly 9 per cent of JSA expenditure could be being claimed fraudulently, equivalent to over 100,000 people given the unemployment level at the end of 1998. Analysis of some of the young New Deal participants suggests that many of them are earning some modest, though none the less strictly fraudulent, amounts of money while claiming benefit. The Department of Social Security always claims to put much effort into reducing fraud and the new Labour administration is no different. The suspicion remains, however, that fraud is still a persistent problem.

GOVERNMENT SCHEMES FOR THE UNEMPLOYED

The scale of both unemployment and the fraud problem has been reduced by successive governments' introduction of work schemes for the unemployed. The work schemes that have been introduced over the last two decades have had a varying degree of carrot and stick – some seemed genuinely to have been designed to offer training and increase individuals' employability, while others looked more like attempts to reduce the unemployment figures. The Community Programme and the Enterprise Allowance Scheme were examples of programmes geared towards job creation. The Job Training Scheme and Youth Training Scheme were geared towards training, while Restart and the Availability-for-work test seemed more geared towards fraudulent claimants. Restart, which was introduced in 1986, interviewed one-and-a-half million people over the following year. It is estimated that about 10 per cent were taken off the unemployment count yet less than half of 1 per cent got jobs directly as a result. It is assumed that many left the count for fear of the consequences if it was found out that they were doing paid work while claiming.

The introduction of the Job Seeker's Allowance in 1996 and the New Deal, welfare-to-work, programme in 1998 and 1999, both of which required claimants to attend interviews with benefit officials, undoubtedly shook off a significant but unknown number of fraudulent claimants from the count. It is difficult for a centre-left government, which is pursuing policies to help the less advantaged, to be seen to be adopting overly draconian policies. It is undeniable, however, that the introduction of schemes usually disrupts the statistical series, derived from administrative sources.

THE UNEMPLOYMENT RATE

The unemployment numbers can be difficult to understand properly if they are not expressed as a percentage. Certainly international comparisons are well-nigh impossible without the conversion into a rate. A percentage is a fraction, with the unemployed as the numerator, but what should the denominator be? Unemployed as a percentage of what?

The largest possible sensible denominator would be the population of working age. For much of the post-war period, the unemployment rate (as measured by the claimant count) was the number of unemployed divided by the sum of employees in employment (now referred to as employee jobs) and the unemployed. Then in 1986 the self-employed and armed forces were added to the denominator. Unemployment was thus expressed as a percentage of the workforce. At the time this change caused a 1.4 per cent drop in the unemployment rate (though all back data were revised). Even though the change was sensible, it introduced a new source of revision into the recent figures. Self-employment is

Table 6.2. Unemployment rates with different denominators

		Million	Unemployment rate
1	Unemployed	1.790	—
2	Employees	23.841	—
3	Total (rows 1 and 2)	25.631	7.0
4	Self-employed	3.200	—
5	Government schemes and family workers	0.245	—
6	Total economically active (rows 3–5)	29.076	6.2
7	Total of working age (16–59/64)	35.881	5.0
8	16–24 year olds	4.595	—
9	Aged 50+	6.607	—
10	Active (row 6) less young and old	17.874	—
11	Unemployed 25–49	0.882	4.9

Source: LFS. Data for UK, seasonally adjusted, Q4 1998, as at April 1999. Row 6 is the official rate.

notoriously difficult to measure and is usually estimated from the LFS. If self-employment is revised, unemployment percentages must be revised too. Table 6.2 shows some alternatives using recent data.

THE TREND IN UNEMPLOYMENT

Although the debate about the definition of unemployment receives plenty of attention, for most commentators and politicians it is the trend in unemployment that is usually most important.

Unemployment seldom went into double figure percentages before the 1980s. There were single years when it was high, but it was only in the 1930s that it was consistently high, peaking at 15½ per cent in 1932, roughly 3.4 million unemployed. During the Second World War and for thirty-five years after it, unemployment was in low single figure percentages. Looking back, it is hard to imagine unemployment having been a problem. Yet at the time modest rises in that low level of unemployment were viewed with concern. It was always a policy goal to reduce unemployment, and it was hoped to do this (often in vain) without boosting inflation or lapsing into balance of payment crises.

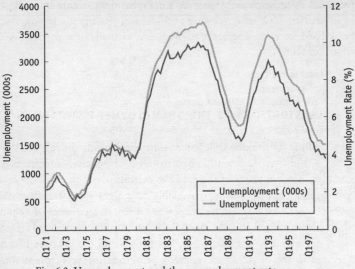

Fig. 6.3. Unemployment and the unemployment rate

In 1950, when the present claimant count series began, there were only about a quarter of a million unemployed. Numbers rose to a peak of just under half a million in 1959, but fell back before rising sharply in the early 1970s to peak at a little below a million in 1972. The short-lived economic boom of 1973 reduced unemployment to half a million, but by the late 1970s the figure had trebled to one and half million. It doubled again to three million, around 11 per cent, peaking in 1985. The rate fell to reach a trough in 1990. The rate then rose, reaching a peak in 1993, close to the mid-1980s peak, before declining over the period to the end of 1998 (see Fig. 6.3).

The eradication of unemployment has been a political goal in many countries. It is most unlikely ever to be achieved, however, for a variety of reasons. There will always be an element of structural unemployment where, within a region or country, the skills of individuals do not match the job opportunities. In the UK, for example, there are many unemployed middle-aged, blue-collar workers in some regions. It is not easy for these people to move and retrain to fill the vacancies that exist in the service sector in other regions. There will also be frictional unemployment as people are always changing jobs and can be temporarily recorded as unemployed. Seasonal unemployment occurs in a number of industries, such as agriculture and tourism. Finally, there will always be a hard core of unemployed who are virtually unemployable, for whatever reason.

DISTORTIONS TO THE UNEMPLOYMENT STATISTICS

The 'fiddling' of the unemployment numbers, mostly during the 1980s, is by far the most frequently cited instance of political interference in statistics. Around thirty changes to the definition of the claimant count have been identified, although arguably only eight were statistically significant (see Table 6.3). Each change was a direct consequence of a change to the benefit system and was defended at the time it was made on grounds of greater accuracy or practicality. Yet because all the changes but one operated in the direction of reducing published unemployment totals, the suspicion lingered that the motive behind the changes was to reduce the damaging political effect of high unemployment in the early 1980s. At the time the unemployment numbers were the responsibility of the Department of Employment, not the CSO. The seven largest changes reduced measured unemployment by over half a million.

Most of the changes reflected the evolution of the unemployment benefit system. This is clearly shown in the example of the largest single change, which occurred in 1982. Up until that date, the monthly unemployment numbers were based on those registered at Jobcentres, which tried to find them jobs. From 1982 it ceased to be compulsory to register at the Jobcentre to claim benefit and the computer count of those claiming benefits through social security offices became the measure of unemployment. Registrations at Jobcentres fell sharply (indeed, to around only 100,000 by 1990) and ceased therefore to be an adequate measure of unemployment. About a third of the fall in the unemployment figure of 190,000 reflected greater accuracy, but about two-thirds of the fall reflected the removal of job seekers not entitled to benefit. Some 23,000 severely disabled were added to the count, who might well have been left out by any criterion other than the claiming of benefit.

Other changes in the definition were less readily justifiable. Around 200,000 claimants aged over 60 were removed from the count in two

Table 6.3. Major changes in the compilation of claimant count unemployment statistics

Date	Change	Effect
October 1979	Fortnightly payment of benefits	+20,000
November 1981	Men over 60 offered higher benefit to leave the working population	−37,000
October 1982	Jobcentre registration made voluntary. Computer count replaces clerical count	−190,000
March 1983	Over 60s given National Insurance credits without claiming unemployment benefit	−162,000
July 1985	Northern Ireland discrepancies	−5,000
March 1986	Two week delay in compilation of figures to reduce overrecording	−50,000
September 1988	New regulations for under 18s	−90,000
July 1989	Change in redundant miners' conditions	−15,500

Source: Employment Gazette, December 1990 and March 1994 employment release.

stages by being given higher long-term benefits. These people were now outside the definition, but not the condition, of unemployment. While claimants over 60 who have been unemployed for some time are not likely to find a job, the appropriate response might well have been to give them priority in the labour market or on training schemes rather than removing them from the unemployment count.

Figures were published by the then Department of Employment for earlier periods on the new basis but not for later periods on the old basis. This apparent failing is defended on the grounds of statistical integrity in that, if a change in definition lowers the registered unemployed, it becomes impossible to track the current status of those who would have been eligible on the old basis. To produce such a measure would involve too many value judgements. In the early 1990s, the Unemployment Unit estimated that unemployment would have been about a million higher if the definitions had not been changed. This issue became progressively less sensitive during the 1990s, due to the fall in the unemployment rate, the growing focus on the LFS measure and the lack of any additional major changes to the definition.

DATA RELEASES

Since the spring of 1998 one integrated monthly release, containing the key labour market data and offering a coherent picture of the labour market, has replaced two separate releases. It brings together data from the Labour Force Survey, employer surveys and the administrative systems of the Benefits Agency and Employment Service. The focal point for the markets and the media tends to be the unemployment numbers, traditionally the claimant count version, and the earnings growth figures. The bulk of the release, however, contains figures derived from the Labour Force Survey. This has less of a following in financial markets because it has always offered less timely information. The integration of the Labour Force Survey data into the monthly release in 1998 has encouraged the markets to look more closely at the LFS data.

The press release tables offer a full break-down of the involvement of the adult population in the labour market. Table 6.4 shows the main break-downs that are available. In addition, the total is split into male and female and by age. There are also tables showing the reasons why temporary employees are working in a temporary capacity and why part-time workers are working part-time and some analysis of workers with second jobs. There is also information on actual and usual weekly hours of work.

The figures shown in Table 6.4 give a good picture of developments in the labour market. They show, for example, that in the year to the fourth quarter of 1998, the number of employees grew (in net terms) by nearly half a million. The three main, and largely equal, 'sources' for these employees were a reduction in self-employment and unemployment and an increase in the population of working age. Although this information is useful for building a picture of what is happening in the economy, the data are presented on a rolling three-month basis with the result there is only modest change from month to month. There is also quite a large sampling error. For these reasons, and that of unfamiliarity as explained above, the financial markets pay relatively little attention to these numbers when they are released each month.

The table is also a useful reminder of the complexities of the labour market. It is not simply a matter of there being employed and unemployed

Table 6.4. Labour market status of the adult population, end 1998

| | Millions | Change over 1998 | |
		Thousands	%
Employed, of which	27.286	304	1.1
Employees, part-time	5.960	157	2.7
Employees, full-time	17.877	332	1.9
Self-employed, part-time	0.693	15	2.2
Self-employed, full-time	2.507	−121	−4.6
Other employed	0.245	−78	−24.2
Unemployed	1.790	−103	−5.4
Economically inactive, of which	17.071	−46	−0.3
Over retirement age	9.467	28	0.3
Does not want a job	5.263	−45	−0.9
Wants a job but not available	1.644	40	2.5
Wants a job and available	0.698	−73	−9.4
All aged over 16	46.147	156	0.3

Note: Totals may not add up due to rounding.
Source: LFS, Q4 1998, UK, seasonally adjusted.

within a fixed labour force. Many individuals will frequently shift between being active and inactive in the labour market. The UK in the last couple of decades (as with many other countries) has seen a large increase in the early retirement of men coupled with a greater proportion of women joining the labour market. Trends such as these can have a much greater impact on economic development than fluctuations in the unemployment rate. It is interesting to note that the participation rate of females varies considerably between countries. In some, such as the US and Scandinavian countries, it can be as high as 70 per cent. By contrast, in other European countries it is below 50 per cent, and in Muslim countries it can be negligible. Note also that migration can at some times in some countries have a dramatic impact.

The press release also includes the data on employment from the employers' survey, the so-called workforce jobs data. These data are available only quarterly and with a lag, but have the advantage that they show employees by industry. The total workforce is broken down into employees, self-employment, the armed forces and government supported trainees. The vast bulk of the workforce, over 85 per cent, is employees and most of the rest is in self-employment. The figures for employees come from either a survey of employers or the so-called centralized returns which are compiled by certain industries for their own purposes. The survey's results can be benchmarked against the Labour Force Survey. The greatest uncertainty about accuracy surrounds the figures for self-employment, which come from the LFS. People are asked whether they consider themselves to be self-employed, regardless of their official tax or National Insurance treatment.

Box 6.3. **Employer surveys**

There are three principal employer surveys. The Annual Employment Survey (AES) is conducted annually in September and samples 450,000 local units covering around one third of the worksites in the United Kingdom. The short-term turnover employer survey (STES) is smaller and is conducted every three months. It provides estimates of quarterly changes in the number of jobs between the annual surveys. It surveys around 34,000 enterprises each quarter. The Monthly Wages and Salaries Survey (MWSS) collects information on gross wages and salaries paid to employees and is used to calculate the monthly average earnings index.

The employer-based jobs series is available back to 1959, though regional and local area data are available over shorter periods. The industry break-down from the employer surveys is generally thought to be more accurate than that from the LFS, but like any sample the results are dependent on the quality of the sampling frame. The sampling frame of the wages and salary survey was discredited as a result of the reviews following the suspension of the earnings data in October 1998. The survey has since been improved. We should bear in mind that the employer survey measures the number of jobs while the LFS counts the number of people with jobs. The two are different as one person can have more than one job.

The industry break-down, as shown in Table 6.5, is a useful additional tool for analysis. The figures for employment in the service sector are particularly useful since the output data for the service industries have been limited. The figures are also broken down by sex. The figures in Table 6.5 show that the economic expansion in the late 1990s was private service sector oriented. In 1998 virtually all the growth in employment

Table 6.5. Employees by industry

		Change over year	
	Thousands		%
Agriculture and fishing	270	−25	−8.5
Energy and water	216	−5	−2.2
Manufacturing	4,123	−32	−0.8
Construction	1,116	100	9.8
Services, of which	18,063	409	2.3
Distribution, hotels, restaurants	5,415	162	3.1
Transport and communications	1,407	69	5.1
Banking, finance and insurance	4,370	152	3.6
Public sector, education, health	5,763	3	0.1
Other services	1,106	23	2.2
TOTAL	23,788	447	1.9

Note: Totals may not add up, due to rounding.
Source: Employer surveys, September 1998, UK, seasonally adjusted.

occurred in three sectors: construction; distribution, hotels and restaurants; and banking, finance and insurance – despite accounting for less than half of total employment.

Monthly employment data are available for manufacturing and the remainder of the production sector – the extraction industries. The figures receive little attention now and it is often argued that they should no longer be published. The fact that more detail is available on manufacturing than services, even though it is a smaller and decreasing part of the economy, is an indication that the ONS has been too keen to hang on to the old and unable to fund the development required to collect and publish the data that many would wish to see.

Most attention is focused on the unemployment figures. There are several tables in the monthly release showing figures from both the Labour Force Survey and from the Benefits Agency, i.e. the claimant count figures. Unemployment is shown by age and duration on both bases. As explained before, the claimant count is more up-to-date and is available on a monthly as opposed to a three-month rolling basis. The tables also show the inflows to and outflows from the claimant count. The main attraction of the Labour Force Survey figures is that they can be related to other changes in the labour market.

EARNINGS GROWTH

After unemployment, the most keenly awaited figure is that for average earnings growth. The earnings index in its present form goes back to 1980. It is based on a monthly inquiry, called the Monthly Wages and Salaries Survey, to a sample of employers. Prior to 1998 the sample structure and the sampling methodology fell short of best practice, but from 1999 the sample was improved as it started to be based on the Inter-departmental Business Register. The monthly press release publishes the whole economy average earnings index for each month and a so-called 'headline rate' showing the percentage change over the year for the latest three months. The series is seasonally adjusted and covers Great Britain. The total is broken down in two ways: by industry sector (production, manufacturing and services) and by ownership (private and public) (see Fig. 6.4).

A break-down of the average earnings figures by detailed industry level (twenty-five components) is available from *Labour Market Trends*. The definition of the detailed break-down was changed from April 1999. From that date, earnings growth at the detailed level excluded bonuses and was presented on a three-month rolling basis aligned to the third month under consideration (rather than under the previous methodology of the centred three-month average basis). It was felt that the previous basis of publication introduced too much volatility into the series.

A crude index of earnings would be very volatile from month to month as seasonal variations in pay, bonuses, arrears or advances of wages resulting from pay negotiations, and the effect of industrial disputes, take their toll. Accordingly, the producers of this earnings series (originally the Department of Employment and now the ONS) have produced an underlying series that attempts to make appropriate adjustments. Acknowledging the uncertainty in the series, the annual growth rate was always published to the nearest ¼ per cent up until 1998, when it moved to the nearest 0.1 per cent.

The average earnings series available from 1999 is superior to its predecessor series, but there are some important features to appreciate. First, earnings should be distinguished from pay settlements. Earnings include overtime, bonus payments, shift premium, incentive payments

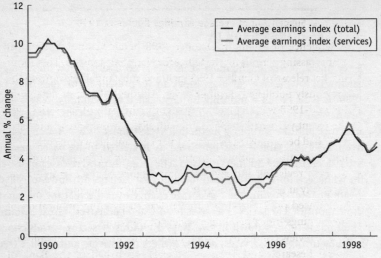

Fig. 6.4. Average earnings growth

and the various forms of wage drift, such as grading drift, which occurs when the proportion of higher graded posts rises. These are not included in settlement figures, which generally show growth of 1–2 per cent less than the earnings figures. There are no official figures for settlements, but some data are available from other sources, such as the CBI and Income Data Services. Second, the earnings index is derived from a survey of gross wages and salaries paid, divided by the number of employees. Accordingly, it is affected by changes in the composition of the workforce, such as employing more or fewer part-timers, and makes no allowance for the number of hours worked.

The ONS also produces the annual New Earnings Survey. It is conducted in April each year and is based on a 1 per cent sample of the employees in employment in Great Britain. The publication of the NES receives little attention in financial markets or the media, but is a useful benchmark and source of additional information on the labour market. It includes information on the hours worked for groups of workers sub-divided by sex, occupation, region and industry. It also has information on the composition of earnings and hours worked.

Box 6.4. **Suspension of average earnings figures in 1998**

A sequence of events in October 1998 heralded one of the most embarrassing periods for the Office for National Statistics. The labour market release of October 1998 included substantial revisions to the previously published earnings series. Although the latest data point for mid-1998 was changed only slightly, the path of the series over the recent years had changed dramatically. Earnings growth in early 1997 had been boosted by nearly 1 per cent and growth in early 1998 had been cut by a similar amount. As a result of the implausibility of these revisions and given the importance of the earnings data, especially at such a critical time of economic management, the ONS announced on 2 November that it was suspending publication of the earnings index pending a review of the series.

The review conducted by the National Institute for Economic and Social Research and Treasury officials, on behalf of the Bank of England and the Treasury, reported in March 1999. It clearly isolated the problems with the original and the revised series and presented a new, improved version of the data. It was clear that the ONS had mishandled the process of revising the series, even if its intentions had been honourable. The scale of the upgrading that was necessary reflected the neglect of the series by the Department of Employment, which had been the guardians of it until responsibility was transferred to the CSO (subsequently the ONS) in 1995. The episode was a stark reminder of the need to review continually and update the samples and methodology used to derive statistical series. The original, revised and final numbers are shown in Fig. 6.5.

VACANCIES

The series for vacancies used to be keenly watched in the 1970s and 1980s, but is of less relevance now. The series has a number of problems. First, it only measures vacancies at Jobcentres, which are a small and probably diminishing proportion of total vacancies as more employers use private

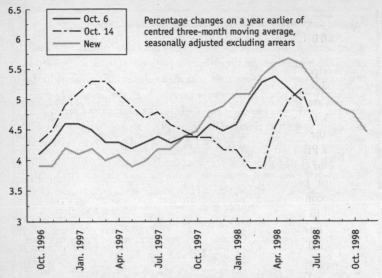

Fig. 6.5. Changes to earnings data following the 1998/9 review

channels. Perhaps only 30 per cent of engagements are made through Jobcentres. Second, vacancies data can be affected by changes in the administrative system. In 1997 the Employment Service announced that vacancy stocks were over-estimated by around 40,000 because of the retention of old vacancies which should have been cancelled. In the same year it also came to light that not all placings were being recorded strictly in line with the Employment Service guidance.

The changes rather than the levels of vacancies may still indicate a trend. Vacancies tend to move in the opposite direction to unemployment. During the course of 1998, for example, the stock of unfilled vacancies rose by 41,000 to 309,000 and unemployment fell by about 100,000. It would be wrong to think that the level of unemployment could be cut if only individuals accepted the advertised vacancies. Most vacancies last only a matter of weeks so the figure indicates the trend of labour market turnover rather than the number of posts that cannot be filled. In December 1998 the stock of unfilled vacancies at 309,000 reflected new notifications during the month of 220,000 and vacancy outflow of 229,000.

PRODUCTIVITY AND UNIT WAGE COSTS

The press release also includes figures for output per head, in other words labour productivity, and earnings per unit of the output, or unit labour costs. Both are given in index form, with the index currently starting at 100 in 1995, in common with most other series. The increase in earnings divided by the increase in labour productivity is equal to the rise in unit labour costs. Productivity growth, therefore, normally reduces the increase in unit labour costs below the rise in earnings. While monthly figures are available for manufacturing, only quarterly data are published for the whole economy. Productivity growth in manufacturing tends to be higher than in the whole economy due to the nature of the activity – it is easier to introduce new technology – and the lower contribution of labour to total costs. As the monthly data are erratic, markets tend to focus on the latest three months compared with the same three months a year before.

It is quite usual for productivity to fall sharply as the economy slows and enters recession. Companies rarely act as if they have anticipated the fall-off in orders, preferring to cut overtime working and build stocks before eventually cutting staff and other costs. Understandably, perhaps, the hope is that the slowdown will be brief and short-lived, and fail to turn into a fully fledged recession. For opposite reasons, productivity generally rises in an economic recovery. As demand picks up companies remain nervous and are generally slow to recruit, boosting productivity.

In the boom years in the mid-1980s, the growth in manufacturing productivity averaged over 5 per cent a year. This would have been an extremely impressive performance had earnings growth not been as high as 9 per cent over the same period. The consequent unit labour cost increase of around 4 per cent meant that inflation was sure to remain higher than desired. Increases in unit labour costs of that order were large compared to Britain's main industrial competitors so industry could remain competitive only as a result of devaluation. The recession played havoc with the productivity record and whole economy productivity turned negative in 1990. A rough rule of thumb is that 2½ per cent inflation is achievable with earnings growth at or below 4½ per cent due to productivity averaging 2 per cent over the long term. Towards the end

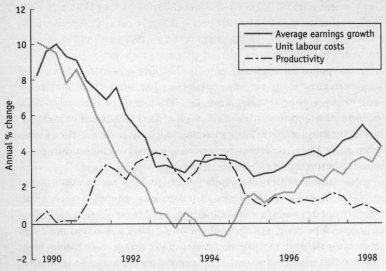

Fig. 6.6. Average earnings growth, unit labour costs and productivity

of 1998, inflation, earnings growth and productivity were all within half of 1 per cent of these numbers (see Fig. 6.6).

The monthly release also includes figures for labour disputes and the educational status of young people. There are limited regional summaries and international comparisons. There is a wealth of information about the labour market beyond that published in the monthly release. The ONS publication *Labour Market Trends* is an invaluable source of information (for both statistics and analysis) and there are regional monthly releases for the LFS data. The ONS monthly publications, *Economic Trends* and the *Monthly Digest of Statistics*, offer additional information such as regional unemployment numbers, weekly and hourly earnings data, and some employment data by sector (including civil service, local authorities, the armed services and agriculture).

TRENDS IN EMPLOYMENT

Table 6.6 shows how the composition of the labour market has changed over the last two decades. The time periods shown reflect the peaks in employment – in 1979 and 1990 – and the troughs – in 1983 and 1993. In the earlier periods the data are very unlikely to catch the precise peaks and troughs as the Labour Force Survey was conducted only once every two years, in contrast to its current quarterly frequency.

Several points are, however, of note. The first concerns the impact of economic growth on employment levels. The number of employees dropped by around 2 million, about 10 per cent, in the early 1980s' recession and then rose by a similar amount during the economic expansion of the mid- to late 1980s. Employment fell again, by about 1 million, in the early 1990s' recession before rising by over 2 million during the economic expansion of the mid- to late 1990s.

Second, the trend in total employment has been rather more muted than that of employees, reflecting the trend in self-employment. Self-employment doubled during the 1980s to about 3½ million before falling by about 10 per cent in the recession of the early 1990s and remained remarkably stable during the remainder of the decade. Self-employment – at least that which is declared in the survey – seems to be less responsive than employment to changes in overall demand in the economy. It appears that many of the reforms and liberalizations of the labour market during the 1980s did increase the attractiveness of or the scope for self-employment.

Table 6.6. Changes in labour market, 1979–1998

	Spring 1979 million	Spring 1983 million	Spring 1990 million	Summer 1993 million	Winter 1998 million	Change since 1990	Change since 1993
Employees	22.6	20.4	22.5	21.4	23.8	1.3	2.4
Self-employed	1.8	2.3	3.5	3.1	3.2	−0.3	0.1
Total employment	24.4	23.1	26.4	25.0	27.3	0.9	2.3
Unemployed	1.5	2.9	1.9	2.9	1.8	−0.1	−0.9
Economically active	25.8	26.0	28.3	27.8	29.1	0.8	1.3
Economically inactive	15.3	16.4	15.6	16.4	17.1	1.5	0.7
Total aged 16+	41.1	42.4	44.0	44.2	46.1	2.1	1.9

Source: LFS, seasonally adjusted, total employment also includes minor categories not shown.

Third, it is interesting to note that over half of the increase in employment between 1993 and 1998 reflected new entrants to the labour market rather than a fall in unemployment. During that period the number of over 16s increased by 1.9 million, of whom 1.3 million entered the labour market. Many of the remainder will have entered full-time education. Unemployment fell by less than 1 million, illustrating the fact that, skill-wise, the pool of unemployed does not necessarily closely match the jobs that become available.

The different trends between men and women regarding full-time and part-time work are also of interest. As Table 6.7 shows, part-time employment for both men and women grew more strongly than full-time employment in the six years of economic recovery after the trough in employment at the beginning of 1993. A longer run of the series would show that the number of full-time male workers is currently about 1 million below the peak level seen a decade earlier while the number of full-time female workers is roughly back at the level seen then. These differential trends partly reflect lifestyle choices but also the changing nature of the job market – the greater emphasis on services and flexible working hours tends to encourage more women into the labour market and create more part-time jobs.

The statistics show what is happening but they do not explain why or offer any qualitative assessment. We do not know, for example, whether more jobs have been created on a full-time equivalent basis or whether the labour market as it is now offers increased well-being. In general, the statistics suggest that the employment situation is healthier now than it

Table 6.7. Trends in employment by sex and status

	Q1 1993 million	Q1 1999 million	Change Million	%
Male full-time	13.1	13.7	0.7	5.1
Male part-time	1.0	1.4	0.3	30.0
Female full-time	6.4	6.8	0.4	6.0
Female part-time	5.0	5.5	0.4	8.5
TOTAL	25.6	27.3	1.8	7.0

Note: Totals may not add up due to rounding.
Source: ONS.

was two decades ago as more jobs have been created and activity rates have risen. That said, the changes in the labour market have been quite dramatic and have given rise to a range of social and regional problems that were neither forecast nor intended.

THEORIES AND POLICY

Although the control of inflation has been central to macro-economic policy for the last decade, for much of the twentieth century full employment, synonymous with the near eradication of unemployment, was central to policy. There has been much debate as to whether unemployment is due to a deficiency of demand in the economy, too high a real exchange rate, the price of labour being too high, or is an inevitable result of technological progress.

There has also been much debate among economists about the so-called 'natural rate' of unemployment, often known as the NAIRU, or the non-accelerating inflation rate of unemployment. At this rate, the demand for and supply of labour are said to be in balance with no net effect on inflation. In essence, the theory states that an increase in growth can be translated into higher employment up to the NAIRU. Any further increase in demand will lead to higher wages and therefore higher inflation, as employment cannot expand. Estimates for NAIRU are highly subjective and vary considerably between countries and over time. By the late 1990s it was widely accepted to be around 5 per cent, having been probably around 8 per cent a decade before. As the NAIRU is affected by many factors including, for example, the structure of the labour force, social benefits, taxes, the minimum wage and rates of trade union membership, it offers a useful framework for discussion but is of little practical use for forecasting.

The Bank of England's quarterly inflation report presents the most comprehensive assessment of how the labour market affects policy. The labour market constitutes one of the four key chapters of the inflation report, the others being money and financial markets, demand and output, and costs and prices. It is clear that average earnings growth is central to concerns about inflation though this sits alongside an assessment of the general tightness in the labour market. As the Bank's report indicates, a thorough assessment of tightness requires all available data to be assessed. The Bank, in common with analysts in the financial markets, looks not only at the official data discussed above but also any private sector survey data that is available. It is also important to consider the impact of any changes in legislation brought by the government. Assessing the inflationary impact of the legislation from the Labour Government, such as the New Deal and the Working Time Directive, is complex and necessarily arbitrary.

7 | Consumers

Consumer activity – personal income, expenditure and saving – is the largest and arguably the most important sector in the economy. Personal consumption accounts for nearly two-thirds of UK GDP. Personal income is a better guide to living standards than total GDP as it includes not only incomes from employment, but also transfer payments such as social security benefits and bank interest, which are not part of GDP because they are not value added. Despite the importance of consumer income and expenditure for the economy, the official data are not amongst the most timely. The initial estimates of GDP and industrial production are available many weeks before the initial estimates of consumers' expenditure.

Personal incomes are either spent – becoming incomes for others who in turn spend and save – or saved – providing the investment finance for future production, income and consumption. Accordingly, changes in incomes – specifically real household disposable income – or in the spending and saving activities of consumers are vital to understanding both short-term and long-term developments in the economy.

The activity of consumers is influenced by many factors, including:

- Interest rates. A rise in interest rates not only increases the cost of existing variable rate loans and discourages new borrowing, but also improves savings rates and encourages saving. Together, these effects reduce spending by more than the higher interest income will increase spending.
- Wealth. An increase in asset values, most notably housing and the stock market, will increase wealth and encourage spending.

- Product cycle. The relatively sudden availability of new products can increase spending. The best examples in the UK from recent years are mobile phones and personal computers. There was a strong demand for many 'western' consumer products in Eastern Europe in the early 1990s, following the opening up of those markets.
- Financial deregulation. For commercial or legal reasons, it is still difficult to obtain credit in many economies. Whenever constraints are eased, there is usually a surge in credit demand and with it higher spending. There is little doubt that financial deregulation was one of the main causes of the UK economic boom in the second half of the 1980s.
- Price expectations. In the short term, consumers will tend to bring spending forward if they expect the price of goods to rise, and conversely to delay spending if they expect prices to fall. If higher inflation is expected to be sustained over the longer term, there is some evidence that saving will increase so that individuals can maintain the real value of their accumulated savings.
- Demography and life cycle. The young tend to borrow and spend, the middle-aged tend to save for retirement and the old tend to spend their accumulated savings. Accordingly, the performance of economies can be affected where there are major shifts in the demographic profile.

Each of these factors will have a different impact at a different time.

As in other areas of economic statistics, terminology has become a little confused, due to loose usage of words and the unavailability of data on one consistent definition. Accordingly, some of the concepts do not mean quite what common sense would lead us to suppose. Consumption is indiscriminately described as being by the household, consumer, private or personal sector, even though, strictly defined, these sectors are all different.

There is some hope that the concept of the household will eventually dominate, following the recasting of the national accounts onto an ESA basis in 1998, which prompted UK statisticians to produce more data on the household basis. Households are defined as small groups of people who share the same living accommodation, who pool some, or all, of their income and wealth and consume certain types of goods and services collectively, mainly housing and food.

The UK national accounts used to publish figures for the personal sector which included not only the household sector, but also life assurance and pension funds, unincorporated businesses and non-profit making institutions. Since 1998 unincorporated businesses, or partnerships, have been classified in the national accounts as non-financial or financial corporations. Private non-profit making institutions are shown separately in their own sector. Life assurance and pension funds are allocated to the financial corporations sector. Sole traders, however, will continue to be recorded as part of the household sector as their accounts are not readily separable from those of households. People living in institutions, such as retirement homes, hotels or prisons, comprising about 1½ per cent of the population, are also included in households. The clearer identification of households will make analysis of the consumer sector much easier in the coming years than it has been in the past.

The bulk of the quarterly personal income and expenditure data is published in the quarterly series of national accounts press releases and publications described in Chapter 4. The annual *Blue Book* is also a rich source of information, but offers data only on an annual basis. Data for some of the key variables, such as consumers' expenditure and saving, go back to 1946. The *Blue Book* publishes data for the latest ten years and the tables in the quarterly GDP press releases offer between three and ten years of data. Most of the data are available in current and constant price form and are almost invariably presented and assessed in seasonally adjusted terms.

Although more and more domestic information is becoming available on the consumer sector, international comparisons of the sector remain extremely difficult. The boundaries between public and private sectors and the nature of the vehicles for the provision of pensions, social benefits, savings, insurance etc. are very different in different countries, with the result that even when there are common statistical definitions, the numbers might not strictly be comparable. The considerable variation in the level of the household savings ratios between countries often has more do with statistical definition than economic realities. This is another example of where it is more fruitful to follow trends in indicators than to compare levels. The arrival of the common ESA definitions should improve the scope for international comparisons.

THE HOUSEHOLD ACCOUNTS

Table 7.1 sets out a summary of the household sector accounts. The term 'compensation of employees' is the remuneration, in cash or in kind, received by employees in the household sector as payment for the services of labour. It includes wages and salaries and employers' social contributions. Other income, about a quarter of total income, includes rental income, that part of income from self-employment relating to sole traders, and receipts in respect of ownership of financial assets. The balance of primary income, the sum of compensation of employees and other income, represents household income as a result of participation in the production process.

The balance of primary income is then adjusted by the net impact

Table 7.1. Summary of the household sector account

Component	ONS code	£ billion, 1998
1. Compensation of employees	D.1	463.6
2. Of which, wages and salaries	D.11	401.7
3. Other income	B.2, B.3, D.4	159.3
4. Balance of primary income, gross (1+3)	B.5g	622.9
5. Current taxes on income, etc.	D.5	−103.9
6. Social benefits (net) and other transfers	D.61, D.62, D.7	48.1
7. Disposable income, gross (4+5+6)	B.6g	567.1
8. Adjustment for equity reserves	D.8	15.7
9. Final consumption expenditure	P.31	542.0
10. Saving, gross	B.8g	40.8
11. Total resources (7+8) = Total uses (9+10)	TR/TU	582.8
Memo item – Saving ratio (10/ 11*100)	—	7.0%
12. Capital transfers (net)	D.9	2.4
13. Change in liabilities and net worth (10+12)	B.10.1g	43.2
14. Gross fixed capital formation	P.51	34.8
15. Other adjustments (net)	P.52, P.53, K.2	0.7
16. Net lending/borrowing (13−14−15)	B.9	7.7

Source: ONS national accounts press release and Economic Accounts, Q4 1998.

of current taxes, social benefits and some other relatively modest current transfers, such as some insurance claims and grants from overseas. Current taxes on income (which includes taxes on profits and capital gains) and so-called other current taxes (including vehicle excise duty and council tax) take about 15 per cent of total incomes. Deductions from income for social contributions (mainly pension contributions, actual or computed, compulsory or voluntary, from the employee or employer) are even larger (at £134 billion in 1998). These are offset for the household sector as a whole by the receipt of social benefits (£172 billion). Including some other minor transfers, the net result is households' gross disposable income.

A technical adjustment is made to reflect the net equity of households in pension funds, leaving 'total resources' available to households. This is the sum of money that the household sector has to spend or save. By definition, total resources must equal total uses, the sum of expenditure and saving. Final consumption expenditure, or individual consumption expenditure, is the total current expenditure of the household sector on goods and services, including spending abroad (see below).

That part of total uses that is not spent is saved. It is important to emphasize that saving is derived as a residual in the accounts, so the accuracy of the figure depends on the accuracy of all the items of household income and spending. As it is the comparatively small difference between two large numbers, errors in income and spending data can have a large impact on the estimate for saving. Accordingly, the series often moves erratically and is revised as later data become available. The figures for saving, which are net of borrowing, are also vulnerable to any changes in definition of what is included in consumption and income. The level of saving is often expressed as a ratio – the saving ratio – defined as saving as a percentage of available household resources.

There was a noticeable fall in the saving ratio between 1980 and 1988. This reflected the rise in borrowing, associated with the housing market, that occurred during the economic boom, rather than a fall in savings as such. The ratio rose rapidly from around 4 per cent in 1988 to 11 per cent in 1992, the trough of the recession. After hovering around 10 per cent for some years, the ratio declined in the late 1990s to reach 7 per cent by the end of 1998 (see Fig. 7.1).

The capital account shows how these savings and capital transfers are used to finance the acquisition of non-financial assets. Capital transfers are relatively modest. Receipts include investment grants from local

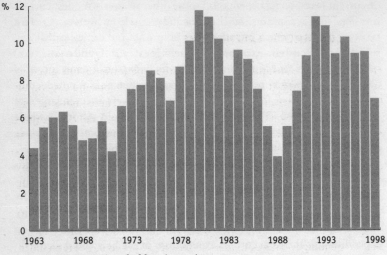

Fig. 7.1. Household saving ratio

authorities, and payments include capital taxes, most notably capital gains tax. The bulk of investment spending is gross fixed capital formation, which in the household sector is primarily investment in dwellings. It also includes a smaller amount of additional tangible investment by farmers, professional people and sole traders. The main intangible fixed assets are entertainment, and literary and artistic originals. There are also modest changes in inventories (included in the 'other adjustments' row), relating to the stocks held by traders included in the household sector and even smaller amounts relating to the net change in ownership of valuables, such as precious stones, antiques and works of art. Consumer durables are not included in this category, as the ONS assumes that they are 'consumed' in the period.

The financial account (not shown in the table) includes changes in financial assets, such as holdings of bonds and shares, deposits with banks and loans (mainly mortgage lending), and in financial liabilities.

CONSUMERS' EXPENDITURE

Household final consumption expenditure is the formal name given to consumer spending. It includes not only traditional consumer spending but also imputed rent for the provision of owner-occupied housing and consumption of own production. It includes household expenditure overseas, and excludes spending by non-residents in the UK. In recent years these two numbers have been similar. The 1998 *Blue Book* shows overseas spending by UK residents to be £16 billion and spending by non-residents to be £13 billion in 1997, compared to household spending of £500 billion in that period.

Table 7.2 breaks down spending into the main components by commodity, as they are commonly shown. Durables make up about 10 per cent of spending and non-durables a little over 40 per cent. The remainder, services, is nearly half of total consumer spending. It is noteworthy that spending on services grew fastest in 1998. The proportion of consumer

Table 7.2. Break-down of consumer spending figures, 1998

Component	Spending		% change, 1998/1997
	£bn	%	
Durables, of which:			
Vehicles	28.5	5.4	6.1
Other durables	22.9	4.4	3.5
Non-durables, of which:			
Food	53.9	10.3	1.3
Alcohol and tobacco	41.7	8.0	1.9
Clothing and footwear	31.8	6.1	1.2
Other non-durables	93.7	17.9	2.7
Services, of which:			
Rent, water and sewerage	69.4	13.3	4.9
Catering	47.6	9.1	10.6
Transport and communication	50.0	9.6	6.4
Other services	84.1	16.1	9.5
Total household expenditure	523.5	100.0	5.0

Source: ONS national accounts press release, March 1999. Current prices.

spending on services has been rising steadily for many years. Data are available quarterly in current and constant price form, two months after the end of the quarter, as part of the GDP sequence of press releases.

The *Blue Book* also shows annual figures for household consumption broken down by purpose or function. The classification used, COICOP (the Classification of Individual Consumption by Purpose), is designed to indicate the socio-economic objectives that individuals aim to achieve through various kinds of outlays. The introduction of ESA95 coincides with the re-definition of these classifications and data will be available on this basis for all European Union member states. The break-down is useful, but with the data only being published annually they are not closely followed by financial markets.

There is a wide range of sources for consumers' expenditure data, including:

- Sample surveys of spending by households and individuals
- Statistics of retail and other traders' turnover
- Other statistics of supply or sales of particular goods and services
- Administrative sources
- Commodity flow analysis.

The ONS tries to find the best estimate for each good or service from the various sources which are available. In general, the quality of data for spending is higher than that for incomes or saving.

Three continuous surveys provide much of the quarterly information. Two of them, the Family Expenditure Survey and the National Food Survey, both surveys of households, will be merged into a single Expenditure and Food Survey from 2001, subject to successful testing. The third, the International Passenger Survey, is a survey of individuals, both resident and non-resident, conducted at entry points; it seeks information on holiday and travel expenditure. The ONS also uses some business surveys, notably the annual inquiries into distribution and service trades and the monthly retail sales inquiry, in the estimation of household consumption. Specific sources and administrative information embrace, for example, the privatized utilities and similar industries, government tax data and certain trade association sources.

Household expenditure surveys make an important contribution to the measurement of consumer spending. Spending is normally recorded over a one- or two-week period. The attraction of this kind of approach is that the information collected usually covers spending across a comprehensive range of items. But there are certain disadvantages in this approach, including:

- Suspected under-recording of expenditure at the top end of the income range.
- Under-recording of certain items of expenditure, such as betting, alcohol and tobacco.
- Difficulties in allowing for the spending on large and infrequently purchased items, such as cars and furniture.
- The near-impossibility of measuring certain items, such as financial services and insurance, in a way that is consistent with economic accounts concepts.
- Difficulties allowing for the expenditure of foreign tourists, juveniles and people living in institutions.
- Survey sampling and participation which may not be fully representative.

A key role for the ONS statisticians is to identify the importance of these problems and allow for them in the estimates. This presents a number of complex statistical issues related to the grossing up of household expenditure to national totals, in addition to normal problems such as seasonal adjustment.

Most of the information is collected in cash (i.e. current prices) form. The constant price figures are derived from a mixture of deflated values and direct or indirect volume estimates. Most of the price information used for deflation is provided by the ONS retail prices index, but certain other sources are used, particularly for services. Deflation is undertaken in as much detail as possible with the aggregate estimates being derived through a process of summation of the estimates for individual goods and services.

The adoption of the new national accounting framework in 1998 gave rise to coverage changes for household expenditure. There are two important additions to household consumption, which, at the time of writing, had not been implemented by the ONS (or any other statistics office) – changes to the measurement of the output of financial institutions and an explicit coverage of illicit expenditure, such as that on drugs. By contrast, among the exclusions were domestic rates (but not council tax) and vehicle excise duty paid by households, both of which were part of consumption but now count as taxes on income and wealth. There were many other smaller changes, but the balance of the inclusions and exclusions had the effect of reducing household consumption compared to the previous definition of the personal sector.

RETAIL SALES

One of the earlier indications of the trend of household expenditure is given by the monthly estimate of retail sales published by the ONS two to three weeks after the end of each month. The retail sales release covers only a modest part, about 40 per cent, of total consumers' expenditure. The value of sales covered by the indicator was a little under £200 billion in 1998, compared to total household consumption of around £500 billion. It is not easy to say exactly what is included in both retail sales and consumer spending as the two surveys use different definitions. The main difference, however, is that the retail sales survey does not cover services, such as utilities, catering and transport, which account for nearly half of total consumer expenditure. The other notable component of consumer spending not included in the retail sales survey is vehicles. Retail sales relate to GB while consumers' expenditure relates to the whole of the UK.

The retail sales data cover either a four- or five-week period rather than a calendar month. The figures are published in index form, based on the reference year (1995 at the time of writing) when sales values in pounds were calculated. They are categorized by type of retailer. This presents a problem: it means, for example, that an article of clothing sold in a food shop will count as a sale by a food retailer. Food and furniture sold in Marks & Spencer counts towards the sales of a clothing store. This categorization is increasingly irrelevant as stores sell an ever wider range of items. The advantage of this analysis, however, is that contributors need to provide only one figure each month, limiting the form-filling burden and increasing the timeliness of the data.

The press release contains three indices. The most useful index, particularly for comparison with the consumers' expenditure figures, is that which gives the volume of retail sales, seasonally adjusted. Another index gives the current value of sales, not seasonally adjusted. (A seasonally adjusted version is available on request from the ONS.) Since 1994 the

ONS has been publishing a third series, which shows a break-down of sales by commodity as opposed to type of retailer. The series is in value terms, is not seasonally adjusted and is based on a small sample (just forty or so in early 1999) of the largest retailers. As the commodity break-down is subject to greater revisions than the other data, the percentage change figures are presented only to the nearest whole number.

Financial markets tend to focus on the monthly and annual change in the volume of sales, viewing it as the best short-term indicator of consumer demand. There has recently been some doubt cast on the worth of these numbers. Many retailers have said that value, as opposed to volume, figures would be more meaningful in times of intense high street competition, fickle consumers and low inflation. The month on month change is highly dependent on the choice of seasonal adjustments, which are by no means easy to estimate as retailing and spending are constantly changing. (A massive seasonal adjustment is applied to December and January, for example, as sales in some sectors can halve between the two months.) Accordingly, it is common to look at the trends in the latest three months compared to three months before, to smooth any erratic data.

Despite the weaknesses of the break-down (by food and non-food retailer) of the data, the market will look at the split with a view to excluding the food component, where short-term fluctuations are not so relevant to the prospects for the economy. The additional break-down of non-food (into retailer categories of clothing and footwear, household goods, non-specialist and other goods) is sometimes of interest. The commodity break-down has not yet attracted much attention. Some analysts will look at the difference between the growth in the value and volume series, to gauge the pressures on high street inflation.

The retail sales data are obtained by the ONS from a panel of approximately 5,000 retailers. It aims to survey all the very large retailers (defined as those with a turnover of £5 million or more in 1995) but also includes a sample of the smaller independent retailers, who account for a quarter of retail sales. In 1992 the inquiry became compulsory and its size increased from around 3,000, in an attempt to improve reliability. (The survey panel had included over 6,000 retailers in the 1970s but cuts in funding had reduced that number by over half by the early 1980s.)

The data collected refer to the value of retail sales, which is then deflated by (in large part) the appropriate component of the RPI, to derive the volume series. The information used in the first estimate covers around

Table 7.3. Break-down of retail sales figures, volumes, 1998

Component	Weight		Index (calendar year 1998, 1995=100γ)	% change 1998/1997
	Sales*	%		
Total	3205	100	111.7	2.9
Food stores	1441	45	108.8	2.7
Non-food	1600	50	114.3	2.8
Clothing/footwear	502	16	112.0	0.7
Household goods	380	12	125.2	6.8
Non-specialized	289	9	111.5	0.0
Other	428	13	109.2	3.3
Non-store retailers	165	5	111.6	5.6

Notes: *Sales are average weekly sales in 1995, £ million. Components may not add to total due to rounding.
Source: ONS February 1999 press release.

three-quarters of all retailers by turnover. Although a significant part of the total data set is missing, revisions to the initial estimates, when all the data are available, have usually been modest – around 0.2 per cent. Data go back to 1955. Table 7.3 shows the main break-down given in the press release.

Every two years the retail sales index is re-weighted to reflect the changes in the pattern of expenditure, the size of businesses and the types of goods sold, as seen in the fuller Annual Retail Inquiry carried out in that year. The index continues to be referenced on the same base year, however, for reasons of convenience. The process of re-weighting the retail sales series can cause the level of the index in the recent period to fall or jump. This largely reflects the differential price movement of goods which are changing weights over time.

The seasonally adjusted series attempts to adjust for the timing of bank holidays, but trends in the data around peak spending periods such as Easter (the date of which can move by some weeks) and Christmas should be treated with some caution. Seasonal adjustment appears particularly difficult for retail sales due to the variable timing of sales periods. Recent years have seen the summer sales, which traditionally took place in August, move to the earlier part of summer. January sales have moved forward, in some cases to the pre-Christmas period. The impact of unseasonal changes in the weather on spending patterns can also be considerable, as can changes in tax rates. Seasonal adjustment does not necessarily mean that the resulting series will be smooth. Monthly retail sales figures can be volatile for any number of reasons. The death of Diana, Princess of Wales, in 1997 and the 1998 World Cup in France are examples of events which disrupted the pattern of sales (see p. 51).

The growth of retail sales was reasonably robust during most of the 1990s. In the six post-recession years (1993 to 1998), growth averaged about 3 per cent. The weak year, 1995, was compensated for by the strength of 1997, which was boosted by the windfalls from building society demutualization (see Fig. 7.2). It is interesting to note that sales by non-food retailers tend to be much more responsive to the economic cycle than total sales. In 1992, for example, non-food sales actually fell while food sales remained reasonably robust, growing by 2½ per cent. In 1997, the strongest year of the 1990s, non-food sales growth was nearly 7 per cent compared to 4 per cent in food sales.

Consumers' expenditure tends to move in line with retail sales despite its wider coverage. Not surprisingly, some parts of consumers' expenditure, such as spending on services and some discretionary or luxury goods, such as cars, tend to rise more strongly in periods of strong growth and fall more sharply in recessions. This is compensated for in the total by relatively stable demand for some other components, such as utilities. The net impact of all these variations is shown in Fig. 7.2.

There is always considerable interest in high street inflation trends. Although the retail price index inflation numbers are the principal source, analysts will often compare current and constant price versions of the consumer spending and retail sales data in search of a different angle on recent events. The implied deflators for the components of consumer spending or retail sales can reveal interesting information about the pressures faced by retailers in different sectors.

CBI DISTRIBUTIVE TRADES SURVEY

The CBI began publication of a monthly distributive trades survey in 1983. The structure is similar to its industrial trends survey described in Chapter 8. The survey covers the so-called distributive trades, breaking down the responses into retailing, wholesaling and the motor trades. Most of the market attention is focused on the retailing component. The

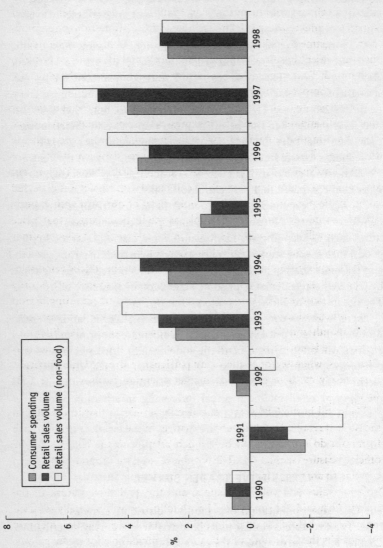

Fig. 7.2. Consumer spending and retail sales – growth rates compared

normal survey comprises four variables: sales volume; volume of orders placed with suppliers; volume of sales for the time of year (a form of seasonal adjustment); and volume of stocks in relation to expected sales. A larger survey is conducted quarterly and includes additional questions on employment, investment, business sentiment and expected prices. Respondents give the present position in the current month, and the expected position next month. Each question allows for three possible answers: the same, up, or down, compared with the same month a year before.

The survey gives the percentage of respondents giving each answer for that month and the next month. It expresses these percentages in balance form, showing the difference between the 'ups' and 'downs', and ignoring the 'sames'. The press release shows the balances for each month over the previous year and attempts to discern trends from them. The present position for the current month is also compared with what it was expected to be in the previous month. The comparison of out-turn with expectations can be revealing. For example, it might be expected that price reductions will be unusually aggressive in the sales period if sales volumes in the previous months fell short of expectations.

The sample size is only a fraction of that used in the official retail sales survey and, as the survey is not compulsory, the response rate is only around 50 per cent. The survey does not cover the same reporting period as the official measure as it is generally conducted in the last two weeks of the month and the first week of the following month. The difference in coverage is normally only significant at certain times of year, such as Christmas, when seasonal effects are particularly strong. Unfortunately, it is usually at these times that market attention focuses on the CBI survey.

The trend in the CBI survey is generally similar to that in the official measure of retail sales, although the changes in the balances from month to month do not appear to bear much relation to the changes in the official measure (see Fig. 7.3). The possible reasons for the poor short-term correlation are many, including sample size, sample structure, difficulties isolating value and volume changes, and the qualitative nature of the survey. That said, the survey does have a following as it is usually released a day or two before the official measure of retail sales. The commentary provided by the CBI, alongside the survey results, also adds useful colour.

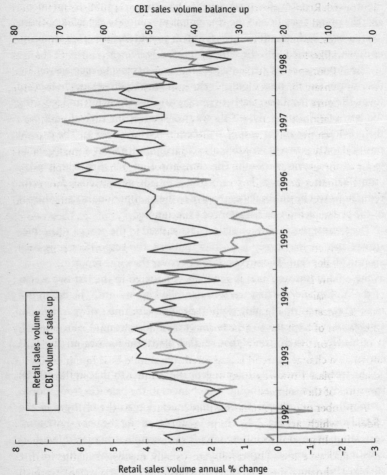

Fig. 7.3. Retail sales – government and CBI figures compared

OTHER SOURCES

The British Retail Consortium (BRC) sales monitor is published at the start of the second week of each month. Retailers report the value of their sales in the latest month and in the equivalent period a year before, on both a total and like-for-like basis, with the latter removing the effect of changes in retail floor space. The data are neither seasonally adjusted nor deflated to compensate for price changes. The non-seasonally adjusted sales value growth figure from the ONS usually lies between the two BRC series.

The relationship between the BRC series and the official measure is erratic from month to month. This could be due to the lack of seasonal and calendar adjustment in the BRC data and the lack of small retailers in the survey (even though the monitor covers half of retail sales). The qualitative commentary on a dozen sub-sectors provides interesting colour and background. The survey is a recent addition to the information set and data are available from 1994 but the figures only go back two or three years in the monthly release. The BRC also produces a Shop Price Index, which measures high street inflation, and launched a monthly Scottish sales monitor in 1999.

The John Lewis Partnership, which accounts for about 2 per cent of UK retail sales, publishes weekly sales values. These figures, published in the *Gazette*, their publicly available in-house magazine, give some indication of both food and non-food sales. Financial markets normally only focus on this source at times of uncertainty, such as around Christmas or when a change in trend is suspected. We should bear in mind that the data are biased towards spending in the south of England, due to the location of their outlets.

A number of polling organizations conduct surveys of consumer confidence which are used by some analysts as indicators of consumer spending. In general, more optimistic consumers are more likely to spend more and save less. The results are usually presented in the form of balances showing the percentage of consumers feeling more optimistic minus the percentage feeling less optimistic. Over the short-term, optimism can be affected by many factors such as political crisis or the outbreak of war, but these indices do provide a useful guide to economic developments over the medium term.

Table 7.4. Household financial accounts and balance sheet, 1997, £bn

	Inflow (+)/ outflow	Total holding	Change in value, yr/yr
Net acquisition of assets:			
1. Deposits with UK financial institutions	33.9	433.6	36.1
2. Other	5.4	106.1	6.8
3. Total deposits (1+2)	39.3	539.7	42.9
4. Medium/long dated gilts	−6.1	7.6	−9.2
5. Other securities (not shares)	0.8	12.4	0.8
6. Total securities (4+5)	−5.3	20.0	−8.4
7. Quoted UK shares	−11.7	293.1	103.5
8. Unquoted UK shares	−0.4	180.9	41.2
9. UK mutual fund shares	6.4	91.1	10.4
10. Other shares	0.1	12.5	0.6
11. Total shares (7 to 10)	−5.6	577.6	155.7
12. Life assurance and pension funds	41.2	1300.1	220.6
13. Other	0.7	72.2	−0.9
14. Total assets (3, 6, 11 to 13)	70.2	2509.7	410.0
Net acquisition of liabilities:			
15. Short-term loans	10.0	93.1	9.5
16. Mortgages	23.7	430.0	21.2
17. Other long-term loans	3.6	13.0	1.4
18. Total loans (15 to 17)	37.4	536.1	32.1
19. Other liabilities	1.1	50.9	1.5
20. Total liabilities (18+19)	38.4	587.0	33.6
21. Statistical discrepancy	−8.3	—	—
22. Net financial assets (14−18+21)	23.5	1922.7	376.4

Source: 1998 *Blue Book*.

THE FINANCIAL ACCOUNT AND BALANCE SHEET

The *Blue Book* publishes annual data for the household financial accounts and balance sheet. These data are not market sensitive but are useful for understanding developments in the consumer sector. It is useful to be able to see the assets and liabilities (both the stocks and the flows) and to estimate the impact of interest rate changes on behaviour. We should note that interest rate changes have markedly different effects on households of different ages and incomes. Table 7.4 shows the household financial accounts and balance sheet in 1997. The *Blue Book* sets out these numbers in more detail and over a nine-year period.

Several points are noteworthy:

- Net assets vastly outweigh liabilities (due mainly to pensions).
- Actual investment in any given year is not the same as the change in the value of the outstanding stock, as the existing assets or liabilities change in value during the year.
- Roughly half of household savings are in pensions and life assurance, with the bulk of the remainder split between bank deposits and shares.
- Contributions to life assurance and pension funds are much more stable than the contributions to other savings vehicles, primarily because each year represents the continuation of a long-term agreement. There has been a net outflow from equities, quoted and unquoted, in recent years, possibly reflecting the reduction in buying following the decline in privatizations. Even so, the value of existing shareholdings has been rising rapidly.
- The main destination for discretionary saving is deposit accounts held at banks and building societies, though the amounts fluctuate markedly over the years, primarily in response to interest rate changes.
- Roughly three-quarters of loans are mortgages. The appetite for non-mortgage loans disappeared in the recession of the early 1990s, but had returned by the second half of the decade as a result of stronger economic growth and the prospect of sustainable lower interest rates. The increased use of in-store credit and interest-free offers as marketing tools has probably also boosted credit growth.
- The stock of mortgages is broadly equivalent to the total of high street bank and building society deposits.

Companies are a major influence on the whole economy. The performance of the other sectors depends on whether industry and commerce are in advance or in retreat. Companies account directly for less than a quarter of GDP through their profits and other income, yet they account for three-quarters of output and provide about three-quarters of all employment incomes through the wages and salaries they pay their employees. They undertake about two-thirds of all fixed capital investment. They are responsible for virtually all British exports of goods and services and they are major users and sources of finance for the banks and the capital markets. It is in this sector that we might see the 'animal spirits' that strongly influence the health of the economy.

Official statistics about companies are notoriously difficult to compile, and, although there have been many improvements in recent years, the data are still incomplete, subject to later revisions and extremely tricky even for experts fully to understand. The financial press and those working in the stock market are more influenced by the results of individual companies than by the aggregated official figures, which come out later and use different accounting concepts.

The value of official statistics is that they give a broader and more balanced picture than any results of individual companies, however large, and are a better guide to the performance of the economy as a whole. The problem is that extraordinarily little is published on a monthly basis. The only statistic of any note published monthly by the ONS is the index of output, and this is only for the production industries, i.e. excluding the output of the service industries. All the other information that we might want to know about corporate behaviour, such as profits, investment and employment, is available only quarterly or annually, or from private-sector surveys.

It is not clear how this situation of poor data came about. It is true to say, however, that a vicious circle of apathy and disinterest had arisen. Macro-economic commentators in the UK have devoted surprisingly little attention to the dynamics of the corporate sector and company profits compared with their counterparts in the US. The post-war interest was in demand-led Keynesian economics. Similarly, politicians were more interested in welfare issues than large companies, many of which were nationalized. There was also a relatively low priority traditionally attached to the theory of the firm and profits in UK academic culture. There was, accordingly, little need for statistics and little concern that they were of poor quality.

There is no simple answer to the question, 'How many businesses are there in the UK?' The Inter-departmental Business Register of the ONS is the most comprehensive source and holds information on around 2 million businesses. The register is limited to traders registered for VAT (1.6 million) and additional businesses with taxed employees. Of the 2 million, 600,000 are registered companies: the rest are predominantly sole proprietors and partnerships, although central and local government and non-profit bodies are also included. The IDBR misses the many businesses below the VAT threshold (£51,000 turnover a year, in 1999) that also have no taxed employees. Using the Labour Force Survey and Inland Revenue data, the ONS and DTI publish estimates annually: the latest suggests there are 3.7 million businesses in the UK, but those very small businesses not on the register account for less than 2 per cent of gross domestic product.

It is important to appreciate that the number of businesses is volatile, rising during times of economic prosperity and falling during recession. There is also an enormous turnover of businesses with over 10 per cent closing each year and a similar number being created. At any one time, half the businesses in the country will have been in existence for less than five years. The vast majority of businesses are small, with only 3,400, less than a tenth of 1 per cent, employing 500 or more people and 78,000 with between 20 and 499 employees. Attention tends to be focused on the few thousand large companies, or corporates, which tend to be public.

The corporate sector includes those companies that are defined as resident in the UK, rather than British-owned. In a national accounting sense, there are three types of company. First, UK private-sector companies. Second, UK affiliates of foreign companies (foreign affiliates of UK companies are excluded). Third, public corporations (PCs), such as the Civil Aviation Authority and the BBC. The act of privatization or nationalization of a company will distort the sectoral break-down of the statistics.

Analysis of the corporate data of the 1980s is fraught with difficulty as a result of the extensive privatization programme. Since 1979 around fifty large and many more smaller companies have been privatized, reducing the nationalized industries' share of GDP from 11 per cent in 1979 to barely 2 per cent in the early 1990s. The number of employees in the nationalized industries fell from nearly 2 million in 1979 to 300,000 in 1998, representing a fall in the share of workforce jobs over the period from 7 per cent to 1 per cent. The gross trading profits of the public corporations fell during the second half of the 1980s while those of the non-oil private sector broadly doubled.

More generally, the quality of the data in the corporate accounts was very low in the mid- to late 1980s, but the review of government statistics started in 1988 led to many changes. Key among these changes are: the establishment of the IDBR (Inter-departmental Business Register); improved surveys for company finance, capital formation, investment; a new quarterly survey for company profits; and the concentration of statistical work in the ONS. The coverage of the service sector was also improved.

In recognition of the old weaknesses, one of the targets set for the CSO as part of its new Agency status in the early 1990s concerned the size of the corporate sector balancing item. The balancing item effectively shows the extent to which the accounts do not add up. In the period 1983 to 1989, the balancing item of the industrial and commercial companies sector averaged around 2 per cent of GDP. The equivalent figure for the current definition of the corporate sector (non-financial corporate sector) has averaged below 1 per cent in the 1990s and has been under ½ per cent in most years. This strongly suggests that there have been improvements to the quality of the data. As analysts' confidence in the data grows, it is quite likely that corporate accounts will attract growing attention.

DATA RELEASES

The ONS publishes the quarterly corporate data as part of the sequence of GDP releases described in Chapter 4. The only major monthly data specific to the industrial sector is the index of output. A limited amount of other monthly aggregate data relating to the corporate sector – on prices, employment, tax receipts and overseas trade, for example – is dealt with in the respective chapters of this book. The ONS, either on its own or in partnership with other organizations, also publishes monthly press releases on usable steel production, vehicle output, machine tools and engineering turnover and orders. Some of the data are published in the ONS's monthly compendia of statistics but because of their specialized nature are of little interest to those studying the state of the macro economy.

Largely due to the paucity of data about the industrial sector, a large number of private-sector sponsored surveys have arisen in recent years. It would be fair to say that in the short-term economic commentary conducted in government, the markets and press, it is the monthly data on output or survey news on sentiment that are discussed most. The monetary policy debate has that as a background but also focuses on the global trade environment, the exchange rate and any other evidence that sheds light on likely corporate behaviour. The quarterly data on the corporate sector remain, however, a vital part of longer-term econometric forecasting, which is largely carried out on a quarterly basis.

THE QUARTERLY GDP RELEASES

The quarterly information about the corporate sector is progressively released in the three GDP releases each quarter (which are described in Chapter 4). The initial estimate of GDP is based on the monthly industrial output figures (see below, p. 181), but the release gives almost no break-down of what is happening in each sector. The second release, a month later, is more interesting. It gives a full break-down of output by industry sector and the first estimate of the gross operating surplus of corporations, as part of the income break-down of GDP, and investment, as part of the expenditure measure of GDP.

It is only on publication of the third GDP release that a picture of the corporate sector worthy of analysis emerges. As part of the income measure of GDP, the gross operating surplus of corporations (which was published in the second GDP release) is subdivided into financial and non-financial corporations and by public and private sector. More importantly, however, the third release sees the first publication of the accounts of the private non-financial corporation sector. The sources and methods for the collection of this quarterly data set are described in Chapter 4, which explains how the full GDP estimates are derived.

A sample account using 1998 data appears in Table 8.1. The primary account shows how total resources, or incomes, are derived. Rental income (amounts payable for the use of fixed assets) and property income (amounts accruing from lending or renting financial or tangible non-produced assets including land) are added to the gross trading profits.

Table 8.1. Private non-financial corporations' account, 1998

		£bn
Primary income account:		
1.	Gross trading profits	152.9
2.	Rental of buildings	10.6
3.	Inventory holding gains	0.6
4. (1+2+3)	Gross operating surplus	164.1
5.	Property income receipts	50.0
6. (4 + 5)	Total resources	214.1
7.	Total payments	117.2
8. (6–7)	Gross balance of primary incomes	96.9
Secondary distribution of income account:		
9.	Social benefits, transfers, etc. received	12.9
10.	Taxes	−25.6
11.	Social benefits, transfers, etc. paid	−13.2
12. (8+9+10+11)	Gross disposable income	70.9
Capital account:		
13.	Gross fixed capital formation	89.2
14	Inventories	3.0
15.	Other changes	0.4
16. (12–13–14–15)	Net lending (+)/borrowing (−)	−21.3

Source: ONS quarterly national accounts press release, March 1999.

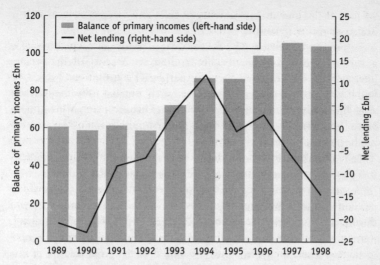

Fig. 8.1. Corporate sector financial balance and net lending

Various payments, mostly dividends and interest, are netted off to leave the gross balance of primary incomes. The secondary distribution of income account nets off taxes and other incomes and expenditure (mainly social security, transfers and insurance) to leave gross disposable income. The function of this gross, or undistributed, income is to finance capital expenditure, which is mostly investment, but also includes inventories or stocks, which are shown in the capital account.

The corporate accounts are complex and many of the numbers can be volatile from year to year. The annual *Blue Book* sets out the structure of the corporate account in six tables over just three pages. These tables show clearly how all the components fit together. Following the revisions to the structure of national accounts in 1998, much of the terminology is unfamiliar even to seasoned analysts. Many of the detailed break-downs in the *Blue Book* are published on only an annual basis, though some of the series can be derived. (In this area, as in many others, it is always worth approaching the ONS to see if data are available even if they are not formally published.)

Fig. 8.1 summarizes the experience of the corporate sector during the 1990s. The gross balance of primary incomes shows how tough the early 1990s' recession was. The reduction in interest rates and the fall in the value of the pound at the end of 1992, following sterling's exit from the exchange rate mechanism, had a dramatic effect and heralded a much more prosperous period. The financial strength of the corporate sector is summarized in the chart by net lending. After several years of very large deficits, the corporate sector experienced a run of surpluses. The years 1997 and 1998 were, however, much tougher. The pound had strengthened, the economy was slowing, yet expenditure on investment was continuing to grow rapidly. As a result companies again became large net borrowers.

The official statistics and much of the economic analysis tend to focus on non-financial corporations. This largely reflects their relative importance in the economy. Non-financials are 60 per cent of GDP, pay 77 per cent of salaries and make 60 per cent of investment. The contribution of the financials sector is 6, 10 and 4 per cent respectively. There are, however, many financial corporations in the economy and they are fully covered in the key publications, such as the *Blue Book*. The financials sector is split into monetary financial institutions, other financial intermediaries and financial auxiliaries, and insurance corporations and pension funds. In national accounting terms, the accounts of financial corporations are structured in the same way as their non-financial counterparts, but the differences in their businesses mean that they can look very different. For example, the interest payments and receipts of financials – in many cases a core component of the business – dwarf those of non-financials.

There is also much less distinction drawn today between the oil and non-oil sectors of the economy. The oil and gas sector is now referred to in the national accounts as the continental shelf company sector. The last decade has seen both the output and the average price of North Sea production fall so that the contribution to the economy is much less than it was in the early 1980s.

INVESTMENT AND STOCKBUILDING

Investment, in national accounting terminology, is referred to as gross capital formation (GCF). This roughly equates to gross fixed capital formation (GFCF), what would normally be called investment. Formally, however, gross capital formation also includes the change in inventories

Table 8.2. Gross capital formation, £bn

	1989	1994	1996	1997	1998
Gross fixed capital formation	122.2	113.0	122.0	130.5	141.3
Change in inventories	3.1	4.8	1.8	3.7	3.6
Change in valuables	—	0.1	−0.2	−0.2	0.3
TOTAL	125.5	118.0	123.7	134.0	145.1

Note: Constant 1995 prices.
Source: 1998 *Blue Book* and national accounts press release, March 1999.

(often referred to as stockbuilding or destocking) and the 'acquisitions less disposals of valuables' (large value items such as precious stones, art and antiques). Table 8.2 shows data for some recent years and compares them to the peak year for constant price GCF in the last cycle, 1989. In 1998, GCF was 19 per cent of GDP.

GFCF is defined as the acquisition less disposals of fixed assets and the improvement of land. To qualify, an asset must be used repeatedly or continuously in the production process for more than a year. It would include buildings and other structures, vehicles and other plant and machinery, and also plants and livestock which are used in production. It also includes intangible assets such as computer software and artistic originals. Investment is not always easy to define. For example, 'ordinary repairs and maintenance' are not investment while 'improvements' are. Qualification as investment also depends on the owner and the use. For example, a car sold to a company is investment while the same car sold to a household is not.

The initial estimate of GCF, in current and constant prices, is published in the second of the GDP releases (coming towards the end of the second month following the end of the quarter). The first detailed break-down of GCF (in constant prices) is released a month later in the third of the GDP releases. One table shows the break-down of investment (GFCF) and another shows the break-down of inventories. Table 8.3 shows the two break-downs of investment – by sector and by asset – with illustrative figures for 1998.

The break-down of investment and stockbuilding shown in the GDP release is insufficient for any serious analysis of trends. Fortunately there are additional releases, one devoted to each topic, which do provide the

Table 8.3. Break-down of investment, 1998

By asset:	£bn	By sector:	£bn
Transport equipment	15.1	Business investment	102.0
Other machinery	59.7	General government	10.1
Dwellings	23.7	NHS trusts	1.4
Other buildings	39.0	Other public corporations	0.3
Intangible assets	3.8	Private sector	27.5
TOTAL	141.3	TOTAL	141.3

Note: Constant prices.
Source: National accounts press release, March 1999.

necessary detail. The detailed release on investment is called 'Business investment' and, as the name suggests, it provides no break-down of public sector investment or investment in dwellings. This is unfortunate but not a major shortcoming. As Table 8.3 shows, business investment is the bulk of total investment (accounting for over 70 per cent of investment in 1998) and, in any case, it is private-sector business investment which is subject to the more interesting trends.

The detailed release breaks down business investment into thirteen industry groups and shows it in current and constant prices. It also shows a break-down of private-sector manufacturing investment by asset. Oddly, the business investment release has traditionally been released the day before the third GDP release. Since it offers detail of one of the components in the third GDP release, it would seem to make more sense to release it simultaneously (ideally in the same release). The ONS defends the current practice as it gives more weight to the need to avoid a clustering of press releases on one day. Publication on the day after the GDP release would make it impossible for those with econometric models fully to update their data on the day of GDP release.

Initial estimates of inventories are published in the second of the GDP releases, and again, in revised format, in the third release. The detailed break-down of stockbuilding is no longer released in the form of a press release. (It was until 1998.) Instead it is published as a so-called *Quarterly Volume*, roughly two weeks after the third GDP release.

Private sector gross fixed capital formation is highly dependent on the state of the economy. Indeed the capital expenditure cycle is more pronounced than that of GDP as a whole. Table 8.4 shows the current

Table 8.4. Gross fixed capital formation, £bn

	1990	1992	1994	1996	1997
Private sector	94.3	80.4	87.7	109.1	118.4
Of which:					
Dwellings	16.9	16.2	18.3	20.5	22.6
Transport equipment	9.3	7.0	10.0	11.3	13.4
Machinery and equipment	33.1	31.6	35.0	46.6	48.5
Public corporations	5.5	5.7	5.6	5.3	4.8
General government	14.6	14.2	14.1	11.3	10.5
TOTAL	114.3	100.3	107.4	125.7	133.7

Note: Current prices.
Source: 1998 *Blue Book*, table Sup2.

price investment figures for 1990, the peak year for investment in the last economic cycle, for 1992, the trough for investment, and for some of the recent years, which have seen renewed strength. It shows that investment in transport equipment is the most volatile. In percentage terms, investment in transport fell most sharply in the early 1990s and rose most sharply in the late 1990s. The main engine for investment growth in the second half of the 1990s came from the service sector. It is noteworthy how investment in the public sector is not related to the economic cycle.

Stockbuilding played a modest part in the economic picture of 1997 and 1998 (as the numbers in Table 8.5 testify), adding less than ½ per cent to GDP growth in each year. It is important to remember, however, that the level of stocks remains high (see first column in Table 8.5). As GDP was around £800 billion in 1997, it needs a shift in stocks of £8 billion between years to impact on GDP by 1 per cent.

Occasionally stockbuilding has had a dramatic impact on the aggregate economic figures. The whole of the 1980 recession, for example, was accounted for by the change from a positive to a negative stock build of 1 per cent of GDP from 1979 to 1980. The other components of demand were generally unchanged in real terms. In 1988, at the height of the economic boom, stockbuilding contributed two-thirds of 1 per cent to the total expansion in the economy of 5 per cent. In 1990, the year of greatest destocking, the run-down of stocks accounted for a decline of four-fifths of 1 per cent of GDP, in a year when there was barely any growth in the economy.

Table 8.5. Inventories, £bn

| | Level at end 1997 | Change in: | |
		1997	1998
Mining and quarrying	0.8	—	−0.1
Manufacturing	54.8	−0.1	0.4
Electricity, gas and water	1.8	0.1	−0.1
Wholesalers	24.2	0.7	0.4
Retailers	19.1	0.9	0.7
Other industries	31.9	2.0	2.2
TOTAL	132.6	3.7	3.6

Note: Constant prices.
Source: National accounts press release, March 1999.

Inventory levels are not spread across business sectors in proportion to output. Manufacturing, for example, holds two-fifths of inventories in the economy yet produces only one-fifth of the output. On account of the importance of manufacturing, total inventories for that sector are split into three categories: materials and fuel, work in progress and finished goods. Each component comprises roughly a third of the total but the change in any period can be dramatically different in each. This breakdown, plus the subdivision into the various industry groups, allows some conclusions about stockbuilding to be drawn.

The figures for stockbuilding are, however, both highly volatile and among the least accurate of government economic figures. Accordingly, they tend to be given relatively little attention when they are released each quarter. While stock figures have little impact on economic policy on a month to month basis, trends in stockbuilding become important when making an economic forecast over the next year or two.

For the sake of simplicity, the change in stocks is usually expressed as a percentage of GDP. It is rarely over 1 per cent and usually less. To gauge the impact of stock changes on GDP changes, we have to take the difference in stockbuilding as a percentage of GDP between one year and the next. This most useful figure is still surprisingly absent from most official statistics.

Perhaps the easiest way to view the trends in stocks is by reference to stock ratios. The monthly ONS publication *Economic Trends* publishes manufacturing stocks as a ratio to manufacturing production, retail stocks relative to retail sales and total stocks to GDP. In general, stock ratios have declined, as firms have become more efficient at controlling stock levels. The decline during the mid- to late 1990s, however, was modest, as the generally lower level of interest rates has made it less expensive to carry stocks.

THE CLASSIFICATION OF INDUSTRY

It is important to be aware of the existence of the Standard Industrial Classification, as it is the basis for the classification of business establishments. The SIC was first introduced in Britain in 1948, but has been revised on a number of occasions since, most recently in 1992. Revision is necessary from time to time to allow for the introduction of new products and the evolution of industrial structure.

Over the years there have been great efforts to compile a single classification usable in all countries. This has been only partly achieved. The United Nations introduced one system, called ISIC, in 1989, while the EU agreed their system, called NACE, in 1990. While there are many similarities between the two classifications they are not the same. The UK's SIC is based exactly on the NACE system, but adds some extra sub-divisions for additional detail. The SIC has a hierarchical five-digit system. At the highest level of aggregation, SIC(92) is divided into seventeen sections, each denoted by a letter. For example, section D, which includes divisions 15 to 37, is manufacturing and within that, sub-class 17.40/1 is the manufacture of soft furnishings.

The SIC categories and the corresponding break-down used in GDP(I) and the monthly index of output of the production industries are shown in Table 8.6.

Fig. 8.2 shows the weights of the various industrial categories in GDP, at 1995 prices. The traditional references to industrial sectors as being primary, secondary or tertiary are not often used these days. That said, in broad terms the first two components, agriculture and mining (A–C), would correspond to the primary category. Manufacturing, utility supply and construction (D–F), would correspond to the secondary category. This leaves the service sector (G–Q), roughly two-thirds of the economy, as the tertiary sector.

Table 8.6. Classification of industry

SIC categories	GDP(I)/IOP categories
A Agriculture, hunting and forestry B Fishing	Agriculture, forestry and fishing
C Mining and quarrying	Mining and quarrying
D Manufacturing	Manufacturing
E Electricity, gas and water supply	Electricity, gas and water supply
F Construction	Construction
G Wholesale and retail, repairs H Hotels and restaurants	Distribution, hotels and catering, repairs
I Transport, storage and communication	Transport, storage and communication
J Financial intermediation K Real estate, renting and business activities	Business services and finance
L Public administration, defence and social security M Education N Health and social work O Other community, social and personal services P Private households with employed persons Q Extraterritorial organizations and bodies	Government and other services

There is enormous disparity between the growth rates of different industrial sectors. The index numbers for output in any recent period show this with great clarity. The star performer in the second half of the 1990s was the category of transport, storage and communication. It grew by an average of about 6 per cent in each year. Over the same period manufacturing, by contrast, hardly grew at all.

It could be said that there are three different kinds of industrial sector. First, the output of some industries is closely related to the economic cycle, for example, distribution and retailing. Construction is a sector that exaggerates the cycle with more marked booms and busts. Second, some sectors seem largely immune to the cycle and experience steady growth, come what may. The utilities and government services, such as education and health, are good examples. Finally, there are industrial sectors such as agriculture

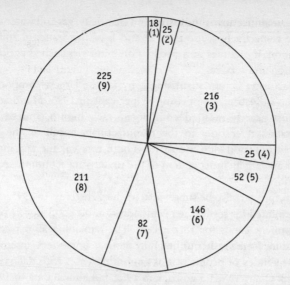

Key 1 Agriculture, forestry and fishing
     2 Mining and quarrying
     3 Manufacturing
     4 Electricity, gas and water supply
     5 Construction
     6 Distribution, hotels and catering, repairs
     7 Transport, storage and communication
     8 Business services and finance
     9 Government and other services

Fig. 8.2. Shares of GDP by industrial category

and mining that experience their own pronounced cycles, which are usually largely independent of the broader economic cycle.

THE INDEX OF OUTPUT OF THE PRODUCTION INDUSTRIES (IOP)

This monthly indicator from the ONS comes out some twenty-six working days, just over a month, after the end of the month. The production industries, all of which are covered by the survey, made up 27 per cent of GDP in 1995. The production industries comprise mining and quarrying, manufacturing industries and electricity, gas and water supply. These are respectively sections C, D and E of the Standard Industrial Classification. It excludes non-production industries such as agriculture, construction and services.

Manufacturing is, not surprisingly, by far the largest component of production industries, comprising 81 per cent in 1995. Manufacturing is the most eagerly awaited component each month. Indeed, many commentators refer only to the manufacturing result as the energy component of production industries is both very volatile and moves in ways that are largely independent of the underlying economic trends in the economy.

Total output can also be subdivided by market sector. In 1995, durable goods accounted for some 5 per cent, non-durable goods for 21 per cent and investment goods for 18 per cent. The remaining 55 per cent was accounted for by the rather unhelpfully named component 'intermediate goods'. The index of production is a monthly series with data available from 1968. Quarterly data go back to 1952 and annual data to 1948.

The index of output of the production industries is compiled from around 250 separate indicators from different sectors of industry. Most are available monthly but some are available only quarterly. Most are obtained by the ONS but the Department of Trade and Industry provides some of the information on the energy sector and the Ministry of Agriculture, Fisheries and Food provides data relating to the food industries.

The purpose is to measure net output or value added, that is, total outputs less inputs, in constant prices. Sales information is deflated to base year prices using price indices compiled by the ONS. Home sales are converted using the output producer price index for the appropriate industry. Export sales are deflated by export price information collected directly in those industries which are most important to the IOP. All the figures are seasonally adjusted then combined into broader categories and then into the three SICs which make up the production industries.

The seasonal adjustment is important as some of the series have strong seasonal patterns reflecting factors such as the weather, Christmas, August car registrations (up until 1998) and summer holidays. The seasonal factors are re-estimated every month for the current and latest month, contributing to the frequent revisions of the data. (The most recent months are also revised as the initial estimates are based on partial information.) Once a year new factors are employed for a long span, generally in the autumn in the quarterly round after the *Blue Book*. Unadjusted data are available from the ONS.

The quality of the output data has greatly improved over the last decade and the last few years have seen relatively modest revisions and little bias. This is in marked contrast to the situation prevailing in the mid-1980s when the initial estimates of the data were always being revised up to show stronger output growth. These errors contributed to the fundamental rethink about official statistics discussed in earlier chapters, and led to the many improvements in collection and processing. The index of production is one of the earliest and now most accurate components of GDP and therefore influences the initial estimates of GDP perhaps more than any other single indicator.

A number of improvements in data collection are worthy of mention. First, the IOP has become progressively dependent on the Monthly Production Inquiries (MPI) which have been enlarged to industries where reliance had previously been on quarterly data or on trade association information. The current MPI sample size is 9,000. Second, data collection has been dramatically improved with respect to stocks. The quarterly stocks inquiry was enlarged and made statutory in the early 1990s. Subsequently, monthly stocks inquiries were introduced for companies operating in the computer, aerospace and shipbuilding industries, which have particularly large and volatile stock holdings. Third, there have been substantial improvements to the methodology associated with exports.

The five-yearly re-basing, which was last carried out in 1998 to put the series on 1995 weights, can lead to a more substantial re-writing of history than the normal revisions. The revisions usually led to a stronger trend in output, largely because the more distant the last re-weighting, the greater the weight given to declining industries and the smaller the weight given to expanding industries.

Table 8.7 shows how the weights of industrial production have changed over the last decade or so. By far the most dramatic change since the 1985 weights were introduced has been the decline in the importance of oil and gas extraction. The other primary industry, mining and quarrying, has also seen its share of the total fall. Most of the other components have experienced a corresponding rise, though it is clear that some of the traditional industries, such as textiles, have declined relative to others, such as chemicals.

Table 8.7. Industrial output: evolution of weights

		Parts per 1000		
		1985	1990	1995
C	Mining and quarrying	215	77	96
CA	Oil and gas extraction	180	59	80
CB	Mining and quarrying	35	18	16
D	Manufacturing	706	844	812
DA	Food, beverage and tobacco	91	110	108
DB to DC	Textiles and textile products	47	47	44
DF	Coke, petrol, nuclear fuel	18	23	18
DG	Chemicals and manmade fibres	72	86	91
DJ	Metals and metal products	63	73	93
DK to DM	Engineering (various)	258	302	251
_*	Other*	157	202	208
E	Electricity, gas and water	79	79	92
C+D+E	Production industries	1000	1000	1000

Note: *'Other' includes, for example, wood, paper and printing, rubber and plastics, non-metallic minerals, SIC sub-sections DD, DE, DH, DI and DN.

There is always a healthy debate about the current state of manufacturing industry and its ability to satisfy domestic and export demand. The intensity of the debate reflects not only the experience of the last thirty years, which, as Fig. 8.3 shows, has been anything other than smooth, but also the lobbying power of some of the companies and their representative organizations.

The 1970s was a grim and volatile time which saw output expand by an average of less than 1 per cent in each year. The recession at the start of the 1980s caused a 15 per cent fall in manufacturing output. The trend was then firmly up for a decade prior to the commencement of the recession in 1990. Although the early 1990s' recession was as deep as that of a decade before, the manufacturing sector was less severely hit. All recessions are different and that of the early 1990s was prompted primarily by high interest rates that hit consumers directly rather than the corporate sector. Also, by the late 1980s, industry was leaner and fitter than in the 1970s and more able to withstand a slowdown.

Due to their nature and despite the quality improvements, the data

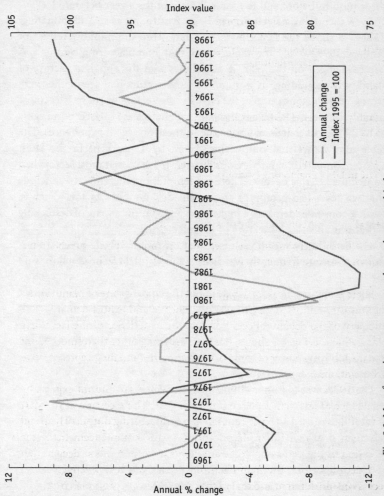

Fig. 8.3. Manufacturing output – annual growth rate and index

can be highly erratic from month to month. Accordingly, it is common amongst analysts to look at trends in terms of the format in the monthly press release, i.e. output in the previous three months compared with the three months before and the same three months a year before.

Even then the data release can be as frustrating as it is illuminating. Table 8.8 shows the key growth rate data from the monthly release of January 1999. While the table shows that manufacturing output was barely changed on the year, it also shows that the apparent picture of stability is misleading, as a number of the sectors had seen either very strong growth (for example, the engineering sector) or sharp falls (most notably textiles). The text accompanying the release offered no insights as to the factors that were giving rise to these divergent experiences. The table also shows that output had fallen by 1 per cent in the latest quarter compared to the previous quarter. It seems that most sectors had contributed to this decline. There is a temptation, therefore, to conclude that whatever had prompted this recent decline was a factor – such as weaker consumer demand, a higher exchange rate or a spate of destocking – that was affecting all sectors of manufacturing.

Of the industry specific releases, that on motor vehicle production is one of the more frequently watched. It shows total car production, split

Table 8.8. Trends in production industries' output

	Latest quarter compared to:	
	3 months before	3 months a year ago
Production industries	−0.9	0.7
Mining, quarrying, extraction	−0.6	4.5
Electricity, gas and water supply	0.2	3.9
Manufacturing	−1.1	−0.1
Of which:		
Coke, petrol, nuclear fuels	−3.0	−6.7
Chemicals and manmade fibres	−0.7	1.5
Basic metals	−3.2	−3.0
Engineering	−0.2	3.4
Food, drink and tobacco	−0.8	−2.3
Textiles, etc.	−4.6	−9.1
Other	−0.9	−0.5

Source: ONS. Figures from the January 1999 release of the November 1998 data. Data are published in greater break-down in the ONS *Monthly Digest*.

according to whether it is for the domestic or export market, and total commercial vehicle production. There are times when information about this industry, one of the largest in the country, can be of interest. The release is not, however, very expansive and the more detailed information that would be needed for any serious analysis is published in the monthly *Business Monitor* on motor vehicle production.

In the late 1990s, the ONS introduced a new quarterly press release called *Distributive and Services Trades*. The release results from new inquiries launched in 1991 and 1992 as a result of the initiatives to improve the quality of data and evolved from the now-defunct *Business Monitor SDQ10*. The release shows turnover data for thirteen main components of the service sector and a number of sub-divisions. Business services, for example, are broken down into eight categories including advertising and industrial cleaning. In the year to the fourth quarter of 1998 some components, such as courier activities, software consultancy and motorcycle sales, saw turnover grow by over 20 per cent, while car repair, adult education and some wholesaling activities saw turnover fall. In 1999 the ONS started publishing prototype monthly figures for services output.

PRIVATE-SECTOR SURVEYS

There has been an explosion of private-sector surveys in the last decade. Many of these are still quite new and as we do not yet have data for a full economic cycle, their real value is hard to judge. The main plus and minus points of surveys in general are summarized at the end of this chapter. It is noteworthy that the Bank of England's quarterly inflation report – the forecasting and analytic benchmark – typically refers to a number of the surveys. Several of the more prominent surveys are now considered, starting with that produced by the Confederation of British Industry (CBI), which is probably followed more thoroughly than any of the others.

The vast majority of private-sector industry surveys are presented in the form of a diffusion index. That is, the questions offer a three-way answer of up, same or down. The results are normally presented in terms of a single number, a positive or negative balance between 'ups' and 'downs', ignoring the 'sames'. Some of the surveys claim that a positive number should be interpreted as a rise in what is being measured and a negative number as a fall. But this is by no means universal as the numbers do not necessarily have any significance, so the diffusion approach means that it is especially important to look at the trend in recent months or quarters.

CBI INDUSTRIAL TRENDS SURVEY

Once a quarter the CBI sends a questionnaire to a weighted sample of 1,200 to 1,500 manufacturing firms. A shorter questionnaire is sent out to the same sample in the intervening months. Thus, usually in the fourth week of the month, the CBI issues either a monthly or a quarterly industrial trends survey. The results are published only two weeks after the closing date for replies and only four weeks after the questionnaires first reach companies, so the results offer an up-to-date assessment of the state of the economy.

The survey covers both the situation during the period prior to the questionnaire being filled in, and the expectation for the following period. Although the replies are qualitative rather than quantitative, they do make it possible to assess developments in manufacturing industry before the official statistics are available. The CBI surveys are published with a commentary by the organization's economics staff.

The monthly inquiry asks five questions covering total order books, export order books, stocks of finished goods, the volume of output and average prices. The quarterly inquiry's thirty or so questions also cover optimism about the business situation and exports, capital expenditure, numbers employed, new orders, deliveries, stocks of raw materials and work in progress, the length of order books, factors limiting output and exports, adequacy of capacity and the factors limiting capital expenditure. Full results are available for eleven sectors and around fifty sub-sectors within manufacturing. Results are also given split by company size, and for Scotland and Wales.

On release of the quarterly survey, attention is initially focused on the business optimism index. The breadth of the survey does, however, lend itself to rather more detailed analysis. Accordingly, in the hours and days that follow its release, commentators use this survey to enhance their picture of the state of manufacturing industry. The monthly survey is easier to summarize as there are only five questions. Attention tends to be focused on the output and prices balance.

The survey is also interesting as it allows out-turn to be compared with expectations. An out-turn balance in one survey can easily be compared with the corresponding expectations balance from the previous survey. If expectations have run ahead of out-turn over several surveys, it would be reasonable to expect a sharper fall in the months ahead to realign the two.

The CBI research suggests that the level of the balance is better correlated with changes in the level of the corresponding official statistics than with the levels themselves. In other words, if 20 per cent more businessmen think output will go up rather than down month after month, the implication is that output is rising by the same amount each month, rather than that it is staying at the same level each month without rising.

The survey was introduced in 1958. (It became quarterly in 1972 and the monthly survey was introduced in 1975.) The resultant long run of results gives the survey a track record that is not shared by the more recently introduced surveys. The CBI survey played a very important role in the mid- to late 1980s, when the quality of the official data was at its lowest. Indeed, government statisticians used the results of the CBI survey as a check on the official output data.

Although there is usually a close relationship between the trends in the official data and the CBI survey, this is not always the case. In particular, over the short term, from quarter to quarter, there can be significant divergence (see Fig. 8.4). The survey, in common with most of the surveys, is most useful when help is needed in providing support for the view that a turning point in the economic cycle has been reached. One strength of the CBI survey data is that there are no revisions. This is an important asset especially at the turning point in the cycle. There have been instances where the official data have not initially shown a turning point, which appeared only after subsequent revisions.

One of the principal reasons why the CBI survey is the most closely followed of all the surveys is the 'honesty' with which it is presented. The CBI is keen to ensure that the survey's results are correctly interpreted. To aid this process they periodically conduct 'questionnaires on the

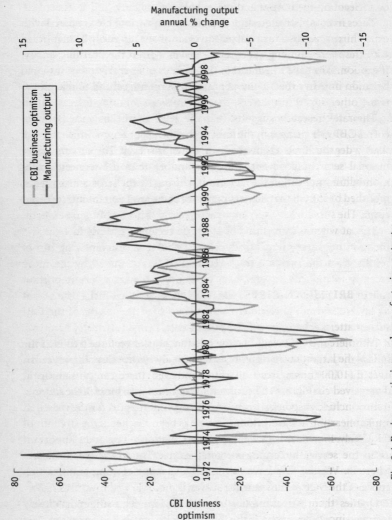

Fig. 8.4. Business optimism and manufacturing output

questionnaire'. The latest of these was conducted during the summer of 1998 and threw up a number of important observations. First, over 90 per cent of respondents said that the survey was completed at a senior level. Second, even though there is some ambiguity and a variety of practices in completing questions, there is stability in these practices over time. Third, the question on capacity working has a number of dimensions so the response cannot just be interpreted as a direct measure of capacity utilization. The CBI's reports on the surveys offer many other insights which do improve the quality of any analysis of the results. Unlike most of the other survey producers, the CBI makes economic forecasts that incorporate their survey results.

The CBI also publishes a number of additional surveys which are, to varying degrees, linked to the industrial trends survey. The surveys cover financial services; consumer, business and professional services; small and medium enterprises; the regions; and property. Each of these surveys is published by the CBI in partnership with a company from the appropriate sector. The surveys have varying structures and histories but can be worth looking at when information about the given sector is desired.

BRITISH CHAMBERS OF COMMERCE

If size mattered, the *Quarterly Economic Survey* from the British Chambers of Commerce (BCC) would be the one that markets followed most. The BCC is the largest business representative body in the UK and represents around 110,000 businesses in all sectors and of all sizes through its network of approved chambers. The survey for the fourth quarter of 1998 was the first to include responses from over 10,000 companies, which together employ nearly 1 million people.

Roughly 40 per cent of respondents are manufacturers and 60 per cent are in the service sector. Of the total sample, around 40 per cent are exporters. While the sample covers a wide range of company size the nature of the BCC means that the survey is more skewed towards smaller companies than, for example, the CBI surveys. The survey has been running since 1985.

The survey is conducted during the final month of each quarter with results being published in the first month of the following quarter. The survey is conducted by individual Chambers of Commerce and then collated by region. The national summary is then brought together by the BCC. The survey is thorough, asking a wide range of questions about home and export orders, employment, cashflow, investment, confidence and prices. The results are split by manufacturing and service sector and are available by region. Unfortunately the survey document publishes data for only the latest and preceding quarters. While it also includes some charts covering a longer time horizon, the numbers required for analysis are not always to hand (though they are available from the BCC).

The impact of the survey on financial markets is probably limited by the fact that there is no co-ordination of the release among regions. This means that the regions will usually publish their local results in the week up to the publication of the national result. The drip-drip approach probably raises media coverage but it reduces the market impact.

PURCHASING MANAGERS

The Chartered Institute of Purchasing and Supply (CIPS) is the national body representing supply chain professionals. The members of the Institute determine the needs of enterprises, identify reliable and economic sources of supply, and control the performance of services and flow of goods through corporations. As such, it is felt that its members are well placed to gauge the health of the UK corporate sector. CIPS is the UK sister organization to the National Association of Purchasing Management in the US.

The report on manufacturing has been published monthly since 1992. Questionnaires are sent to a stratified sample of around 500 companies. Survey responses reflect the change, if any, in the current month compared to the previous month based on data collected mid-month. For each of the indicators the report shows the net difference between the number of higher/better responses and lower/worse responses. A diffusion index reading above 50 per cent indicates an overall increase in that variable, below 50 per cent indicates an overall decrease.

The 'headline' Purchasing Managers' Index (PMI) is a composite indicator designed to provide an overall view of activity in the manufacturing sector and act as a leading indicator for the whole economy. It is a weighted combination of the responses to the questions on new orders, output, employment, suppliers' delivery times and stocks of items purchased. The three additional regular questions asked concern prices, stocks of finished goods and the quantity of purchases. The aggregate index is the most important single figure, but responses to each of the individual questions can be of equal interest depending on the circumstances prevailing in the economy. The series are available seasonally adjusted and unadjusted. The former is subject to revision as the estimation of the seasonal factors changes over time.

The CIPS also publishes a longer leading indicator in its report on manufacturing. This is designed to indicate turning points in economic activity one year in advance. The series has helped to plug a gap left when the ONS decided to cease publication of its leading indicators in the late 1990s. The CIPS index includes job vacancies, television advertising, retail sales, interest rates, consumer credit, economic optimism, house prices and share prices.

The purchasing managers' report, as it is called, is one of the more helpful and thorough of the non-official surveys. While the detail that it provides helps to add 'colour' to the economic picture, the predictive power is, as with many of the surveys, subject to much debate. The PMI can certainly claim some successes, but it has also given some false steers. The CIPS should be congratulated for honesty, openness and helpfulness as it includes in its monthly report a number of comparisons of its series with official series. As a result, the reader is much clearer about what is being offered and what can sensibly be claimed. By way of illustration, Fig. 8.5 compares manufacturing output as measured by the CIPS with

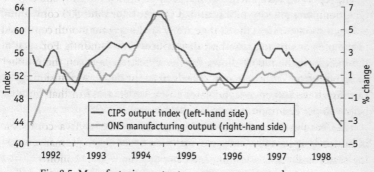

Fig. 8.5. Manufacturing output – measures compared

the ONS version. The CIPS version has been advanced by two months and both are plotted as three-month moving averages.

The CIPS also produces monthly reports on construction and services, the latter excluding retail and wholesale businesses. The surveys help to fill gaps in the ONS data set and provide helpful background information, but as both are still relatively new (having started in 1997 and 1996 respectively), they have yet to build up a useful track record.

3i UK ENTERPRISE BAROMETER

3i, the venture capital company, has been conducting a quarterly survey of companies since 1988. The core questions are the same in each survey. The first three questions attempt to assess the overall business and political climate. Questions concerning the desirability of starting a new business, expanding an existing business or embarking on growth by acquisition, are combined to derive the headline Index. There are also regular questions on the topics of employment, turnover, investment and profitability. All of these questions, bar the last, have been running since 1988. Various break-downs of the total, according to the age of the business, the business sector and the turnover are available.

Each survey is supplemented by topical questions on, for example, interest rates, the role of non-executive directors or various government initiatives. While some of these questions, for example on skill shortages and European integration, are repeated periodically, the data set is inevitably less complete.

Questionnaires are typically sent out towards the start of the first month of each quarter. The cut-off date for responses is normally four weeks. The survey results are published during the second month of each quarter. Unusually for a survey, there can be revisions to earlier data as late responses from earlier surveys are added to the database. Questionnaires are sent to a random sample of 1,000 UK companies in which 3i has an investment. The response rate for the November 1998 survey was 40 per cent. Their portfolio of companies is approximately 3,000 and individual companies are usually mailed no more than twice each year. The sample is large enough to give some confidence in the trend and the aggregate responses, but inevitably the sample sizes for break-downs are small.

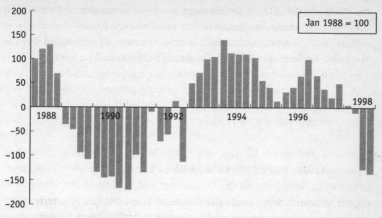

Fig. 8.6. Business sentiment – 3i Index

3i claims that their Index did predict the emergence from recession in mid-1991 and the decline in growth from mid-1994. The survey also showed a sharp fall in output during 1998. The survey is not, however, in common with all other surveys, a foolproof aid to predicting the course of the economy. The level of the Index can be highly volatile from quarter to quarter. For example, the Index recorded a sequence of −133, −8, −68, −55, +14, −111, +49 and +72, over the two-year period from the third quarter of 1991 to the second quarter of 1993. Over the same period the annual change in GDP went from minus 2 per cent to plus 2 per cent. While the trend in the Index was clearly right, the quarter to quarter fluctuations made interpretation very difficult. For example, the very sharp fall in the fourth quarter of 1992 (to −111) reflected sterling's exit from the Exchange Rate Mechanism. Business sentiment was clearly severely hit, but the path of output was unaffected. This illustrates the difficulty of using surveys of sentiment for predicting real economic activity. Similarly, it was hard to know what to make of the very sharp fall in the Index in the third and fourth quarters of 1998. Output did not fall as sharply as suggested. (See Fig. 8.6.)

The survey does act, however, as useful corroboration of emerging trends and the break-downs within it help with the 'picture painting' and 'story telling' side of forecasting. It was interesting, for example, that from 1995 onwards the survey showed that manufacturing companies experienced less of an improvement in the business climate than their non-manufacturing counterparts. The new business balance has also been a good lead indicator of new business creation as measured by, for example, the NatWest measure based on bank account activity.

DUN AND BRADSTREET

Dun and Bradstreet (D&B) is a provider of commercial credit and business marketing information. The quarterly survey of UK business expectations is driven by the US parent and is carried out in eighteen countries worldwide. It asks questions on sales, profits, prices, employment, new orders, exports and inventories. It has been running since 1988, although some of the questions were added more recently. The results are available by region.

The survey is conducted in the first two weeks of the final month of the quarter, with the results being published in the middle of the first month of the following quarter. The sample is selected by size, sector and region from over three million companies on the D&B database. Although the response rate, at around 20 per cent, is low, the survey still has 1,500 to 1,800 responses and has the benefit that Dun and Bradstreet is an 'independent' company.

ENGINEERING EMPLOYERS' FEDERATION

The Engineering Employers' Federation presents the results of its business trends survey in a quarterly document called *Engineering Trends*. The survey is conducted through the federation's network of thirteen regional associations covering the whole of the UK. It is conducted during the second month of the quarter with the deadline for responses at the beginning of the third month and publication at the end of the quarter. The sample size fluctuates around 1,700 with a response rate of typically 50 per cent.

The national figures are derived by weighting results from each region according to the number of employees in its member companies, and are presented as a diffusion index. Questions are asked about output, new orders (domestic and export), employment, capital expenditure plans and full capacity working. The survey has been running since the early 1990s.

The survey provides useful information about the engineering sector, which is the largest single component of manufacturing (about a third). Media and financial market interest in the survey fluctuates according to the plight of manufacturing. Accordingly, in the second half of the 1990s, when there was considerable debate about the level of the currency, the survey was of interest. The survey is presented alternately with a supplement on either the economic outlook or employment prospects.

SO ARE THE SURVEYS WORTH FOLLOWING?

Perhaps surprisingly given the importance of the suite of surveys, there has been little real analysis of their merits. Some of the major pluses and minuses are clear. The advantages of surveys are:

- Timeliness. The official data on output and prices in manufacturing industry are reasonably timely, but much of the other information, on profits and inventories, for example, and especially anything on services, is far less timely. The surveys therefore provide an early insight into what is happening in the economy.
- Forward looking. Official data are by definition backward looking. Surveys are less historic and are often more forward looking. If a survey can boast respondents who occupy senior positions in the company, the results can be illuminating.
- Corroborative information. It is always dangerous to rely on one single source or series. It is reassuring to have several surveys which support either each other or the trends shown in the official data, especially at turning points.
- New information. While some of the information might not be too useful or of great interest to a macro-analyst, it is always good to have additional descriptive 'colour' when assessing the state of the economy. Surveys do in general promote understanding, add value and offer unusual break-downs and anecdotal support for trends seen in official data.

● Popularity. The surveys have a following in the markets and media, so they can prompt market reaction even if the reaction is not justified! The popularity is based on several survey 'successes'.

Possible problems are:

● Balances (see p. 187) are meaningless. The questions seek qualitative and not quantitative responses with the consequence that the resulting balances have no meaning in isolation. While such surveys make the job of respondents easier, it is clear that they imply a loss of information. We never know whether a response of 'higher' means just a little higher or very much higher. Some fairly complex interpretation is often required to relate diffusion indices to the official series of monthly and quarterly statistics.
● Confusion over time periods. Most of the surveys ask their questions relative to different periods. Some ask about the latest month compared to the preceding month, some about the last four months and others about the latest month compared to the same month a year before. Even then, as research has shown, respondents fail to understand precisely what is being asked of them and can answer a 'different' question. In the CBI survey, for example, respondents are asked about the trend 'over the past four months'. CBI research shows that while most view this as meaning the last four months as a whole compared to the preceding four months, some interpret it as the trend during the four-month period, or in the last four months compared to the same four months a year before.
● Imperfect samples. The samples are often far from perfect. They can be self-selecting – and clearly are to the extent that the sample is usually comprised of members of an organization. The surveys are voluntary and sometimes have low response rates. The official series based on a business register and with compulsory response is likely to be better.
● What is 'the same'? It is not uncommon for a very large minority or even the majority of respondents to answer a question as 'the same'. It is, however, most unlikely that whatever is being measured will be exactly the same as in the previous period. CBI research, again, has shown that some respondents feel that fluctuations of over 5 per cent are still worthy of the answer 'the same'.
● Seasonal adjustment. Tests have shown that whether respondents are asked for answers seasonally adjusted or unadjusted, some will answer

'adjusted' regardless. CBI research has shown that respondents tend either to take account of seasonal variation in giving their response or to make no attempt on the grounds that seasonality is not significant. In this sense, many of the surveys are partly seasonally adjusted even if they claim to be unadjusted. While the survey should be largely free of seasonal influence, careful examination shows that some of the balances in some of the surveys do reveal a seasonal pattern. Business optimism in the CBI survey, for example, is nearly always higher in April than in January. This so-called 'spring effect' is attributed to the introduction of the New Year prices and passing of the spring Budget.

● Sentiment distortions. It is both the strength and weakness of these qualitative surveys that they are affected by sentiment. A number of factors, such as changes to the timing of the government's annual Budget and sterling's exit from the exchange rate mechanism, have affected survey results over the years. Such events have ultimately had little impact on the real economy as reflected in official statistics. It is, of course, impossible to tell how much of the survey to survey volatility reflects factors which will not influence real activity.

9 | Overseas Trade

The monthly trade figures were probably the most important of all the economic indicators in the post-war period, certainly up until the 1980s. During the Bretton Woods period of fixed exchange rates up to 1972, a deficit or a series of deficits in the trade figures was regarded as the signal for a rise in bank interest rates. This would both bring in capital to finance the deficit and slow down the growth of the economy, reducing the demand for imports and switching resources into exports and saving. If this treatment did not work, bad trade figures could trigger off speculation about devaluation. (Devaluation of the pound against the dollar only actually happened twice under Bretton Woods, in 1949 and 1967.)

When the UK and other countries moved to floating exchange rates, the trade figures became a signal of changes in the exchange rate, which, once removed, led to changes in interest rates, particularly if a persistent fall in the currency was developing. In the economic boom of the late 1980s, the trade figures came to the fore as a large deficit on the current account appeared. It was only when the UK moved towards current account balance during the first half of the 1990s, and there was a reduction in the volatility of the figures, that the trade figures took a back seat. At least, that was, up until early 1999, when a deficit once again seemed to be emerging.

In broad terms, there are two ways to reduce an external trade deficit. First, it is possible to pursue policies to reduce the volume of imports desired in the deficit country by reducing the rate of economic growth. Lower domestic demand will also encourage producers in the economy to seek export markets. Second, it is possible to change relative prices by devaluing the exchange rate. Following devaluation, imports become more expensive and exports become cheaper, tending to depress the demand for imports and boost exports. There is thus both a price effect and an income effect.

The practice of importing and exporting is also central to the concept of economic development. At one level, imports of goods and services are attractive because either they are products that cannot be produced domestically or there is a comparative quality or price advantage in buying them from abroad. But too many imports or the wrong sort of imports may displace domestic production and strain financial resources. It is common practice to measure import penetration for a country. Imports of goods and services, measured as a percentage of GDP, are a crude measure of the degree of dependence on imports, with a higher figure indicating that an economy is more vulnerable to changes beyond its borders. Japan and the USA have below average import penetration of around 10 per cent of GDP. Other countries, such as Sweden or The Netherlands, have higher figures of over 40 per cent. The EU average import penetration is around 25 to 30 per cent, depending on definition, roughly in line with the UK's. On the whole, it should be obvious that, the smaller the country, the higher the percentage of imports and exports. Exports generate foreign currency earnings, improve product quality through global competition and boost GDP growth.

TERMINOLOGY AND CONCEPTS

As in some other areas of statistics, the terminology associated with the balance of payments can make the statistics difficult to understand at first sight. The balance of payments is a collective term for the accounts of a country with the rest of the world. Once it is appreciated that the figures are nothing more than an accounting record of international flows, built up in a series of layers, the accounts become easier to understand. As with the main economic accounts of the country (and the introduction of ESA95), the structure of the balance of payments figures was also overhauled in 1998, and brought into line with the IMF *Balance of Payments Manual*, fifth edition. (A summary of the main changes is presented in the introduction of the 1998 edition of *United Kingdom Balance of Payments*, known as the *Pink Book*.)

Box 9.1. **Double entry accounting**

The accounting conventions are simple in that the accounts are double entry – every transaction is entered twice. In theory, every credit entry in the current, capital and financial accounts should be matched by a corresponding debit entry so that the total current, capital and financial account credits should equal total debits. Double entry accounting conventions used in the balance of payments figures consist of:

Credit entries	*Debit entries*
Exports of goods and services	Imports of goods and services
Income receivable	Income payable
Transfer receipts	Transfer payments
Increases in financial account liabilities	Increases in financial account assets
Decreases in financial account assets	Decreases in financial account liabilities .

For example, a British export of a good, recorded as a credit entry on the current account, would be matched by a debit entry such as:

● An increase in UK assets abroad (e.g. an increase in UK residents' deposits with banks abroad).
● A decrease in UK liabilities abroad (e.g. a fall in sterling deposits from abroad with UK banks).
● In the case of a barter transaction, by imports of a similar value.

For the first two, a current account credit is matched by a debit in the financial account while for the third, both halves of the transactions are recorded in the current account.

The trade account between one country and another, or more typically between one country and the rest of the world, can be struck at any one of a number of levels. The usual aggregates are (and are qualified in Table 9.1):

● The visible trade balance. Exports of goods less imports of goods, i.e. the net export of goods.

- The trade balance. The visible trade balance plus the services balance, i.e. the net exports of services such as travel, transportation and insurance.
- The current account balance. The trade balance plus the net impact of the inflows and outflows of 'invisible' income, from earnings mainly from investments and government grants. Investment income is broken down into four categories: direct investment, portfolio investment, other investment (such as earnings on trade credit) and reserve assets.
- The capital account. This comprises the transfers of ownership of fixed assets, transfers of funds associated with the acquisition or disposal of financial assets and cancellation of liabilities by creditors without any counterparts being received in return. (This definition of the capital account was a new arrival as a result of the 1998 recasting of the accounts.) The main components are migrants' transfers, EU transfers relating to investment, and debt forgiveness. The magnitude of these transactions is small compared to the current and financial accounts and, at the time of writing, the capital account had yet to be embraced by market analysts.
- The financial account. This comprises flows of direct and portfolio investment, and bank loans and deposits (and broadly corresponds to the old definition of the capital account). The current account surplus or deficit is, by accounting convention, offset by a corresponding deficit or surplus on the capital and financial accounts. A current account surplus necessarily gets invested abroad, and a deficit has to be financed by foreign borrowing. If the UK sells more to foreigners than it buys, it has to lend them the money, and if it buys more than it sells, it has to borrow the money. This leads to an increase in UK assets or liabilities *vis-à-vis* foreigners.

Table 9.1. Main balance of payments balances, 1997, £bn

	Credits	Debits	Balance
Goods balance	171.8	183.6	−11.8
Goods and services balance	228.7	229.3	−0.6
Current account	354.2	346.2	8.0
Capital account	1.1	0.8	0.3
Financial account	248.1	256.2	−8.1
TOTAL	603.4	603.2	0.2*

Note: *Net errors and omissions.
Source: ONS *Pink Book*, 1998, table 1.1.

Only by coincidence is the current account (or any other balance) likely to be in balance, with the two amounts equal. It is generally in surplus or deficit. Most analysis of the balance of payments is conducted in terms of the first three of the balances set out above, but the increased importance of investment flows has led to more attention being focused on the financial account.

HISTORICAL TRENDS

According to the Royal Economic Society's figures, the UK's largest ever current account surplus was in 1913. The surplus, which had been only 1 per cent of GDP in 1901, rose to 10 per cent by 1913. The war converted the surplus into a deficit but by 1920 there was again a surplus of 6 per cent of GDP. By 1931 the account had moved back into deficit and stayed there throughout the 1930s. In 1940 the deficit ballooned to 12 per cent of GDP and remained high until 1947.

In the post-war period, the UK current account has been in surplus slightly more often than it has been in deficit. Up to and including 1998, there have been twenty-four years of deficits and twenty-nine years of surpluses since the present run of figures began in 1946. The surpluses were generally larger than the deficits up to the mid-1980s, but the size and apparent durability of the deficits during boom times, especially in the late 1980s and early 1990s, was at the time a concern to policy-makers and financial markets (see Fig. 9.1).

Even though the current balance has often been in surplus, the UK has had a surplus on the balance of visible trade in goods in only six of the fifty-three post-war years. Conversely, there has been a surplus in services in forty-six years. The visible trade deficit has usually outweighed the surplus on services, leaving a goods and services deficit in thirty-seven years. Deficits on invisibles are rare, however, leading to the relatively large number of current account surpluses. This pattern is shown for recent years in Table 9.2. In both 1997 and 1998 the trade deficit in goods was largely compensated for by a trade surplus in services, to leave a small deficit on trade (row 7). But a large surplus on investment income, partly offset by a deficit on transfers (mainly contributions to the European Union), delivered a current account surplus in both years.

Box 9.2. **Value, volume and terms of trade**

The initial assessment of the latest trade figures will focus on the latest month's or quarter's cash figure, perhaps an underlying version of the total. But it is not particularly illuminating to analyse the movement of exports and imports over a year or from year to year in current pounds, since so much of the change can be due to price inflation.

It is inappropriate to deflate import or export figures by the RPI, because their composition is so different from that of the basket of goods used to calculate it. It is possible to scale the figures by relating them to GDP in each year; for example, in 1998 total UK exports of goods were 20 per cent of GDP and total imports were 22 per cent of GDP. The usual method for obtaining volume figures is to deflate the cash figures for exports and imports by unit value, or price, indices (which are given in the monthly press release). The ONS calculates the price indices from information derived from its statistical inquiries. Most analysis of trends in trade is conducted in terms of the volume series.

Analysts will often refer to the 'terms of trade'. This is a measure of the ratio of export prices to import prices, indicating the volume of imports that can be bought with a unit of exports. The terms of trade are said to improve if export prices rise more rapidly than import prices. For example, if export prices rise by 4 per cent and import prices rise by 1 per cent, the terms of trade have improved by 3 per cent. The terms of trade indices are constructed from the import and export unit value indices.

The composition of the current account balance has undergone many changes in the last thirty years. In the early 1970s there was normally a surplus in manufactures and invisibles, together often exceeding the deficit in food, raw materials and fuels. In 1974 the oil price rise increased the fuels deficit, pushing up the current account deficit to nearly 3 per cent of GDP. By the early 1980s the development of the North Sea oil and gas fields had switched the fuels account into surplus. As surpluses continued in manufactures (because of the recession) and in invisibles, the UK had a current account surplus as large in relation to GDP as the deficit of some years earlier.

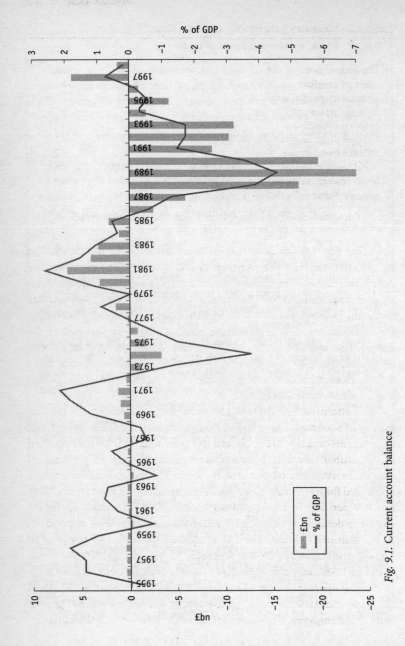

Fig. 9.1. Current account balance

Table 9.2. Summary balance of payments, £bn

	1997	1998
1. Exports of goods	171.8	163.7
2. Imports of goods	183.7	184.3
3. Balance in trade of goods (1−2)	−11.9	−20.6
4. Exports of services	57.3	61.8
5. Imports of services	45.4	49.1
6. Balance of trade in services (4−5)	11.8	12.7
7. Balance in total trade (3+6)	−0.1	−7.9
8. Total income (mainly investment income)	11.1	15.8
9. Total current transfers	−4.8	−6.4
10. Current balance (7+8+9)	6.3	1.5

Source: ONS balance of payments Q4 1998, first release, March 1999.

During the 1980s trade in manufactures crossed over into deficit, but by 1985 the fuel surplus had grown so that it covered the manufactures deficit twice over. The current account surplus survived, though on a smaller scale, until 1986. The halving of the oil price in 1986 and the economic boom of the late 1980s, with the associated import of manufactured goods, led to a large current account deficit by the end of the decade. The recession of the early 1990s helped to correct the deficit and, in general, the 1990s was a period of much more stable current account figures, close to balance. The aggregate impact of these trends in services and goods is shown in Fig. 9.2.

The pattern of visible trade has evolved considerably over the last quarter of a century. The principal change has been the fall in importance of food, fuel and raw materials and the growing importance of finished manufactured products. Manufactured products were 50 per cent of exports in 1976 but 60 per cent by 1998. The proportion of imports accounted for by manufactured goods rose much more sharply, doubling from 29 per cent in 1976 to 60 per cent by 1998. The most significant change in destination or origin of trade has been the growing importance of the European Union. The EU accounted for under 40 per cent of imports and exports in 1976 and roughly 55 per cent in 1998.

In late 1998 and early 1999, the balance in traded goods showed signs of deteriorating and recorded the largest deficit for nine years. Much of the trade deterioration came on the export side where volume growth had turned negative. The reason for this deterioration was threefold:

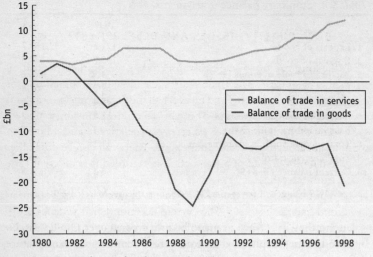

Fig. 9.2. Balance of trade in goods and services

- The appreciation of the pound by 25 per cent in the two years to the middle of 1998.
- The squeeze on manufacturers' competitiveness following the rise in unit labour costs.
- The Asian and emerging market crisis (in 1998) which caused those countries collectively to cut their imports from Britain by about a third.

There are relatively few comprehensive non-official sources for trade data. Two of the more important surveys of exports – those from the purchasing managers' report and the CBI monthly trends survey – both suggested some recovery in export prospects in early 1999. Even if export volumes stop falling, the balance can continue to deteriorate before improving, due to the so-called J-curve effect. This occurs when a weakening of the currency leads to a fall in export prices before contributing to a rise in volumes, causing export values to fall further before improving.

DATA QUALITY, ISSUES AND DEVELOPMENT

While the long-run trends are easily discernible, the short-term position is not always so clear. The trade figures are difficult to compile – it is simply impossible to identify and measure all the flows. Some transactions are concealed for tax reasons or by organized crime, or just misreported, while some of the capital items, especially speculative financial flows for example, are almost impossible to measure. There can also be difficulties with the data if one half of a transaction is recorded in a different time period from the other.

The reputation of the balance of payments figures was rock bottom in the second half of the 1980s. The current account deficit widened from next to nothing in 1986 to over £22 billion, 4 per cent of GDP, in 1989. The trends being revealed by the data were of intense policy and market interest, yet the data were inaccurate. In 1990, the balancing item – the extent of unaccounted flows or the mismatch between the current account and capital and financial accounts totals – in the overseas accounts for 1989 was £15 billion compared with a current account deficit then estimated at £19 billion. The invisibles data had become much harder to measure, especially in the wake of financial liberalization in the 1980s. The scrutiny report of government statistics, published in 1989, said that the 'invisibles balance is subject to frequent, persistent and substantial revision'. The quality of the data has improved as a result of the various initiatives taken by the ONS over the last decade.

That said, the initial balance of payments figures for the full year 1998 showed net errors and omissions of £7 billion, compared to a current surplus of £1½ billion. In the context of total debits (imports) and credits (exports) of around £350 billion, the error is not so large, but when the accounts are close to balance such an uncertainty, if resolved, could make a large difference to the appearance. (The unidentified balance for 1997 was much smaller, only £1½ billion, in mid-1999.) In most countries, discrepancies in the accounts are set out as an unidentified balancing item and when the unidentified component of the accounts is large it is wise to interpret the figures with caution. Professional statisticians suspect that the bulk of the error occurs in the capital and financial, not current, side of the account. The problem of accurate recording is a global one –

some studies have shown that world imports exceed world exports by up to $100 billion a year!

Not surprisingly, the published figures are subject to frequent, and occasionally substantial, revision. The balance of payments in any particular quarter or year has often turned out to be quite different from that originally published. By that time, of course, any damage may have already been done, because market reaction to the original figures is seldom reversible. A good part of the problem is that the current account balance is the difference between the two much larger estimates of credits and debits. As Table 9.3 shows, in 1998, for example, total credits and debits on the current account were up over £350 billion. A small change in either estimate would have a disproportionate impact on the balance, which in that year was close to zero.

There was a major change in the source of the monthly trade numbers in 1993. The arrival of the single European Market in 1993 did away with border controls at the internal frontiers of the European Community countries and, as a consequence, the need for the so-called customs declarations, leaving EU nations with the task of finding a new source. The last monthly trade release on the old basis was that for December 1992, published in January 1993. There then followed a period, lasting for much of 1993, when there were no monthly trade data for intra-community trade. Figures for trade with countries outside the EU continued to be published as before, three weeks into the following month. The new method for collecting intra-community trade data is referred to as Intrastat and is common to all EU members. It is based on the control of VAT collection in the member states as opposed to customs declarations at the point of import or export.

In 1994, when the Intrastat data started to be published, there were two separate press releases for UK trade, one showing the trade balance with non-EU countries and the other showing trade with EU countries. The data for trade with the EU were published much later than the other

Table 9.3. Overseas account figures for 1998, £bn

	Total credits	Total debits	Balance
Goods and services	225.5	233.4	−7.9
Total current account	354.9	353.4	1.5

Source: ONS balance of payments press release for Q4, 1998. March 1999.

release, roughly ten weeks after the end of the month. This reflected the fact that the Intrastat data came from businesses' own premises instead of being collected from the port of arrival or dispatch.

Financial markets and policy makers had the double irritation of having to do without trade data for several quarters and having data published later than had been the case before. There was some criticism of the EU authorities for not running the new and old data collection systems in parallel for a period as a check on quality. It was very unfortunate in the case of the UK, as there was increased interest in the trade data at that time after the currency devaluation in September 1992 following the departure of sterling from the exchange rate mechanism.

Due to the lack of public confidence in the Intrastat data, the CSO together with Customs and Excise conducted a quality audit of the data. The results of this exercise, published in May 1994, revealed some weaknesses, notably in the value and volume splits, and some bias in the early estimates resulting from under-recording. The exercise provided some reassurance about data quality but there is a clear break in the data at the end of 1992 and some relatively minor concerns about the data quality remain. The revisions and uncertainties are probably modest in relation to the usual variability of the trends shown in the series.

Most of the trade data are now published on a 'balance of payments' (BoP) basis. Until the second half of the 1990s data were often presented on an 'overseas trade statistics' basis (OTS). Conversions between the bases require two adjustments to be made. The first is to deduct the c.i.f. (insurance and freight) component of imports. The second adjustment concerns coverage and cost, for example, and allows for UK-made items delivered to UK owners abroad and items where no change in ownership has occurred (such as those going overseas for repair).

WHAT DATA ARE PUBLISHED?

There are two main sets of indicators about the UK's accounts with the rest of the world that appear in press notice form. In the last week of each month, the ONS publishes statistics on the balance of trade with other countries. Reflecting the Intrastat developments described above, the press release, rather confusingly, covers trade with non-EU countries for the preceding calendar month and trade with the European Union for the month before. The release published at the end of March therefore includes non-EU figures for February and EU figures for January. This means that, following the introduction of Intrastat, the country's full trade figures are not available until nearly two months after the end of the month to which they apply.

The trade figures are seasonally adjusted, both to allow for regular annual fluctuations, as with many other statistical series, and to allow for the different number of working days in each calendar month. There remain a number of irregularities which cause some volatility in the figures. To remove some of these, one version of the figures is published without the so-called erratics. Erratics are sometimes known as 'snaps', standing for ships, North Sea installations, aircraft, precious stones and silver. The trade figures are also published excluding trade in oil either as well as or instead of erratics. Even after these adjustments, the figures are erratic from month to month.

There is no one particular figure that the market focuses on when the monthly data are released. There is always some confusion as a result of the figures for trade with the EU being one month behind the rest of the world. That, and the belief in some quarters that it is best to exclude oil and/or erratics from the aggregates, means that a number of figures have to be seen before the initial assessment can be made. Trade figures are often referred to as 'good' or 'bad', depending on whether they are more or less in deficit than the previous month or the recent trend. The key figures from the monthly release (for a full year) are shown in Table 9.4.

The release publishes volume and price indices for trade in goods and a break-down of trade by broad commodity group, in value and volume

Table 9.4. Key trade figures from monthly release, 1998, £bn

	Exports	Imports	Balance
1. Trade in oil	7.0	4.0	3.0
2. Trade in erratics	9.0	10.6	−1.6
3. Trade in goods, ex oil and erratics	147.7	169.7	−22.0
4. Trade in services	61.8	49.1	12.7
Total trade (1+2+3+4)	225.5	233.4	−7.9
Total trade, ex oil and erratics (3+4)	209.5	218.8	−9.3

Source: ONS trade press release for March/April 1999. May 1999.

terms. The total export, import and balance figures are also shown for key countries or groups of countries. The inclusion of a monthly estimate of trade in services is a relatively new development from the late 1990s. The estimates are derived from a number of monthly and quarterly sources, involving an element of estimation. The figures should accordingly be used with appropriate caution, as they are likely to be less reliable than those for trade in goods.

The second main release, published each quarter by the ONS, shows figures for the UK balance of payments. It repeats the figures for trade given in the monthly release, but adds information on so-called invisibles, services, interest, profits and dividends, and both current and capital transfers. It also gives the financial account, which consists of changes in UK overseas assets and liabilities. The bare bones of the current account release were shown in Table 9.1. The current and capital account figures are seasonally adjusted, although the financial account and international investment data are not.

The break-down of services is shown in Table 9.5. It shows that the UK is in a net deficit position for transportation, travel and government (largely contributions to the EU) sectors, but records a large surplus in financial and other business services. Although the individual numbers vary quite dramatically from year to year, the general pattern of trade in services has been constant for many years.

Table 9.5. Trade in services, 1998, £bn

	Exports	Imports	Balance
Transportation	11.4	13.5	−2.0
Travel	14.4	20.0	−5.6
Communications	1.1	1.4	−0.3
Construction	0.8	0.6	0.1
Insurance	2.6	0.6	2.1
Financial	6.5	0.2	6.3
Computer and information	1.7	0.6	1.1
Royalties, etc.	4.1	4.0	0.1
Other business	17.0	6.2	10.8
Personal, cultural, recreational	1.1	0.5	0.6
Government	1.1	1.5	−0.5
TOTAL	61.8	49.1	12.7

Source: ONS Q4 BoP release, March 1999.

Long runs of visible trade data, and more detailed data, are contained in the *Monthly Review of External Trade Statistics*, published as *Business Monitor MM24*. This is generally published two to three weeks after the monthly trade release. Quarterly data analysed by industry according to the Standard Industrial Classification are contained in the *UK Trade in Goods Analysed in Terms of Industries*, published as *Business Monitor MQ10*. The annual publication *UK Trade in Services*, published as *Business Monitor UKA1*, contains detailed information on services components. The annual *Pink Book* publishes detailed figures on the full balance of payments data set, but only for whole years.

FINANCIAL ACCOUNT AND RESERVES

Details of the financial account are given in the quarterly balance of payments release and subsequently in the annual *Blue Book* and *Pink Book*, the *UK Balance of Payments*. The figures for 1998 are summarized in Table 9.6. Direct investment means investment by corporations, often multinationals, in production facilities in other countries. Direct investment in the UK by US, Japanese and European companies has grown strongly for twenty years but has generally been less than the investment abroad by major UK companies. Portfolio investment increased strongly in the outward direction after the removal of exchange controls in 1979, which allowed UK pension and insurance funds to increase the proportion of foreign shares in their portfolios. As Fig. 9.3 (which plots the balance figures from Table 9.6, rows 4 and 7, for earlier years) shows, outflows from the UK have been greater than inflows over the last decade.

OFFICIAL RESERVES

One of the items in the financial account – reserve assets, which used to be called official reserves – reflects the movements in the government's reserves of gold and foreign exchange. From a low point in 1976, reserve assets grew strongly to peak in 1980, before shrinking over the period to 1984. They then grew very strongly in the second half of the 1980s and

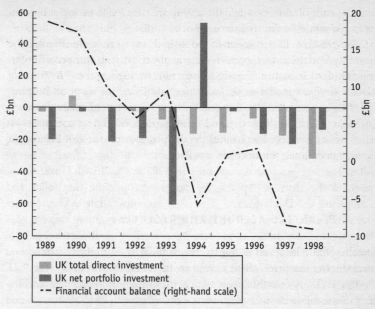

Fig. 9.3. UK portfolio and direct investment abroad

Table 9.6. UK financial account, 1998, £bn

	Investment abroad	Investment in the UK	Balance (credits less debits)
1. Equity capital	48.6	27.5	−21.1
2. Re-invested earnings	15.6	5.0	−10.6
3. Other transactions	4.7	5.6	0.9
4. Total direct investment (1+2+3)	69.0	38.1	−30.8
5. Equity securities	2.8	36.9	34.1
6. Debt securities	32.7	−13.7	−46.4
7. Total portfolio investment (5+6)	35.5	23.2	−12.3
8. Other investment	13.3	47.2	33.9
9. Reserve assets	−0.2	—	0.2
10. TOTAL (4+7+8+9)	117.6	108.5	−9.1

Source: ONS Q4 BoP release, March 1999.

were broadly stable through the 1990s (see Fig. 9.4, which shows the reserves valued in the traditional way in US$).

The principal determinant of the level of reserves is the intervention conducted in the foreign exchange market by the British authorities. Intervention consists either of using foreign currency reserves to buy pounds, with a view to supporting the exchange rate, or of selling pounds to buy reserves, to prevent the exchange rate rising to or at an undesirable rate.

For much of the post-Bretton Woods period, official intervention was used only for short-term smoothing purposes. In the second half of the 1980s intervention was being used as much as in the days of fixed exchange rates. The reserves rose dramatically in 1987 as the British Government pursued the aims of capping the pound, supporting the dollar and shadowing the Deutschmark. The most significant fall in the reserves occurred in the second half of 1992, when the Government was engaged in the eventually futile attempt to keep sterling in the exchange rate mechanism. The reserves fell by many billions of dollars over several months, but the government moved swiftly to rebuild them (see Fig. 9.4).

The Treasury monthly press notice, published on the second working day of the following month, gives the end of month level of reserves and the change during the month. The data are not seasonally adjusted. The change in the month cannot be equated with the amount of official intervention during the month, because other items, such as the repayment of debt or interest earned and paid, can result in a change in the reserves. That said, markets have traditionally viewed the underlying change in reserves as a proxy for foreign exchange intervention, when the markets were interested in measuring it. Much of the guesswork was removed following a decision by the Government in 1997 to publish, as part of the release, the actual amount of intervention carried out in that month. Since then, the amount of intervention has been negligible.

Step changes in the level of reserves occur each March when revaluation takes place. There was also a partial revaluation of reserves at the end of 1998 arising from the process of Euro conversion. A good part of the fall in reserves in 1997 and 1998 reflected the rise in the value of the US$ (and the pound) against the European currencies in 1996 and 1997. About three-quarters of the foreign exchange holdings are in the form of securities, mostly bonds and notes, with the remaining quarter in the form of currency and deposits. Virtually all of the foreign currency holdings are in European currencies (55 per cent) or US dollars (40 per

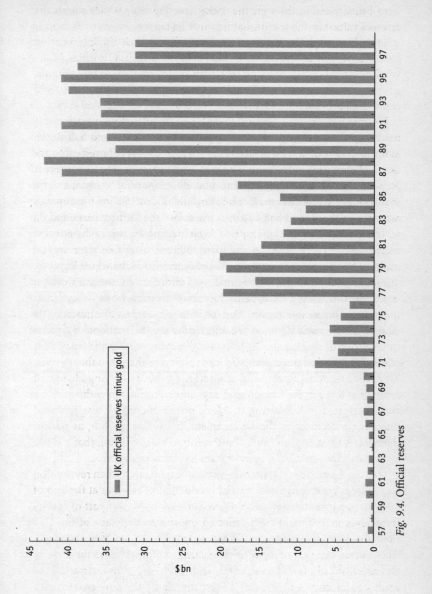

Fig. 9.4. Official reserves

cent), with the remainder mostly in the Japanese yen. Of the roughly one quarter of reserves not held in the form of currencies, most is held in gold or reserves at the IMF.

EXCHANGE RATES

Exchange rates are the price of one currency in terms of another. They are not the subject of a press notice, since they are available in real-time and are published daily by the press. They are, however, published for the record in a number of official publications including *Financial Statistics* and the monthly Bankstats from the Bank of England. Table 9.7 shows the average exchange rates of the pound against the dollar, the Deutschmark and the effective rate index (ERI). The ERI, which is also known as the effective exchange rate (EER) and the trade-weighted exchange rate, measures the value of one currency against a basket of other currencies whose composition is supposed to mirror the make-up of different currencies used in external transactions, i.e. broadly equivalent to trade flows.

There is no simple explanation of what determines the rates in the market. Supply and demand are affected by the international payments

Table 9.7. Key exchange rates

	$/£		DM/£		£ERI	
	Rate	% change	Rate	% change	Rate	% change
1988	1.78	8	3.12	5	105.4	5
1989	1.64	−8	3.08	−2	102.3	−3
1990	1.79	9	2.87	−6	99.6	−1
1991	1.77	−1	2.92	1	100.7	1
1992	1.76	—	2.75	−6	96.9	−4
1993	1.51	−15	2.48	−10	88.9	−11
1994	1.53	1	2.48	—	89.2	—
1995	1.58	3	2.26	−9	84.8	−5
1996	1.56	−1	2.35	4	86.3	2
1997	1.64	5	2.84	20	100.5	16
1998	1.66	1	2.91	3	103.9	3

Source: ONS and BoE publications

associated with trade flows and capital flows shifting around the world's financial markets in search of higher investment returns. The traditional approach to exchange rates suggests that they move in line with international purchasing power. If inflation is higher in one country than another, the currency of the former will fall by the differential in inflation rates to maintain the so-called purchasing power parity. This theory provides a good guide to currency movements in the long term, but can be over-ridden in the short term by portfolio pressures. If one country has higher interest rates than another, investors will tend to buy that country's currency, unless they expect the exchange rate to fall, even if it has a relatively high inflation rate.

Box 9.3. **Fixed and floating exchange rates**

Prior to 1914 exchange rates were fixed by the 'gold standard'. A country that developed a current account deficit would be obliged to consume its reserves of foreign currency and then start to pay for imports by shipping gold. After the First World War, countries experienced very different rates of inflation leading to the mispricing of imports and exports. Accordingly, the gold standard became unpopular during the 1920s and was abandoned by the early 1930s.

Following a period of much experimentation with exchange rate policy in the 1930s, as countries tried to alleviate the ills of the Depression, a new regime was introduced following a meeting at Bretton Woods in the US in June 1944. Following the meeting, the IMF and World Bank were created with the aim of promoting international monetary co-operation. As part of this, major currencies were fixed to the dollar. The system broke down in the early 1970s, since when most major currencies have been free floating. During the last three decades, there have been a number of agreements to have 'managed floats' or 'bilateral pegging'. The arrival of the Exchange Rate Mechanism (ERM), and subsequently European Monetary Union, was the major development over the more recent period.

When a currency strengthens, it is said to have appreciated if it is a floating rate currency or to have been revalued if it is a fixed rate. Conversely, if a currency weakens, it is said to have depreciated or to have been devalued.

The ERI is the best all-round exchange rate indicator. Various organizations produce indices constructed and weighted in different ways, but that produced by the Bank of England is the 'official' measure. It is based on the pound's bilateral exchange rates against twenty currencies, thirteen of which are EU currencies, weighted according to their importance in UK trade (in 1989–91 for the current index). (The present ERI was introduced in February 1995 with the base year set in 1990.) The introduction of the Euro will alter the composition of the index, but it will continue to show a movement each year between that of the Deutschmark/Euro and the US$, with a bias towards the former as its weight is greater. In financial markets, the movement of sterling is measured against both the US dollar and the Euro with roughly equal importance. During the final years of the 1990s the ECU and then the Euro slowly replaced the Deutschmark as the dominant European currency.

There are many ways of quoting exchange rate statistics. They can be shown as rates at the end of a period, such as a month, quarter or year. This is the most useful statistic for balance sheet purposes in order to translate foreign currency assets and liabilities into sterling on a particular day. Exchange rates can also be shown as averages over a period. This is more help for judging their impact on trade over the period. The yearly averages shown in Table 9.7 are the rates most relevant when making an assessment of the impact of the exchange rate on exports and imports. In the financial markets, traders and analysts will often look at charts of exchange rates showing the extreme points in successive trading periods. Such a representation gives a good indication of volatility in the market.

TRENDS IN THE EXCHANGE RATE

The value of the pound rose in the late 1970s as interest rates were increased and as the oil price rose. The pound then fell through much of the first half of the 1980s, by nearly a fifth on an ERI basis. In 1986 the pound followed what is perhaps the ideal path – it rose against the dollar, which kept import prices down, and fell against the European currencies, which increased export profits. The dollar fell as a result of the so-called Plaza Agreement, named after the G5 meeting at the Plaza Hotel in New York in September 1985, which sought appreciation of currencies against

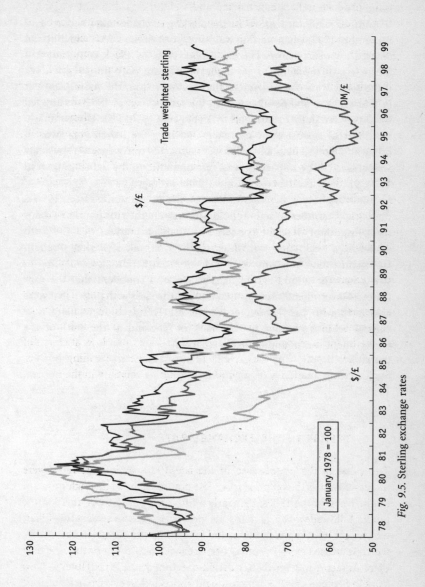

Fig. 9.5. Sterling exchange rates

the dollar. The second half of the 1980s saw a more stable exchange rate profile (see Fig. 9.5).

Another significant move in the sterling exchange rate occurred in September 1992, when sterling was forced out of the ERM, which it had entered two years before. The day is referred to as 'Black Wednesday', if the focus is on the failure to stay in the mechanism, or 'White Wednesday', if the focus is on the benefits to the economy from the subsequent cut in interest rates and devaluation. In the second half of 1992 sterling fell by 13 per cent in ERI terms and by 15 per cent against the Deutschmark. Sterling rose against some currencies, such as the Italian lira, Swedish krona and Finnish markka, which were subjected to even greater speculative pressure. (The impact appears less dramatic in the figures shown in Table 9.7, because the table shows annual averages.)

Finally, in both Table 9.7 and Fig. 9.5, the rise in sterling from 1996 is dramatic. A number of factors combined to strengthen the pound. Perhaps most important were the concerns in financial markets that the Euro would be a weak currency, which is why the bulk of sterling strength was against the Deutschmark. The domestic situation also conspired to strengthen the pound as the markets became confident that the new Labour Government would not take any of the risks with policy that were associated with past Labour governments. The decision to hand over control of interest rates to the Bank of England at the start of the Government compounded this perception.

10 | Money, Public Finances and Financial Markets

Money supply, bank and building society activities, and public borrowing are closely linked, both by statistical definitions and by the way in which British governments have chosen to run policy for a generation. The concepts in this chapter are more difficult to understand than most others in this book, but money is important. It is a measure of value, a medium of exchange and a store of wealth. Money facilitates commercial transactions and the money and securities markets bring together the supply of savings and the demand for borrowing from businesses, government and consumers. In short, 'money makes the world go round', so it is vital to get to grips with the basic concepts.

The evolution of monetary and fiscal policy over the last two-and-a-half decades offers a good insight into how the world and our lives have changed – and how policy has had to change too. Many of the problems that analysts face when using the data discussed in this chapter reflect changes to financial systems. Financial affairs are much harder to measure as a result of the liberalization and deregulation of credit markets, the creation and development of new financial instruments, greater internationalization and the consequences of the technological and telecommunications revolution.

THE EMERGENCE OF MONETARY POLICY

Monetarism as a theory is centuries old, but its application to UK policy goes back to 1976 when the first monetary target was set under the influence of the IMF. It came fully to the fore following the Conservatives' election victory of 1979. From then on, publication of the monthly money supply figures began to displace the trade figures as the key indicator. At its simplest, the theory was that the money supply – the rate of growth of the stock of money – determined the rate of inflation, albeit after a time lag.

At first it was hoped that targets for monetary growth would influence people's expectations about the future rate of inflation. In Germany at the time, trade unions used the government's monetary targets as a key component of their wage negotiations. Monetarism, however, was never really accepted in Britain. There was scepticism both about the Government's ability to achieve monetary targets (i.e. control the growth of money supply) and about the influence of monetary growth on inflation. In a sense, the scepticism was justified, as by the late 1980s the money supply data had no greater status than other releases.

The monetary authorities in a country can attempt to control the growth of money in a number of ways, including changing interest rates, market operations (buying or selling government securities), credit controls, reserve asset ratios (influencing commercial banks' ability to lend) and moral persuasion. Early on, however, the practical difficulties of applying the monetarist theory set out in the government's medium-term financial strategy (MTFS) – first unveiled in 1980 – became clear. The money supply was being driven by bank and building society lending but since the government wanted to encourage free market competition in lending, it could not at the same time limit its growth. Accordingly, without credit controls, money supply growth could only be restrained by short-term subterfuges, such as over-funding (as tried briefly in the 1980s).

The emphasis was therefore gradually switched to the public sector borrowing requirement (PSBR), rather than monetary targets, as the main instrument of the MTFS. Professor Sir Alan Walters, Mrs Thatcher's special economic adviser in the early 1980s, stood the traditional Keynesian view on its head by arguing that a lower rather than a higher PSBR caused the economy to grow faster. Improved and more frequent PSBR data became available in the early 1980s and the indicator came to rank as at least equal in importance to the money supply figures.

Because the PSBR is financed mainly by the issue of gilt edged government stocks, its monthly size was taken by financial markets as a clue to the yields, or interest rates, on these stocks. By contrast, the money supply figures were seen as a guide to short-term interest rates in the money markets, and to the operations of the authorities designed to influence them.

By the late 1980s the exchange rate had become a more important determinant of interest rates. If it fell, interest rates might rise, and vice versa. The British authorities' belief in the exchange rate as the ultimate guide to economic policy reached a peak in October 1990 when sterling entered the exchange rate mechanism (ERM) of the European Monetary System (EMS). The ERM had the apparent advantage of 'locking in' to German monetary policy – the most successful in Europe in the 1970s and 1980s – as the system was essentially a Deutschmark peg. Both the timing (coinciding with German reunification) and the rate (too high) were wrong. Consequently, pressure built up in the system, culminating in September 1992 with the exit of sterling and the Italian lira from the ERM, and a widening of the permitted fluctuation bands for those that remained from 2½ per cent to 15 per cent.

The Government introduced inflation targeting at the end of 1992 and by the mid-1990s it was fully established. Since then the money supply, PSBR and the exchange rate have had no special significance, ranking alongside many of the other variables discussed in this book. Paradoxically, the organization that produces the data, the Bank of England, has assumed greater importance in the policy process, especially since it was given control of interest rates by the Labour Government in 1997. A combination of inflation targeting, semi-independence for the Bank of England and low inflation rates globally, led to the late 1990s seeing the most benign period for UK inflation since the 1960s.

DEFINITIONS OF MONEY

There have been many definitions of money, bank lending and public borrowing in the UK in recent years. Each was chosen at the time to reflect both the changes in the financial system and official policy objectives. At its simplest, money is anything that is accepted as a medium of exchange. This boils down to currency in circulation plus deposits (normally held in banks and building societies). In any developed country, the notes and coin in circulation account for only a small part of the total money supply. The problems arise in defining deposits. A look at definitions chosen in different countries indicates how traditions and structures of the financial system have a large impact.

The various definitions of money can be roughly divided into two categories. Narrow money is notes and coins, and may include deposits used as a means of payment. Broad money generally includes narrow money and, in addition, longer-term interest-bearing deposits used by savers as a store of value. Measures of money supply are known as the monetary aggregates.

The Treasury set targets of one sort or another for monetary aggregates from 1976 to 1997. Through a process of trial and error into the 1980s, the authorities gained experience and many measures of money supply came and went. By the early 1990s, however, the focus was entirely on M0 and M4, which became the authorities' preferred measure of narrow and broad money supply. The target ranges have been given different titles such as 'illustrative ranges' and 'monitoring ranges', reflecting the importance that they had at the time in the policy-making process.

The narrowest kind of money, M0 ('M-nought' or 'M-zero') was introduced in 1982. About 90 per cent of it is notes and coin in circulation with the rest being notes and coin held in bank tills and banks' operational deposits with the Bank of England. (Indeed, analysts usually follow the notes and coin component rather than total M0.) It cannot easily be defined as part of any other monetary aggregate because it is a monthly average, not an end period figure, and includes holdings of money by banks.

M0 was introduced after a public debate as to whether the Bank of England should try to control broad money by influencing narrow money.

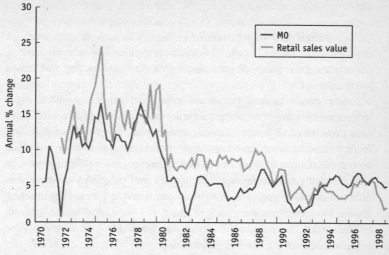

Fig. 10.1. Money supply and retail sales growth compared

The Bank of England cannot, however, directly determine the amount of notes and coin in circulation, as it is determined mainly by consumer spending and interest rates (see Fig. 10.1). If people choose to use notes and coin rather than cheques and plastic cards, M0 will rise. Accordingly, monetary base control, as it was called, was never adopted as an instrument to regulate broad money. But M0 was adopted as a target in its own right, reflecting the link between it and consumer demand – rapid growth in M0 has typically been associated with rapid growth in consumer spending. For many years, however, a monitoring range, as opposed to a target, has been set for M0 reflecting the relative lack of control on it. Although M0 often remained within the target ranges set since 1984, this made little impression on financial markets, as the authorities seemed to pay little attention to it when setting policy.

A more long-standing definition of narrow money was M1, which was first published in 1970. M1 was close to the traditional textbook definition of money as notes and coin plus bank deposits, withdrawable on sight, on which cheques could be written. As in the case of M0, the implication was that money could be controlled by raising interest rates, because this would make it more expensive to keep money in non-interest-bearing bank current accounts. Unfortunately, M1 included sight deposits on which interest was paid, which grew very fast during the 1980s. As a consequence, M1 grew faster than any credible target numbers. M1 was used as a target for two years and then there was some discussion about redefining it as 'retail M1', which would have excluded the interest-bearing wholesale sight deposits. Eventually, in 1990 the Bank of England ceased publication of M1.

A new narrow monetary aggregate called M2 was announced in 1982. M2 comprised the non-interest-bearing components of M1 plus retail time deposits in all banks. It changed definition in 1983 when building society deposits were added, roughly doubling its size. It also became useless for control purposes because building societies offered almost as high interest rates on deposits of less than one month as on their time deposits of longer maturities. M2 was never used as a target in monetary policy. The definition was changed again in 1992 and although it is still published by the Bank of England (as 'retail M4'), it is given little prominence and receives little attention.

The longest surviving definition of broad money was M3. There were several variants of M3 including Sterling M3 (written £M3) and M3c, which included foreign currency deposits. M3 was used in monetary targeting for a decade from the commencement of the policy in 1976. M3 targeting was fraught with difficulties in the first half of the 1980s as private-sector borrowing boomed as a result of companies' need to survive the recession and financial deregulation. During that time, greater attention was progressively paid to public-sector borrowing and the exchange rate, so that when the abandonment of the M3 target was announced in 1986 the financial markets reacted with indifference. (All the target ranges, along with the results, are set out in table 36 on p. 199 of *Measuring the Economy*.)

The drawback of the monetary aggregates is that financial market changes cause liquid assets to move across frontiers between them. For example, when bank interest rates rose higher than building society rates, an increase in M3 was caused purely by a switch from a market which happens to be outside this definition of money (building societies) to one that happens to be inside (banks).

The authorities had recognized this in the late 1970s when they introduced two wider aggregates, PSL1 and PSL2 (PSL stood for private sector liquidity), which were designed to be steadier and more predictable in their growth. PSL2 was used as the target for two years before being

Table 10.1. Break-down of M4

Component	£ billion	
	Change in 1998	Level at end 1998
1. Notes and coin	1.3	23.2
2. Non-interest-bearing bank deposits	−0.7	35.2
3. Other bank deposits	20.8	350.3
4. Building society deposits	9.5	104.9
5. Total retail deposits (sum 1 to 4)	30.9	513.6
6. Total wholesale deposits	28.2	265.8
7. M4 (5+6)	59.0	779.4

Source: Bank of England monetary and financial statistics, February 1999. Seasonally adjusted.

dropped. It was relaunched in 1987, as M5, but a new aggregate, M4, unveiled at the same time, was destined to become the main broad aggregate.

M4 leaves out money market instruments such as commercial bills and National Savings deposits, and sensibly made no distinction between banks and building societies, as the two had become increasingly similar in terms of the accounts offered. The Bank of England still publishes the components of M3 and M5 (and some other liquid assets outside M4) but all attention is focused on M4. Table 10.1 shows the scale of M4, nearly £780 billion at the end of 1998. Over 60 per cent of M4 is held by the household sector and 15 per cent by private non-financial corporations.

Most commentators agree that rigid adherence to monetary targets is unwise against a background of deregulation and innovation in the financial system. It is also clear that there can be no unique definition of money – the various measures are best thought of as being points along the spectrum. Indeed, any division along the spectrum is to some degree arbitrary and likely to be invalidated over time by developments in the financial system.

After twenty years of experience with monetary targeting, the UK is left with a monetary data focus very much on M0 and M4 (and its bank and building society lending counterpart), with neither being given greater importance in policy setting than any other variable. M0 is probably the better short-term indicator of inflation and the best contemporaneous measure of national income, but contains little information for the

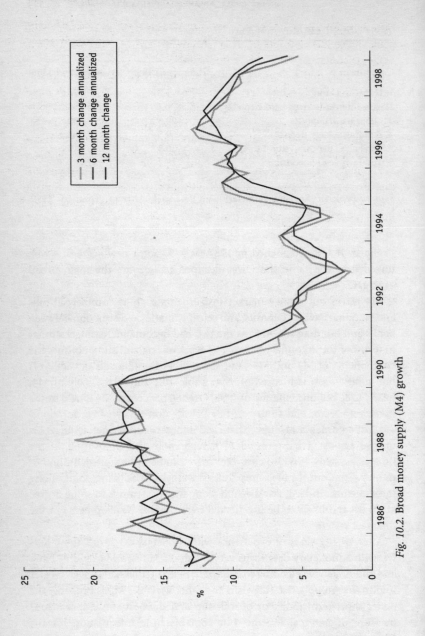

Fig. 10.2. Broad money supply (M4) growth

medium term. M4, or its lending counterpart, is the better medium-term indicator of inflation and nominal output. Fig. 10.2 sets out the history of M4 growth.

In an attempt to overcome some of the difficulties of traditional monetary aggregates, there is periodic interest in index number measures of money supply which weight the components within each monetary aggregate. The underlying assumption is that the components of monetary aggregates are not perfect substitutes. Most attempts apply the Divisia index which allows for the varying transaction properties of monetary assets. The resulting index provides a measure of the quantity of money held in the economy for transaction purposes as opposed to saving. Due to a number of theoretical and practical difficulties, the Bank of England publishes only a quarterly Divisia index.

More recently, the Bank has published a harmonized broad monetary aggregate, called M3H. This is designed to facilitate comparisons among member states when analysing monetary developments in the EC countries. (Indeed, some minor definitional changes were expected to be made to bring this into line with the European Central Bank's version of M3.) The figure is published in a low-key way and no percentage changes are given to help analysis. M3H comprises the components of M4 plus:

- foreign currency deposits held by the private sector with MFIs in the UK, and
- sterling and foreign currency deposits held by UK public corporations with MFIs in the UK.

CURRENT STATUS OF MONEY

In the last decade, as monetary targeting faded in importance, many commentators and officials spent time excusing missed targets. Included in the list of excuses were financial innovation, strikes, sharp rises in taxes (prompting uncertainty and a temporary reduction in consumer spending), and significant or rapid changes in interest rates (lower rates mean that there is less cost, in terms of lost interest payments, attached to holding cash).

The shift in responsibility for monetary policy from the Treasury to the Bank of England (the first major action of the Labour Government following the election in May 1997) led to monetary targets, of any sort, being quietly forgotten. The Budget documents from the Labour Government have not even mentioned money supply. Developments in money supply are still clearly of interest, however, to the Bank of England's Monetary Policy Committee. The quarterly *Inflation Report* discusses the evolving story of the monetary aggregates in reasonable depth. The report looks at the detailed components of the money supply and credit and sets the changes in the context of broader developments in the economy, in financial markets and regarding asset prices, rather than slavishly aiming for a particular growth rate of M0 or M4.

WHAT DATA ARE PUBLISHED?

The money and banking statistics are compiled by the Bank of England by means of frequent and detailed statistical returns from commercial banks and building societies. The main money supply data are released monthly in a sequence of four press releases and a more detailed booklet from the Bank of England. The Bank makes more use of electronic dissemination than does the ONS and much of the data is available on the Bank's web site.

The first release to be published is that for M0. Figures for notes and coin in circulation (which is M0 less the change in bankers' operational deposits with the Bank of England, i.e. the bulk of M0) are available from Bank Returns each Thursday afternoon. The figures apply to the preceding Wednesday. Accordingly, the M0 release is usually published on the Monday, three days after the final Wednesday of the calendar month. The M0 figures are the first official data to be released for each month and, as they are thought to give a good indication of consumer demand, they tend to be closely watched. This is especially so around times of peak activity such as Easter and Christmas, though the normal warnings about the quality of seasonal adjustments at these times apply. The press release focuses on the one-month, three-month annualized and twelve-month seasonally adjusted growth rates, but also presents some additional detail and rates.

Many commentators look at the growth of notes and coin in circulation.

The weekly notes figures can be aggregated to give a good forecast of M0. There are, however, remaining uncertainties relating to the amount of coin in the economy and the seasonal adjustment. Holdings of notes are strongly influenced by holiday periods, when the demand for cash rises sharply.

The Bank press releases normally, but unfortunately not always, highlight any distortions to the data which may affect interpretation. In 1998 and 1999, for example, the press releases set out the distortions to M0 growth caused by the introduction of the new 50p coin (from September 1997) and the issue of the new £2 coin (from June 1998). The estimates of M0 in this release are referred to as provisional: additional data (mainly the final week's figures for Scottish and Northern Irish banks) and updated seasonal adjustments are published roughly three weeks later in the provisional M4 release. The revisions to M0 are typically modest.

The second press release in the monthly cycle is that containing the provisional estimates of M4 and M4 lending (i.e. lending by banks and building societies to holders of M4), and the revised estimates of M0. This release contains a small table showing the counterparts to the changes in M4 in that month and over the previous twelve months, in both seasonally adjusted and unadjusted form. The public sector net cash requirement figure is published two working days earlier in the month in its own press release. Most of the market attention, however, is focused on the M4 and lending growth rates, shown over one month, three and six months annualized, and twelve months, all in seasonally adjusted form. The M4 figure is derived from an end of month stock reading in contrast to the average of the Wednesday figures during a month for M0.

Lending is of interest as it is thought to be a good indicator of personal and corporate confidence and hence of future demand in the economy. Generally, individuals and companies will be more inclined to borrow if they are optimistic about the future. There can, however, be some ambiguity about the interpretation to be put on a change in lending. In the early stages of a recession, for example – and this was particularly so in the early 1990s when the recession was deep – it is never clear whether a rise in borrowing reflects voluntary or distress borrowing and whether any build up in stocks that requires financing is voluntary or involuntary. Table 10.2 shows the main counterparts of M4.

This release gives only a total figure for sterling lending to the private

Table 10.2. Counterparts to changes in M4, 1998

	£bn
1. Public sector net cash requirement (PSNCR)	−7.5
2. Public sector debt sales to M4 private sector	3.0
3. External and foreign currency finance of public sector	−6.2
4. Public sector contribution (1+2+3)	−10.8
5. M4 lending	64.4
6. Other external and foreign currency flows	12.0
7. Net non-deposit sterling liabilities of banks and building societies	−8.2
8. Total M4 change (4+5+6+7)	57.5
Amount of M4 outstanding at end 1998	779.4

Note: Totals may not add up due to rounding.
Source: BoE press release. Seasonally adjusted.

sector. It is necessary to wait for the 'final' release and the accompanying booklet (which is issued – electronically, at least – at the same time) roughly ten days later for a break-down that allows analysis of lending by the economic sector of the borrower. Monthly data are available divided into these broad categories, though quarterly data are available split into around forty industrial sectors. It is unfortunate that this detail is not available sooner as any number of factors can distort the bare monthly lending figures. Sometimes the Bank draws attention to the factors. Typical factors could include: the financing of take-overs, borrowing to pay corporation tax or to take advantage of share issues, and the expectation of a rise in interest rates prompting companies to take advantage of pre-arranged deals at existing rates.

The lending component is of interest in its own right and generally explains the change in M4. All the other components can have a marked influence in any given month, and must therefore be understood, but the trend of M4 will closely reflect the trend in the lending component, as Table 10.2 shows. This has especially been the case since 1986 when the government started to pursue a policy called 'fully funding' public sector borrowing. Since 1994, the Treasury has published annual remits (in March) for the Bank's funding operations in the market. (The Debt Management Office (DMO) took over this task in 1998.) During the second half of the 1990s there were some small changes in the rules, but they have ensured that only the private sector has financed public

Box 10.1. **A brief guide to terminology**

The terminology used in money supply figures, and shown in Table 10.2, can often be confusing. The public sector net cash requirement was previously known as the public sector borrowing requirement and is the net balance between cash expenditure and receipts of the total public sector. Public sector debt includes Treasury bills, certificates of tax deposit, local authority debt, National Savings, as well as gilt edged stock. M4 private sector consists of all UK residents other than the public sector and monetary financial institutions. Monetary financial institutions (MFIs) are the central bank, other banks and building societies. M4 itself comprises sterling notes and coin and all sterling deposits at UK MFIs, held by the M4 private sector.

The external and foreign currency finance reflects the current account of the balance of payments and the M4 private sector's capital account and foreign currency transactions. The public sector component refers to the sale of government debt products to non-M4 counterparties, such as overseas investors, and any currency intervention conducted by the Bank of England. (Since sterling's exit from the exchange rate mechanism in 1992, Bank of England intervention in the foreign exchange market has been negligible.) Net non-deposit sterling liabilities are mainly MFIs' retained profits and issues of long-term securities less some investments and assets. Fuller notes and definitions are available in the monthly publication *Bank of England: Monetary and Financial Statistics.*

borrowing through purchases of National Savings and government bonds.

Two other organizations publish data on the same day as the provisional M4 numbers. The British Bankers' Association (BBA) publishes an analysis of lending by the so-called Major British Banking Groups. (Prior to 1991, similar data were published by the predecessor organization, the City of London and Scottish Banks, CLSB, and before it the Committee of London Clearing Banks, CLCB.) The BBA numbers are consistent with the Bank of England numbers, but the BBA accounts for only around three-quarters of the banks' deposits in M4 and of the contribution to M4 lending. Accordingly, the BBA numbers provide only a partial analysis and break-down of the Bank of England numbers. Comparisons are generally made with the same month a year before. As the industry break-down of the Bank of England numbers is available only quarterly, there is enthusiasm to see this partial picture.

The Building Societies Association (BSA) publishes key building society data based on returns from the largest societies whose assets account for 95 per cent of total building society assets. There is interest in the retail flows, both of savers' money into and out of the societies and borrowers' needs, which are primarily for house purchase. Societies match the gap between the two by funding in the wholesale markets.

The release also gives figures for the number and value of mortgage advances and new commitments to lend. These figures and the various house price indices which are available, are of at least as much interest as the saving and borrowing data. The housing market statistics are of interest in the UK mainly because of the pivotal role that housing has played in influencing consumer demand, through the effect on people's wealth as well as on their purchase of household goods such as furniture and fittings, and inflation.

Interpretation of the building society accounts suffers from the uncertainty that any rises or falls could simply reflect changes in market share between building societies and banks. The problem was particularly acute following the demutualization of many building societies (as they converted to banks) around 1997, as the reclassifications caused considerable disruption to the statistical series. The problems will be less severe going forward as the data series for the smaller (and probably more stable) building society sector builds up.

The third and fourth BoE press releases in the monthly cycle are published together roughly one month after the end of the month to which they refer. One of these releases publishes the final estimates of M4 and M4 lending. The revisions are typically very modest, rarely more than 0.1 per cent on or off any of the growth rates. Several years ago this release also included data on bank balance sheets, a break-down of lending, and various tables recording the Bank of England's operations in the money markets. But following the introduction of the Bank's monthly book of financial statistics, this release has shrunk to a single page.

The fourth release in the monthly cycle publishes figures on lending to individuals. Market attention for this release is divided equally between the cash amount of net new lending in the latest month and the trends

Table 10.3. Lending to individuals

	£bn	
	Lending in 1998	Amount outstanding, end 1998
1. Banks	26.4	393.4
2. Building societies	8.3	107.9
3. Other specialist lenders	5.1	51.6
4. Retailers	0.1	2.7
5. Other	−0.2	3.4
6. Total lending (1+2+3+4+5) (rounded) Of which:	39.7	558.9
7. Secured on dwellings	25.6	457.6
8. Consumer credit	14.2	101.3

Source: BoE *Monetary and Financial Statistics*, seasonally adjusted net lending.

– usually in terms of the three-month annualized or twelve-month rates
– shown in percentage growth terms. The release shows figures for gross
lending as well as net lending, but attention is normally focused on the
latter. The gross credit data can be misleading as much of the 'new' credit
is repaid within a month as many consumers use credit cards simply as
a means of payment. In a typical month in 1998, gross consumer credit
was about £11 billion and net consumer credit was about £1¼ billion.

Table 10.3 shows the key lending figures and the amounts outstanding,
split according to the main sources of funding. There used to be considerable market attention paid to the consumer credit numbers each month.
Until 1994 the CSO published a monthly press release on a narrow
definition of consumer credit. It was decided to cease publication in that
form and to incorporate the data in the Bank of England release with its
broader coverage. The reasons contributing to the demise of the importance of the credit numbers include:

● Consumer credit is, as the table shows, only a modest part of total
personal sector lending. Underlying net credit demand averaged a little
over £3 billion a month in 1998 and only roughly one-third of that
was consumer credit. (It is possible that secured, i.e. mortgage, lending
also finances some consumption either directly or indirectly through
equity withdrawal.)

● Borrowing probably plays only a modest role in driving consumer spending. Net consumer credit in 1998 was about £15 billion compared to household consumption of around £550 billion. Equity holdings rose in value by £150 billion in 1997, and probably had a greater effect on consumer sentiment. The large stock of outstanding credit, much of which is floating rate, suggests that changes in interest rates will have a far greater impact.

- The monthly consumer credit numbers have generally been highly volatile from month to month.
- The trend in consumer credit is subject as much to changes in the relative attractiveness of payment mechanisms and fashions, such as the availability of interest free credit, as it is to changes in consumer sentiment.
- The seasonal adjustment of the consumer credit data is periodically questioned. Lending has traditionally been highest in August when people have borrowed to buy new cars and around Christmas. The first quarter is a time of repayment. Such strong patterns, when they are variable, can make seasonal adjustment hard.

The Bank of England publishes a monthly data book on the same day as the final M4 numbers, called *Monetary and Financial Statistics*. It includes over fifty tables set out under the headings: money and lending; monetary financial institutions' balance sheets; further analyses of deposits and lending; funding, money markets and other central government financing detail; sterling commercial paper, sterling other debt securities, capital issues; and interest and exchange rates. It also includes information about contact points and electronic dissemination of Bank data. The explanatory notes at the back of the publication provide useful information and, where appropriate, additional sources.

The Bank also publishes an annual *Statistical Abstract*, which contains long runs of most of the data in the monthly publication. The document has some useful appendices including the list of references for further information on the statistics and related topics, and a diary of events relevant to monetary statistics over the last thirty years.

The Department for National Savings publishes its accounts, showing the net inflows and outflows, on a monthly basis, roughly two weeks after the end of the month.

DATA PROBLEMS

Notwithstanding the conceptual difficulties associated with money, behavioural changes and the specialist language, the Bank of England statistics are generally well presented and are readily accessible (on the Bank's web site as well as in printed form). The data are probably among the most accurate of the major economic releases as many of the Bank of England returns are comprehensive and compulsory. Even where sampling is required, the Bank's samples often represent over 90 per cent of total business done because much of the business is located in a relatively small number of institutions.

There has, however, been a range of problems that make analysis and comparisons over the longer run very difficult. The section above alluded to a number of these, but there have been many others. For example:

● During the 1970s and 1980s, when the broad money measures were narrower than M4, there were many jumps in the data series as organizations moved into or out of the banking sector.
● Banking figures used to be presented in terms of the banking month, which ended in the middle of each calendar month. In 1986 banking data were converted to a calendar month basis, making them consistent with other economic statistics.
● Until the early part of the 1990s, quarterly lending data covered quarters ending in February, May, August and November, rather than the standard calendar quarters.

The second half of the 1990s saw many changes to the data, giving rise to many data breaks. Unfortunately, the Bank's policy is not to identify breaks in series in the tabulation of the series in the press releases (though some are in the annual *Abstract*). The Bank presents the data in the releases so that the breaks do not distort the flows over the dates of the breaks, but that does not help with analysis over long runs. The best policy when using banking figures is, therefore, to look carefully at the footnotes attached to tables. It is impossible to list all of the changes in this book, but some examples include:

● A review of banking statistics, to bring reporting into line with ESA95 (see Chapter 4 for further details), led to some significant changes in 1997.

- The demutualization of building societies or their purchase by banks, from 1995 but predominantly in 1997.
- The revised SIC92 codes were (belatedly) introduced in 1997.
- A new building society form for monthly reporting was introduced in October 1998 to update to ESA95 standards.
- The introduction of the gilt repo market in 1996 affected M4 and lending.
- The introduction of new coins affects M0.
- The increasing use of securitization and loan transfers, which reduces the size of lenders' balance sheets, and therefore reduces recorded lending, yet leaves the indebtedness of borrowers unaffected, is only partly allowed for in the figures.
- The acquisition and disposal of consumer credit portfolios switches lending between banks and other specialist lenders.

The Bank itself, referring to the break-down of lending data, says: 'A strong health warning must be attached to the long runs of data.' Analysis of those series is thus very difficult. Such significant changes inevitably make it difficult to have complete confidence in the seasonal adjustment factors. Accordingly, seasonally adjusted data should be regarded as less robust than usual for at least a couple of years after a change in the series.

TRENDS IN MONEY SUPPLY GROWTH

The Divisia indices show the growth of money supply over the medium term as well as any other single indicator. There were two main peaks in the aggregate growth rate in the 1970s and mid- to late 1980s and a smaller rise in the second half of the 1990s. It is illuminating to see that a different sector in each period provides the driving force. Borrowing by the household sector grew most strongly in 1979 and 1980. The late 1980s' boom had strong input from the borrowing of non-financial corporations in 1986 and 1987, while the second half of the 1990s saw strong credit demand from financial corporations. The fact that different sectors provided the growth at different times is a strong indication that

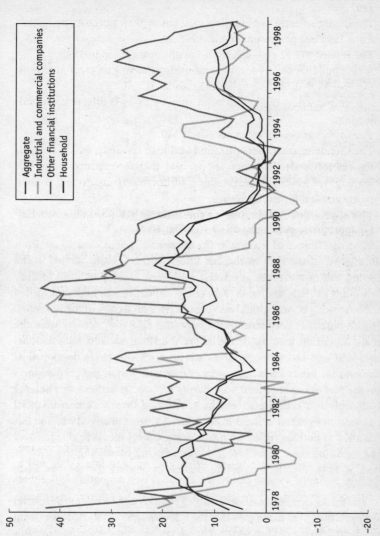

Fig. 10.3. Divisia money supply growth rates

Table 10.4. M4 lending by broad sector over time

	Per cent	
	1978	1998
Financial corporations	7	21
Non-financial corporations	31	21
Personal lending secured on dwellings	49	48
Consumer credit	6	8
Unincorporated businesses	6	2
TOTAL	100	100
Total lending	£68.6bn	£896.1bn

Note: End-year levels.
Source: Bank of England *Monetary and Financial Statistics*.

a monetary policy that follows a single aggregate too closely could lead to inappropriate policy responses (see Fig. 10.3).

The significance of lending in the economic cycle is clear to see from an analysis of the data in the last fifteen years. Lending soared in the second half of the 1980s as interest rates were sharply reduced to their low point in 1988, and taxes were cut. Confidence was high and fuelled the borrowing boom, which was spread across all sectors of the economy. House purchase, corporate investment and take-over activity were the main uses of the lending. At the end of the 1980s, interest rates doubled in a year and recessionary forces set in. A vicious circle developed as demand for funds from borrowers evaporated, just as the preparedness on the part of banks to lend was sharply reduced as earlier loans became bad debts and borrowers went bust. Lending to private non-financial corporations peaked in the third quarter of 1989 at nearly £10 billion but fell away to nothing in less than two years. Companies repaid loans over the following three years before recommencing borrowing towards the end of 1994. Fig. 10.4 plots the change in lending for the five main sectors.

The falling share of total borrowing of primary and secondary industries supports the often-stated view that the UK economy has shifted away from production to the services sector. The data might, however, exaggerate this trend as many companies now lease capital goods, for example, rather than buy them themselves, with the consequence that the leasing company rather than the manufacturer engages in the bank borrowing. Lending

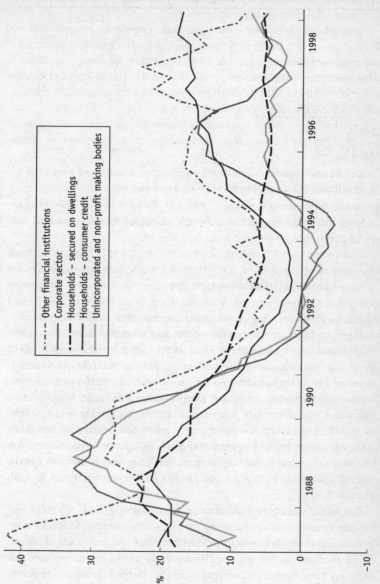

Fig. 10.4. Bank and building society lending by sector

Legend:
- ..... Other financial institutions
- ——— Corporate sector
- —·—· Households – secured on dwellings
- – – – Households – consumer credit
- ——— Unincorporated and non-profit making bodies

%

40

30

20

10

0

-10

1988   1990   1992   1994   1996   1998

to leasing companies and other industry to industry business service companies has risen strongly in recent years.

Personal borrowing for house purchase comprises roughly half of lending, much as it did twenty years ago, although it has been higher and lower in the intervening period. This consistency reflects the continued enthusiasm for home ownership despite the dangers of negative equity (where the mortgage on the house is greater than the value of the house), which was seen so clearly in the recession of the early 1990s. Other data suggest that borrowing behaviour on a personal level is now more cautious and that the early repayment of mortgage capital has become more common.

It is not easy to track lending by industrial sector over time due to breaks in the data series. Fig 10.5, however, shows outstanding borrowing by industrial sector at the end of 1998. As the new survey, which began in 1997, builds up a history, it will be a good source of information.

PUBLIC SECTOR BORROWING

Public sector borrowing is the difference between public expenditure and public revenue. Normally, governments spend more than they receive and need to borrow the difference, but occasionally they spend less than they receive and have a surplus with which to repay some of the accumulated debt. The borrowing requirement is the single most important indicator used to judge how tight an economic policy the government is running. If public borrowing is too high, taxes will rise. Financial markets also watch the borrowing numbers as they indicate the likely quantity of government securities that will be sold to finance the deficit. Behind all the Budget rhetoric, the public borrowing numbers form the heart of the government's annual Budget statement.

The most commonly used statistic for measuring fiscal affairs in the UK has been the public sector borrowing requirement (PSBR). It went from being almost unheard of twenty-five years ago to becoming one of the most important statistics by the end of the 1980s. It was renamed the public sector net cash requirement (PSNCR) by the Labour Government in the late 1990s. Public spending, revenue and borrowing numbers are

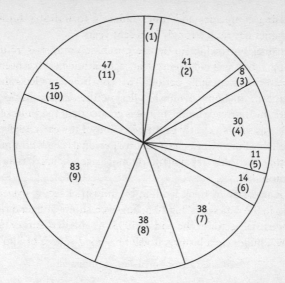

Key
1 Agriculture
2 Manufacturing
3 Construction
4 Wholesale and retail
5 Hotels and restaurants
6 Transport

7 Real estate
8 Leasing
9 Other financial intermediation
10 Insurance and pension funds
11 Unclassified

Source: Bank of England *Monetary and Financial Statistics*

Fig. 10.5. Outstanding borrowing by industrial sector at end of 1998

nearly always presented in nominal terms and are not normally seasonally adjusted.

THE EVOLUTION OF THE PSBR

The PSBR was first used as a concept as recently as 1969. Before that, the central government borrowing requirement (CGBR) was commonly referred to. The PSBR consolidates the local authority borrowing requirement and the public corporations' borrowing requirement with the CGBR, to show how much the whole public sector is borrowing from outside itself. The PSBR excludes transactions within the public sector,

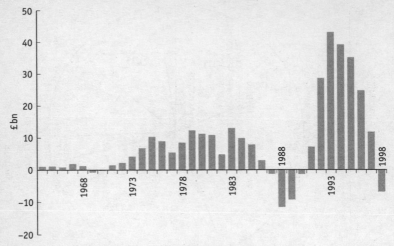

Fig. 10.6. Public sector borrowing requirement

for example on-lending by central government to local authorities and public corporations.

The PSBR was at first calculated on a quarterly basis. Monthly figures exist only from 1981 and were published for calendar months from the end of 1983. Initially, the PSBR monthly figures were published for banking months (mid-point to mid-point of calendar months) as one of the counterparts of the money and banking statistics. This caused much confusion in financial markets, but the move from banking to calendar months for all statistics in 1986 ended this anomaly and consequent difficulties. The PSBR figures still suffer from most commonly being analysed on the basis of the financial year, from April to March, making them difficult to relate to other variables which are mostly aggregated in calendar years. PSBR data figures are published also on a calendar year basis, but they do not have the status of targets, as do the financial year figures.

Figs. 10.6 and 10.7 show the history of the PSBR over the last thirty-five years. Expressing borrowing as a ratio to GDP is far more illuminating than viewing it in cash terms. Given the loss of control of borrowing in the 1970s, which is clear in these charts, it is easier to understand how the control of public finances was such a large issue in the 1980s. The surplus in the late 1980s and the large deficits in the 1990s had more to

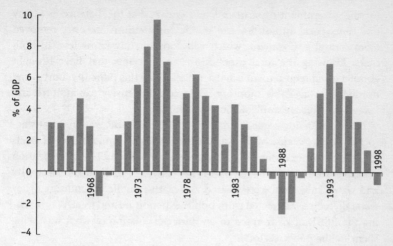

Fig. 10.7. Public sector borrowing as a percentage of GDP

do with the impact of the economic cycle than a more fundamental loss of control.

DATA PROBLEMS

There is a mountain of public finance numbers to analyse, but unfortunately some of the numbers that are most wanted are not readily available. It is possible to analyse public spending and revenues in a number of ways: by the level of government (total public, general, central or local), by department (defence, education, health, etc.), by function, or by economic category. Much of this information is available only quarterly or annually and often well in arrears. Data in the format in which the government plans public spending and revenue in the annual Budget statement are not available until well after the end of the year.

An oddity of the public sector accounts is that the borrowing number is relatively easy to obtain while figures for total expenditure and total receipts are very difficult to obtain. Central government borrowing – by far the largest component – is relatively easy to calculate. This is because the Treasury and the Bank of England essentially keep the bank accounts for the government departments and know what the 'balance' is at any one time. Local authorities and public corporations are once removed from central government, which will consequently know less. In both cases, knowing the total expenditure and receipts that have brought about a given requirement is harder. Reflecting this difficulty, borrowing numbers are available monthly while comprehensive expenditure and revenue figures are available only quarterly.

It was frequently argued in the 1980s that the PSBR was an unsatisfactory concept, because of the way it treated the government sales of assets in public corporations when they were privatized. The privatization proceeds from sources such as British Gas, BT, BP and the electricity and water industries, were treated as negative public expenditure. They were, therefore, subtracted from public expenditure and treated as reducing the PSBR. This resulted in an under-estimation of what was being spent by the public sector.

It was widely argued at the time that it would be more in line with international practice to treat privatization proceeds as financing the PSBR, rather than reducing it. The government defended the accounting procedure by saying that the nationalization of companies incurred public expenditure so the privatization should be counted as negative expenditure. The issue became progressively less sensitive during the 1990s as both the monthly press release and the government forecasts expressed the PSBR both with and without privatization proceeds. Also, the receipts from privatization have become much lower than they were in the peak years of the 1980s. In the second half of the 1980s privatization receipts averaged £5 billion a year.

It was often argued that the actual financial deficit of the public sector (PSFD), the total deficit from current and capital accounts, would make a better measure of the public sector finances. This measure does not take account of any transactions in financial assets and liabilities, such as privatizations. It could be more or less than the PSBR in any particular year. Privatizations apart, the PSFD would normally be within several billion pounds of the PSBR. The PSFD was available only quarterly (until recently – see below) and was analysed following the release of figures, but markets always preferred the higher frequency monthly PSBR numbers. The government also preferred them because the inclusion of privatizations meant that they tended to suggest lower borrowing than the financial deficit.

Another unsatisfactory feature of the PSBR was that it was never expressed as a percentage increase in an outstanding stock of debt. The markets tend to look at the borrowing figure in cash terms on a month by month basis, when in fact it has little meaning or context. Comparison with the same month a year ago gives some indication as to whether the target for the year will be met, but it says little about the significance of the figure for the economy or government policy. A borrowing figure expressed as a percentage of GDP or as a percentage increase in the outstanding debt would be more meaningful. Once again, the principal barrier to this is the relative infrequency of publication of debt and GDP numbers.

NEW LABOUR, NEW FIGURES

The public accounts changed in the late 1990s when the Labour Government revamped the fiscal policy framework in the two years after its election. These changes had knock-on effects – good and bad – on the data.

The Government felt it identified a number of deficiencies in the previous approach. These included:

- Policy objectives were imprecise and subject to change.
- There was insufficient promotion of economic stability and long-term focus.
- Current spending often took precedence over capital spending.
- Tax and spend decisions failed to reflect the impact on future generations.

In 1998, in an attempt to overcome these problems, the government gave statutory basis to its 'Code for Fiscal Stability'. The key part of this was two new fiscal rules:

- The golden rule – over the economic cycle, the Government will borrow only to invest and not to fund current spending
- Sustainable investment rule – public sector net debt as a proportion of GDP will be held stable over the economic cycle.

The Government's *Economic and Fiscal Strategy Report*, published in June 1998, explained that the principal measures in future would be the surplus on the current budget, public sector net borrowing, and the public sector net debt ratio. Historical data for these variables are shown in Fig. 10.8. The fiscal rules are based on the national accounts data, but are not all recognized national accounts variables. The rules are similar to the criteria set out in the Maastricht Treaty but there are some differences:

● They cover the whole of the public sector (whereas Maastricht includes only general government).
● The UK debt measure is net of liquid assets (whereas Maastricht uses gross debt).
● The fiscal rules apply over the whole economic cycle (not to individual years).

The Government also introduced some new public expenditure totals to reflect changes they made to the planning regime. The new public expenditure aggregate is called total managed expenditure (TME), and is divided into two roughly equal parts: departmental expenditure limits (DEL), which will be planned over a three-year period, and annually managed expenditure (AME), mainly social security spending, which will be planned each year. In addition, each government department has been set public service agreements, to clarify their objectives. The Government has also pledged to introduce resource accounting and budgeting (RAB) in the public sector which involves planning, controlling and accounting for departmental spending on an accruals basis.

Only time will tell how successful the new systems for planning and control turn out to be. There is some concern that the new rules, despite being referred to as 'strict' by the government, are too vague. As politicians still control public spending and they are aware of the need to appeal to voters, there is a suspicion that tough decisions will be dodged when the time comes. From the analytical point of view, these changes, with their knock-on effects on the data, show the difficulties of relying on data that come from administrative sources.

A number, but by no means all, of the problems with the data were addressed by the new presentation. Issues included:

● Criticism about the lack of explanation given by the Treasury when it presented the new numbers, along with insufficient back data on the new definitions.

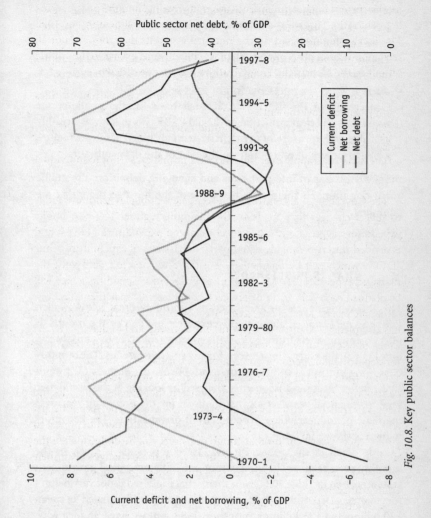

Public sector net debt, % of GDP

Current deficit and net borrowing, % of GDP

Current deficit
Net borrowing
Net debt

1997–8
1994–5
1991–2
1988–9
1985–6
1982–3
1979–80
1976–7
1973–4
1970–1

Fig. 10.8. Key public sector balances

● The treatment of the so-called 'windfall tax' – the one-off tax of around £5 billion levied on the privatized utilities to pay for the government's New Deal, welfare-to-work programme. Some of the public sector accounts are presented including these numbers while some are presented excluding them.

● The surplus on the current budget is a Treasury, not national accounts, definition and includes some capital taxes, mainly inheritance tax.

● There is a less clear presentation of asset sales.

● Concern about the shift to an accruals basis for the public sector accounts – one clear attraction of the old PSBR was that it was a readily available cash measure of the deficit. Accruals based accounts require a greater degree of estimation on the part of the data collectors.

Despite problems of interpretation and changing definition, the public borrowing numbers themselves are some of the most accurate that are published.

WHAT IS PUBLISHED?

The borrowing figures are published in a monthly press release, called *Public Sector Finances*, about two weeks after the end of the month. It offers many numbers from the various government accounts, but throws little light on the underlying reasons for any emerging trends. The monthly borrowing number is compared first with borrowing in the same month a year before. It is most frequently analysed by looking at the cumulative total for financial years set against the total for the preceding year over the same period, excluding proceeds from privatization. The key information is shown in Table 10.5.

Little detail of the public expenditure components is given in the monthly press release. The information available on central government is summarized in Table 10.6. Even then, what is offered is not very helpful for analysis. Departmental spending, for example, fluctuated between £20 billion and £25 billion a month in 1998, but we have no idea why. It is thus hard to know from month to month whether the data are revealing a new trend or just being erratic. There is no monthly spending or receipts information available for local authorities or public corporations.

Table 10.5. Public sector borrowing figures

	£bn		
	1997–8	1998–9	Difference
Net cash requirement (NCR):			
1. Central government (own account)	2.6	−6.2	−8.8
2. Local government	−0.8	−0.6	0.2
3. General government (1+2)	1.8	−6.8	−8.5
4. Public corporations	−0.7	−0.6	0.1
5. Public sector NCR (3+4)*	1.1	−7.4	−8.4
Financial transactions:			
6. Privatization proceeds	1.5	−0.3	−1.8
7. Other adjustments	4.1	2.4	−1.7
8. Public sector net borrowing* (PSNB) (5+6+7) (rounded)	6.6	−5.2	−11.9
Of which:			
9. Central government	7.2	−4.5	−11.7
10. Local government	−0.4	−0.9	−0.5
11. General government	6.8	−5.4	−12.3
12. Public corporations	−0.2	0.2	0.4

Notes: *PSNCR previously known as PSBR. PSNB previously known as PSFD.
Source: Public sector finances press release, March 1999.

Quarterly public sector accounts are published in two phases. Provisional figures are published about eight weeks after the end of the quarter with revised figures appearing alongside the national accounts numbers about twelve weeks after the end of the quarter. The summary figures from this release are shown in Table 10.7, but further break-downs are given. Total receipts are broken down into taxes (three-quarters of the total), National Insurance and other. Total expenditure is broken down into goods and services (nearly half of the total), social benefits, interest payments and other.

Twice a year, the ONS publishes the first release called 'Government deficit and debt under the Maastricht Treaty'. This has been published since 1994. It shows the figures which must be submitted by each member country under the terms of the Treaty of Economic Union, known as the Maastricht Treaty, and submitted to the European Commission. The release shows the deficit and change in gross debt of general (central and local) government over the calendar year and on standard international

Table 10.6. Central government spending and receipts

	£bn		
	1997–8	1998–9	Difference
Cash receipts:			
1. Inland Revenue	117.6	128.2	10.6
2. Customs and Excise	89.8	94.1	4.2
3. Social security	49.3	53.2	4.0
4. Interest	9.5	9.5	0.0
5. Other	20.8	19.6	−1.2
6. Total receipts (sum 1 to 5)	287.0	304.6	17.6
Cash outlays:			
7. Interest payments	27.7	27.0	−0.7
8. Privatization proceeds	−1.8	−0.1	1.7
9. Departmental spending	263.7	271.5	7.8
10. Total outlay (7+8+9)	289.6	298.5	8.8
11. Net cash requirement (CGNCR)* (10–6)	2.6	−6.2	−8.8

Note: *CGNCR previously known as CGBR(O).
Source: Public sector finances press release, March 1999.

Table 10.7. Public sector finances

	£bn		
	Apr.–Dec. 1997	Apr.–Dec. 1998	Difference
1. Current receipts	227.5	244.5	17.0
2. Current expenditure	227.7	235.2	7.5
3. Depreciation	10.4	10.9	0.5
4. Surplus on current budget (1−2−3)	−10.6	−1.6	9.0
5. Net investment	1.0	0.7	−0.3
6. Net borrowing* (5−4)	11.7	2.3	−9.4
Memo:			
7. Net cash requirement	6.4	−1.3	−7.7
8. Net debt (at end of period)	358.0	354.5	−3.5

Note: *PSNBR previously known as PSFD.
Source: Provisional public sector accounts press release, Q4, 1998, February 1999.

Table 10.8. General government financial balances of G7 countries

	1990–4	1995	1996	1997	1998
USA	−3.3	−1.9	−0.9	0.4	1.7
Japan	0.7	−3.6	−4.2	−3.4	−6.0
Germany	−2.7	−3.3	−3.4	−2.6	−2.0
France	−3.8	−4.9	−4.1	−3.0	−2.9
Italy	−10.0	−7.7	−6.6	−2.7	−2.7
UK	−5.1	−5.8	−4.4	−2.0	0.4
Canada	−6.6	−4.5	−2.2	0.9	1.3
G7	−3.3	−3.4	−2.7	−1.3	−0.9
Euro-11 area	−4.8	−4.8	−4.1	−2.5	−2.1

Note: − = deficit. On a Maastricht definition where possible.
Source: OECD.

definitions. We should note that the figures are for general government and not the whole of the public sector, i.e. they exclude public corporations (see Table 10.8).

The Treaty did not determine what constituted excessive borrowing, but a protocol to the Treaty provided a reference value of 3 per cent of GDP for net borrowing and 60 per cent of GDP for gross debt. Accordingly, these are the benchmarks against which countries are judged. This release is not market sensitive as approximations to the figures can be made from data already published. The release of March 1999, showed that general government net borrowing had fallen from a deficit of 4½ per cent of GDP in 1996 to a surplus of ½ per cent in 1998. The debt percentage over the same period had fallen from 53½ per cent of GDP to 49½ per cent. The trends for the UK are shown in Fig. 10.9 and some deficit comparisons with other countries in Table 10.8.

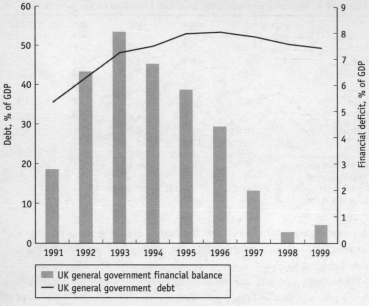

Fig. 10.9. General government debt and deficit

FORECASTS

The PSBR is notoriously difficult to predict. Monthly forecasts are particularly difficult, as the data are highly volatile from month to month. This reflects not only very strong seasonal patterns in government expenditure and tax revenues but also a genuine erratic content. It generally makes no difference to a government department whether it writes a cheque or banks a payment on the first or last day of a month but it will affect the public sector accounts figures.

There is, however, a certain pattern to the PSBR through the year. Tax revenues have traditionally been at their greatest in the first quarter of the calendar year (the last quarter of the financial year) with income tax and corporation tax receipts bunched in January. VAT payments reflect the seasonality of consumer spending. Government expenditure tends to be highest in March as departments spend any remaining allocations,

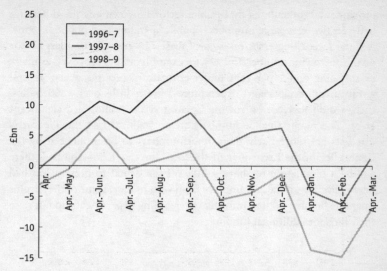

Fig. 10.10. Public sector net cash requirement – cumulative monthly numbers

which they might lose if they were not spent. These patterns change over time, as taxes and payment mechanisms change, and can never be fully allowed for by seasonal adjustment, which is accordingly not applied to the monthly press notice figures. The result is that the cumulative borrowing requirement tends to rise during the year to December, then falls for one or two months, before sharply rising again in March (see Fig. 10.10).

The PSBR is also difficult to forecast for full financial years. The Treasury gives (see Pre-Budget Report from November 1998) average absolute errors (i.e. irrespective of whether the error was positive or negative) for its forecasts. The forecast error for public sector net borrowing in the year just about to start has averaged 1¼ per cent of GDP, a little over £10 billion in today's prices. The error for the forecast three years ahead has averaged 3 per cent, around £25 billion at today's prices. The error on the associated growth forecast accounts for about a third of that error, but the largest part remains an error in the forecast of the public sector accounts themselves.

It is always difficult to know how a period of economic strength or recession is going to impact on government spending and receipts. The fundamental difficulty is that public sector borrowing is the difference between two very large numbers – public spending and public revenue. A small forecasting error on each of these can give rise to a large error on the borrowing number. In 1998, for example, a 2 per cent over-estimate of spending and 2 per cent under-estimate of receipts, when general government receipts and expenditure were a little over £300 billion each, would increase borrowing by around £12 billion – a significant error. The public finance numbers are so political that the Treasury's forecasts are more likely than other numbers to be influenced by the Chancellor of the Exchequer. If the 'real' forecast is looking bad, there will be a temptation to shave a little off the deficit to present less bad news. Similarly, if the accounts are flush with money, some of the surplus might be 'hidden' so that ministers in spending departments do not raise their bids for additional funding.

DEBT

The government publishes various measures of debt. The twice yearly 'Maastricht' press release publishes general government gross debt which is the measure used by the European Union. It excludes the debt of public corporations and measures general government total financial liabilities before netting off short-term financial assets. The public sector accounts press release, in contrast, focuses on public sector net debt. This is approximately the stock analogous to the net cash requirement as a flow. The key debt figures are shown in Table 10.9. Both press releases relate the annual deficit to the debt measure.

The largest and often most volatile component of the public sector's liquid assets is the government's official reserves. These amounted to £21 billion in 1998 and largely comprised foreign currency bonds and notes. (See p. 214 for a fuller description of the reserves.) The National Debt is the most famous measure. Formally, it is the indebtedness of the National Loans Fund. This is not a comprehensive measure of debt but data goes back to 1691, when the Bank of England was founded. It is a little larger than the more popular measures shown in Table 10.9. At the end of March 1998 the National Debt was just under £420 billion. The bulk of this, just under £300 million, was British government stock,

Table 10.9. Public sector debt, 1998

	£ billion	% of GDP
Central government gross debt	403.3	49
Local authority gross debt	51.6	6
General government consolidated gross debt	411.4	50
Public corporations gross debt	25.8	3
Public sector consolidated gross debt	402.8	49
Public sector liquid assets	51.0	6
Net public sector debt (gross debt less assets)	351.8	43

Source: BoE *Statistical Abstract*, table 13.1, 1998. Amount outstanding at end of March.

known as gilt-edged securities. Nearly £60 billion was National Savings debt and just over £10 billion was foreign currency debt. A number of the Bank of England publications give details of the transactions in marketable debt.

INTEREST RATES

Interest rates are not published in a press notice, but appear daily in the press. For longer periods, they are published in the Bank of England's monthly statistics book and in *Financial Statistics* from the ONS. There are many different rates of interest which vary according both to the nature of the institution or person doing the borrowing or lending, and the time period over which the transaction relates.

It is not easy to forecast the movement of rates along the spectrum from short- to very long-term as the influences on the markets are numerous. In general, a combination of real factors – expected inflation, toughness of government policy, strength of the exchange rate, extent of government borrowing, etc. – and market factors – supply and demand for the various products – determine the course of interest rates. Other factors, such as strikes, wars, natural disasters, political crises, along with market euphoria or panic, also influence the markets. Many thousands of people, including a good number of economists, are engaged in the world's money and bond markets trading products which fluctuate according to the expected course of interest rates.

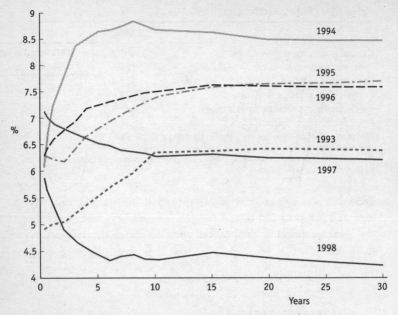

Fig. 10.11. Gilt yield curve at year ends

The monetary authority has much greater control over short-term than long-term interest rates. This is because the Bank of England chooses the base, or repo, rate and can operate in the money markets with considerable effect to bring short-term market rates close to that level. (Setting the short-term interest rate in the UK is now the responsibility of the Monetary Policy Committee of the Bank of England, but prior to 1997 was the responsibility of the Treasury and the Chancellor of the Exchequer.) Longer-term interest rates are influenced more by supply and demand in the market place, and the authorities have only limited control over the course of the variables that the market watches. The government is, however, the biggest sterling borrower, so that the health of the nation's finances strongly influences the supply, and hence the price, of sterling denominated bonds.

The line that plots interest rates against maturity is called an interest rate, or yield, curve (see Fig. 10.11). The normal shape of the curve has longer-term rates at high levels to compensate investors for the extra risk and uncertainty that time produces. There can, however, be extended

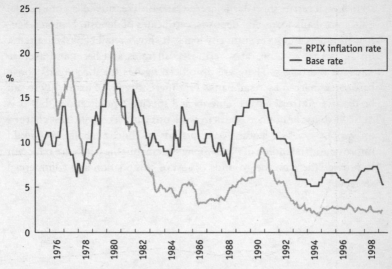

Fig. 10.12. Base rate and inflation rate

periods when the interest-rate curve is downward sloping and said to be inverted. The curve is downward sloping when short-term interest rates are raised to high levels, forcing the front end of the curve up, with the intention of reducing the future rates of inflation, keeping the long end down. In general, a rise in short-term rates will lead to higher long-term rates, but if the rise in rates is perceived to herald a period of slower growth and lower inflation, the curve could pivot with long-term rates falling. Long rates will also fall if, as in the late 1990s, the supply of new government debt is limited by a public sector surplus.

The relationship between inflation and base rates is clear to see: when inflation is threatening to pick up, the monetary authority responds by tightening monetary policy (see Fig. 10.12). The exception was in 1988 when the Chancellor kept cutting rates despite the imminent rise in inflation. The boom was stronger and the subsequent downturn deeper as a result of the delayed action. The 1970s and 1980s experienced much higher average base rates than in the period before and since. The economic cycle of the second half of the 1990s was much less dramatic than those at the start and end of the 1980s.

Financial Statistics publishes yields on gilt-edged stocks and company securities. It carries short-term interest rates on Treasury bills, commercial bills, inter-bank loans and deposits, certificates of deposit, National Savings products and local authority loans. It shows retail banks' base rates, instant access account rates, term deposit rates and basic and average rates for mortgages. There are no official figures for the spreads above base rates charged by retail banks for different types of loans. These can be discovered from advertisements and specialist publications, but it is difficult to use announced rates to work out the average interest charged on various types of lending over periods of time. Such figures would improve understanding of the banking system, but the banks are reluctant to provide them on the grounds of cost of compilation and commercial secrecy.

Sources

General

Economic Trends, ONS, monthly.

Financial Statistics, ONS, monthly.

Forecasts for the UK Economy – A Comparison of Independent Forecasts, HM Treasury, monthly.

Inflation Report, Bank of England, quarterly.

Christopher Johnson and Simon Briscoe, *Measuring the Economy*, Penguin, 1995.

Monthly Digest of Statistics, ONS, monthly.

National Accounts Concepts, Sources and Methods, ONS, 1998 edition.

Daniel Dorling and Stephen Simpson, *Statistics in Society*, E. Arnold, 1999.

The Source (Catalogue), ONS, annual.

UK National Accounts (The Blue Book), ONS, 1998 edition.

Chapter 1   History and Politics

Building Trust in Statistics, White Paper, Cm 4412, 1999.

Business Plans, ONS, annual.

John Pullinger, 'The creation of the Office for National Statistics', *International Statistical Review*, 1997.

Framework Document, ONS, 1996.

Government Economic Statistics, Cabinet Office/HMSO, 1989.

GSS annual reports, annual.

Official Statistics Beyond the Year 2000 (papers from), SUC conference, November 1997.

'Official statistics: counting with confidence', RSS Working Party, JRSS A, 1991.

'Official statistics: governance and consultation', ONS/GSS, 1996.

'Proposed merger of CSO and OPCS, Report of the consultation exercise', CSO/OPCS, September 1995.

'Statistics: A matter of trust', Treasury Green Paper, Cm 3882, February 1998.

'Statistics: A matter of trust', RSS response, May 1998.

Nigel Lawson, *The View from No. 11: Memoirs of a Tory Radical*, Bantam Press, 1992.

Chapter 4 Economic Growth

Compliance Plan, 1998–2000, ONS.

OECD Economic Outlook.

'Quarterly national accounts in the UK', *Economic Trends*, April 1995.

UK Economic Accounts, Q3 1998, ONS.

'UK National Accounts', CSO Methodological paper no. 3, 'Data sources for the quarterly account', April 1995.

World Development Indices, World Bank.

Chapter 5 Inflation

Consumer prices indices, first release, ONS, monthly.

'Development of a final expenditure prices index', *Economic Trends*, ONS, September 1997.

'Harmonised indices of consumer prices', *Economic Trends*, ONS, February 1998.

'Implications of the US Boskin report for the UK retail prices index', *Economic Trends*, ONS, October 1997.

RPI *Business Monitor MM23*, ONS, monthly.

Retail Prices Index Technical Manual, ONS, 1998.

'Seasonal adjustment of RPIY', *Economic Trends*, ONS, May 1999.

'Three year research programme on RPI methodology', *Economic Trends*, ONS, February 1999.

Treasury Committee Reports (of confirmation hearings).

Chapter 6 Labour Market

Guide to Labour Market Statistics Releases, first edition, ONS, April 1998.

'How exactly is employment measured?', ONS.

'How exactly is unemployment measured?', ONS.

Labour Force Survey, Historical Supplement, 1997.

Labour Force Survey, Quarterly Supplement, ONS.
Labour Market Trends, ONS, monthly.
Labour market statistics, first release, ONS, monthly.
'New earnings survey 1998', ONS.

Chapter 7   Consumers

British Retail Consortium press release.
CBI distributive trades survey.
Gazette, John Lewis Partnership.
Guide to Retail Sales Index, ONS.

Chapter 8   Business

3i Enterprise barometer, 3i, quarterly.
40 Years on: How do Companies Respond to the CBI's Industrial Trends Survey?
    CBI Economic trends situation report, November 1998.
Consumer, business and professional services survey, CBI/Deloitte & Touche.
'Employment in the public and private sectors', *Economic Trends*, June 1999,
    ONS.
Engineering Trends, EEF, quarterly.
Financial services survey, CBI/PricewaterhouseCoopers.
Industrial Trends Survey, CBI, quarterly.
Monthly Trends Enquiry, CBI, monthly.
Quarterly Economic Survey, BCC, quarterly.
Regional trends survey, CBI/BSL.
Reports on manufacturing, services and construction, CIPS, monthly.
Size Analysis of UK Businesses, 1998, ONS.
Small and medium enterprise trends report, CBI/Pannell Kerr Forster.
Survey of property trends, CBI/GVA Grimley.

Chapter 9   Overseas Trade

Monthly review of external trade statistics, *Business Monitor MM24*, ONS.
Pink Book, UK Balance of Payments, ONS, 1998 edition.
'Statistics on trade in goods', GSS methodological series, no. 10, ONS.
'UK trade in goods analysed by industry', *Business Monitor MQ10*, quarterly,
    ONS.
'UK trade in services', *Business Monitor, UKA1*, annual, ONS.

Chapter 10   Money, Public Finances and Financial Markets

Budget 1999, HM Treasury, March 1999.

Monetary and Financial Statistics, Bank of England, monthly.

'Monthly statistics on public sector finances', GSS methodology series no. 12, ONS, January 1999.

Pre-Budget Report, HM Treasury, November 1998.

Statistical Abstract (parts 1 and 2), Bank of England, annual.

Index

Numbers in bold indicate Tables; those in italics indicate Figures.